PROPERTY AND PRACTICAL REASON

Property and Practical Reason makes a moral argument for common law property institutions and norms. It challenges the prevailing dichotomy between individual rights and state interests and the related assumption that owners' reasons for action and the good of communities must conflict.

One can understand competing intuitions about private property rights by considering how private property enables owners and their collaborators to exercise practical reason, thereby becoming practically reasonable agents of deliberation and choice who promote various aspects of the common good. The plural and mediated domains of property ownership, though imperfect, have moral benefits for all members of the community. They enable communities and institutions of private ordering to pursue plural and incommensurable good ends while specifying the boundaries of property rights consistent with basic moral requirements.

ADAM J. MACLEOD is an associate professor at the Thomas Goode Jones School of Law, Faulkner University, USA. He wrote this book while a visiting fellow at Princeton University in the James Madison Program in American Ideals and Institutions. His work has been published in the United States, United Kingdom, and Australia. He served as law clerk to justices of the Massachusetts Appeals Court and a judge of the United States District Court, practiced law in Boston, and has held an appointment as a Deputy Attorney General of Alabama.

PROPERTY AND PRACTICAL REASON

ADAM J. MACLEOD

CAMBRIDGE
UNIVERSITY PRESS

CAMBRIDGE
UNIVERSITY PRESS

University Printing House, Cambridge CB2 8BS, United Kingdom

Cambridge University Press is part of the University of Cambridge.

It furthers the University's mission by disseminating knowledge in the pursuit of education, learning and research at the highest international levels of excellence.

www.cambridge.org
Information on this title: www.cambridge.org/9781107095762

First published 2015

A catalogue record for this publication is available from the British Library

Library of Congress Cataloguing in Publication data
MacLeod, Adam J., author.
Property and practical reason / Adam J. MacLeod.
pages cm
ISBN 978-1-107-09576-2 (hardback)
1. Right of property. 2. Property. I. Title.
K721.5.M33 2015
323.4′6–dc23
2015008276

ISBN 978-1-107-09576-2 Hardback

To Katie, who has shared my many plans
of action with grace and love

CONTENTS

ACKNOWLEDGMENTS

I began and completed this project while teaching at Faulkner University, Jones School of Law. I did most of the writing during a year-long visiting fellowship at the James Madison Program in American Ideals and Institutions at Princeton University. Both Faulkner Law and the James Madison Program provided essential support. I am grateful for the helpful comments of those who read drafts of various chapters – Paul Carrese, Eric Claeys, Jonathan Den Hartog, Matthew Franck, Robert George, Richard Izquierdo, Daniel Mark, Ted McAllister, Bradley Miller, Chaim Saiman, David Tubbs, Grégoire Webber, Bradford Wilson, three anonymous reviewers secured by Cambridge University Press, and twelve undergraduate fellows of the James Madison Program. The work also benefited from conversations with generous scholars and friends who helped me develop and hone the ideas, especially Mitchell Crusto, Jeffrey Hammond, Jeffrey Jones, Robert McFarland, J. Stanley McQuade, Jeremy Rabkin, Charles Rhodes, James Stoner, and Matthew Vega. Ned Swanner has provided indispensable research assistance throughout this project and my time at Faulkner Law. I also enjoyed expert assistance from research librarians Gigi Panagotacos at Faulkner and David Hollander at Princeton. I thank Finola O'Sullivan, Richard Woodham, and their team at CUP for their professionalism. Finally, I am grateful for mentors and teachers who have encouraged me to think critically about the relationship between morality and law, especially Timothy Sherratt, Charles Rice, Gerard Bradley, Christopher Armstrong, Lewis Babcock, Neil Gorsuch, and the late Benjamin Kaplan.

Introduction

The moral case for private property

This book makes a moral case for private property. Specifically, it argues that institutions of private ownership are justified, and in many communities are required, by a basic moral principle. That principle is equal respect for human beings as agents of practical reason. The principle gives rise to norms that require communities and their members to establish, honor, enforce, specify, and limit rights of exclusive use and disposition. Institutions of mediated dominion (private property ownership in the common law tradition) have significant instrumental value because they enable humans to exercise practical reason in such a way as to bring about desirable states of affairs consistent with the requirements of practical reasonableness, and thus to become practically reasonable people.

In summary, the argument runs this way: Human beings make plans for the use and management of those things that are under their dominion and control. And they make those plans not arbitrarily but for reasons. The human capacity to make plans for *reasons*, and not arbitrarily or merely to satisfy preferences or appetites, is what makes human beings unique and entitled to special moral respect. Respect for the reasoned plans of others gives rise to strong moral reasons to exclude oneself from things owned by others and not to interfere with any of those plans that do not cause unreasonable harm. From those duties are derived rights of exclusive use and management of things.

The moral norms underlying property are not all moral absolutes, like prohibitions against killing, raping, and maiming. Some of them, such as the duties not to enslave, are absolute while others are specified only in complex, context-dependent judgments. Nevertheless, the norms of property have moral foundations. They are grounded in human goods and requirements of practical reasonableness. Their authority is not derived entirely from positive law. We all have reasons to honor our duties to exclude ourselves from things that are not ours, not to cause unreasonable harm with our things, not to commit waste, and so forth. And where we honor those duties, *someone* enjoys the liberty that corresponds to our self-exclusion and abstention. The question for us is who will enjoy that freedom and responsibility under law. In a communist society, the state (and therefore the elite segment of society that controls the state) has all the freedom. In a society with private property, people have at least some of the freedom that correlates with property duties.

The demonstration of the moral force of property norms begins by observing how people use things. People use and manage things according to plans, which they adopt and execute for reasons. A philanthropist plans her financial expenditures in order to make the lives of her recipients better. A farmer makes a plan for the use of his fields to grow crops. A concert pianist makes plans to use her piano for practicing and memorizing concertos. Parents plan a schedule for use of the car to accommodate the activities of their children.

Some people consume things or exercise control over things mindlessly. But mindless use is a peripheral, non-focal instance of what we mean by "use." The central case of use – what we generally mean when we speak of the use of things – is deliberate use, which is done purposefully in order to realize some good end. It is exercising dominion over things according to a plan of action. Plans of action for the use and management of things are adopted and executed for reasons, goals that are valuable.

When human beings adopt and execute plans of action, they exercise practical reason, which can be distinguished from theoretical reason. Theoretical (or speculative) reason is what one uses when inquiring whether there is a God, or considering the nature of an atom, or doing calculus, for the purpose of knowing the truth. One employs practical reason to attain knowledge of truth in order to solve practical problems and to achieve successes in life. Practical reason is what one brings to bear on the myriad choices one faces on a daily basis, which affect one's short-term and long-term well-being, and the well-being of one's family, friends, neighbors, associates, and fellow citizens. The capacity to exercise practical reason – to deliberate about what to do, to choose a goal for one's action, and to formulate a plan to achieve that goal – makes human beings unique. It is the foundation of our inherent and equal dignity. Human beings are worthy of respect by virtue of being the kind of beings who are reasoning agents. And the plans that humans make are worthy of respect because they are made by reasoning agents.

When human beings make reasoned choices and adopt plans pursuant to those choices, they act as creators. They create new states of affairs and conditions of being, which would not have existed but for their choices, their formulations of plans, and their committed execution of those plans. The philanthropist makes poorer lives richer. The farmer makes food come into being where only weeds grew. The concert pianist replaces silence and noise with beautiful music. Parents raise healthy and well-rounded children. Humans who make plans for the use and management of things make particular instances of well-being come into existence. To interfere with those creative acts would be to risk destroying their fruits.

Yet, there is an even more fundamental, if often misunderstood, reason to exclude oneself from others' things. In the process of acting pursuant to plans, people make and remake themselves. The wealthy business woman makes herself into a philanthropist when she formulates plans to use her assets to enrich others' lives. The man on the tractor makes himself into a producer of food, a feeder of thousands. In an important sense, people constitute themselves while using and controlling things. And as they constitute themselves around their plans for things, those things become tied up in their plans of action, and therefore in the identity that owners create for themselves by executing their plans of action. The farmer's identity becomes tied up to his farm; the concert pianist's identity becomes tied up to her piano. To steal the piano therefore would constitute a wrong in a general and a specific sense. Generally, it would fail to respect the pianist as a being who made her plans, that is, as a human being. Specifically, to steal the thing is to steal a locus in which the person has constituted her identity by acting on her plans.

We can go farther. That humans make plans for the use and management of things is not only a reason for other members of the community not to interfere with their possession and use, but it is also a reason for those in authority not to interfere, and to secure possession and use with the force of law. Because the exercise of practical reason requires freedom and authority over things, political communities have reasons to extend legal protections around domains of private ownership.

Political authorities should protect the private property both of individuals and of communities of individuals. Plans of action have moral significance for both individuals and communities, such as families, universities, and religious associations. Indeed, the common plan of action is what makes a group's identity. The moral value of those plans of action gives political authorities strong reasons to establish, respect, and enforce rights of exclusive use. These are not the only reasons; private property institutions promote many goods other than practical reasonableness. But the moral value of practical reasonableness is a reason to prefer private property to collective or state ownership – the former enables practical reason whereas the latter cuts it off.

The moral case for private property ownership is also an argument for the limitations on property rights that emerge in the common law tradition, primarily from institutions of private ordering and, when necessary and appropriate, from posited law. Just as the freedom to exercise practical reason with respect to things enables owners and their collaborators to realize good states of affairs, it also frees them to make unreasonable choices. Property in the common law tradition meets this challenge, though imperfectly. Property rights have limitations built into them as a result of centuries of experience and the practical judgment of those who have lived with them. Those limitations exert normative force on the deliberations and choices of those who interact with property and create incentives for people to act reasonably. For example, use rights are limited by the standards of reasonableness that inhere in common law doctrines governing nuisance, waste, and riparian water consumption. These and other doctrines create incentives for owners and their collaborators to act reasonably, and enable judgments on unreasonable uses by that great common law institution of practical judgment, the jury.

This case for private ordering entails that common law judges do not make property law in the first instance. Rather, property law emerges from judicial decisions as courts give juridical force to those private duties and rights that are not unreasonable, and refuse to give juridical force to those duties and rights that cannot be reconciled with the requirements of reason. Judicial authorities are expected to enforce the reasonable (or not-unreasonable) judgments of private institutions – owners, their families and collaborators, neighbors, commons and quasi-commons communities, juries, adverse possessors, etc. – and to decline to lend juridical force to those judgments that are unreasonable, such as abuses of rights, harmful nuisances, and violations of moral norms prohibiting slavery, racial discrimination, and other never-reasonable uses of property. Common law institutions of property enable moral agency without giving owners absolute rights to do as they please.

Definitions

This book is a principled defense of common law institutions of property, which produce what I will call the *mediated dominion* of private ownership. Mediated dominion consists of *domains*, within which owners exercise control over things both as individuals and as communities of individuals. Those domains are *mediated*, by which I mean that freedom to exercise dominion is limited according to standards of practical reasonableness.

Some additional working definitions might help. The conception of *property* that comprises the subject of this book is the common law notion of dominion over a thing, governed and protected by law. *Private property* on this view is dominion over a thing exercised by some person or group of persons other than the political community and its authorities. Private property can thus be exercised by an individual; spouses, siblings, or an entire family; a church, mosque, or synagogue; a university or charitable organization; or any other group, association, or intermediary institution.

This conception departs from many contemporary accounts, which view property as an individual right. That atomization of private property is both unnecessary and unhelpful. Common law institutions of private property enable people to own things both as individuals and in communities – in families, religious associations, civic associations, and in other cooperative forms. Within these institutions of private ordering, communities of people together deliberate and decide how to use and manage the resources available to them, and courts ratify those judgments, or not, according to reason. In well-formed institutions, the authority exercised within the family (or the church or synagogue, or the family business) is exercised for the common good – the set of conditions that enables each and all to realize good states of affairs – and therefore authoritative deliberations will take the well-being of each and all into consideration.[1]

Of course, authority within private groups and institutions is sometimes abused. But the record of private property, the family, religious assemblies, and other intermediary institutions measures up well against the records of collectivist ownership systems, especially over the last century. Furthermore, collectivist strategies for managing resources cut off the deliberation and choices of private property's plural institutions

[1] See John Finnis, *Natural Law and Natural Rights* (2nd edn, Oxford: Oxford University Press 2011) [hereinafter NLNR], especially chapters VI and IX.

of ordering.[2] I mean private property to be ownership that allows individuals and private communities to plan the use and management of things insulated from collective decision-making. In other words, private property is simply property that is owned by private persons and groups of persons. I thus mean to contrast private property with systems of collective property governance and with systems of collective distribution.

This book avoids where possible the misleading term "common property." Some of what is mistakenly called common property is really private property that is governed by a group of people. Much of it is in fact collective property, which is controlled by the state. True *common property* is owned by the entire political community but not controlled by political institutions. In light of how much attention the concept receives in scholarly literature, there is surprisingly little common property in the real world. The seas, navigable servitudes and, in some jurisdictions, beaches are common property, and both the state and private citizens have duties not to interfere with those resources in important ways. Intellectual property that has passed into the public domain is common in a different way. The idea of common property is theoretically interesting, but does not tell us much about how most resources are managed and used.

Practical reasonableness in mediated dominion

To sum up: As mediated dominion promotes human flourishing in its various aspects, it particularly serves one architectonic aspect of human well-being, namely the basic human good of practical reasonableness. Practical reasonableness both justifies domains of private ownership to enable its realization and specifies the boundaries of property rights and duties consistent with its basic requirements. The first part of this book explains and defends the claims that mediated dominion does this work better than alternatives, especially collective systems of resource management, because it supplies the preconditions that are required for the realization of practical reasonableness. It examines the way in which practical reason operates within the core of the owner's domain, and explains how property can promote the practical reasonableness of all, even those who do not hold title to things.

Practical reasonableness is a complex good. It subsumes personal autonomy, reasoned choice, and integrity, among other aspects. It is an

[2] NLNR, 168–69; John Finnis, *Collected Essays of John Finnis, vol. III: Human Rights & the Common Good* (Oxford: Oxford University Press 2012), 79–80.

expensive good. It requires institutions and practices that produce a variety of valuable options and incentivize good choices over bad ones. And it requires laws that support those institutions and practices. So its realization depends on a number of conditions. We will focus on four. Because practical reasonableness is a reflexive good, it cannot be instantiated except (1) freely – insulated from coercion – and (2) in favor of good options. Also, because practical reasoning involves the making and carrying out of plans of action, it requires (3) stability of enforceable expectations and (4) commitment.

Private ownership in the common law secures these conditions. It insulates owners and their collaborators from coercion, thus securing freedom. It results in a greater number of good options and more expensive goods than collective property regimes have produced. It creates the stable conditions necessary for people to execute complex plans of actions with respect to things. And by internalizing the externalities of property use and management, private ownership generates motivations for owners to remain committed to their plans of action.

The second part proposes some limitations that must be placed on ownership if the law is not to endorse practically unreasonable choices and actions. Just property institutions refuse to enforce exercises of property liberties that are abusive or undertaken purely out of spite; they allow recovery for unreasonable harms; they ratify otherwise-unlawful adverse possessions against hoarders; they extinguish the title of those who commit waste against future interest holders. These ideals have not always been met in practice. What follows will reveal that the common law of property is quite good, though not perfect. Common law institutions, employing the standards of reasonableness that are embedded in maxims and doctrines, rule some uses of private property beyond the right of the owner.

It is commonly thought that the central concerns of property are efficiency and material prosperity and that, if morality and practical reason are concerns at all, they do their work only at the margins. One purpose of this book is to challenge that view. Though moral concerns appear most clearly in hard cases, they are nevertheless at work in property's core, silently and invisibly. This book does not challenge utilitarian insights about the efficiency of private property for promoting material prosperity. But it also does not accept the premise, so essential to utilitarian and other consequentialist theories, that basic human goods are commensurable with each other, or the claim derived from that premise that goods can be maximized on any single scale.

The argument here is neither deontological nor utilitarian. It understands deliberation and choice to be rationally directed to objectively knowable human goods. It also takes those goods to be incommensurable. Therefore, in this book, private property is understood as an institution that supports robust, but not infinite, pluralism. Mediated dominion can reasonably be used to pursue as many different life plans, projects, and collaborative endeavors as there are property owners, and the law has no reason to choose one of those pursuits over others, even, or especially, when collective institutions and lawmakers fail to perceive value in a chosen course of action. But the law need not secure to owners powers to use their property to cause harm without reason. Private property is reasonably limited by rules that are genuinely and transparently grounded in protection of the common good of a community.

The argument for mediated dominion does not rest on the claim that humans have natural rights in their own labor. This is neither an account of the origins of property nor a theory justifying initiation of property institutions where they did not exist before. As John Tomasi has observed with respect to economic liberties generally, the nature and dignity of human beings should determine what laws the state enacts and which economic liberties it secures. Because the political community has reasons to secure economic liberties, "the requirements of economic liberty help define the shape and limits of the state, even without being radically prior to it."[3]

The subject of this book is the practical reasoning of those who live in a world that has institutions of property and law already up and running. In other words, this book is concerned with the world that we inhabit. On the other hand, the argument can also be abstracted, and the actual law removed from it, and the moral force of the argument would remain. The norms of property are normative because human beings are the types of being that they are: beings who exercise practical reason. Human beings would be that kind of being no matter what their political arrangements. Some political arrangements are more consistent with human nature, and therefore with the requirements of practical reason, than others.

An outline of the argument

First part: the case for domains of private ownership

Chapter 1 describes two conflicting intuitions about property. The first is that freedom to use property must be robustly protected against

[3] John Tomasi, *Free Market Fairness* (Princeton: Princeton University Press 2012), 98.

outsiders, but especially against encroachment by political communities, such as large, public corporations and governments. The competing intuition is that property rights must not be exercised unreasonably or abusively. These intuitions correspond to the competing demands of practical reasonableness, a good that law reasonably promotes in order to help human beings live flourishing lives. The chapter then briefly explains the idea, skillfully developed in recent decades by perfectionist thinkers such as Joseph Raz, John Finnis, and Jeremy Waldron, that law can and should take into account moral concerns such as flourishing and moral duties.

Chapter 2 takes a cut at the common law's solution to the basic problem. Common law institutions and norms of property employ different mechanisms to support and direct the practical reasoning of people who encounter, use, and manage things because the basic principles and requirements of reason are irreducible. The architecture of property is therefore complex. But certain patterns emerge to view when one considers the various ways in which property norms show themselves to different audiences.

Because moral rights must be universalizable, just institutions of ownership must create opportunities for everyone to exercise reason with respect to things. A general *eligibility* to own property is precisely the sort of right that Jeremy Waldron argued could not be derived from an argument based on positive liberty or free choice. Waldron thought the argument from positive liberty is necessarily an argument for a general right to *possess* property, that this right entails redistribution of property, and thus undermines private ownership. Challenging Waldron's argument, Chapter 3 clarifies an important feature of mediated dominion that is often overlooked, namely its use cooperatively within groups and intermediary institutions such as families, for-profit and nonprofit businesses, religious assemblies, and quasi-commons. Mediated dominion enables cooperative deliberation and action among people who have various ownership interests in the domain.

Chapter 4 turns to developing more fully the argument that mediated dominion over things is justified on moral grounds. To explore the moral significance of exercising dominion over things, this chapter adopts the internal point of view of the practically reasonable person. This person acts for reasons, many of which she adopts as conclusive reasons for her future actions. From her perspective, we can discern one sense of Aquinas' insight about self-constitution in the order of the will: that as they deliberate and choose according to reasons, human beings constitute themselves in a real, though incorporeal, order. To the extent that these projects of self-constitution involve dominion over things, those things become bound up in the projects. To trespass against or interfere with an owned thing is therefore to do violence to the user's plan of action, and to fail to respect that person as an agent of practical reason.

Second part: the case for limitations on owner dominion

If understood as a human good, practical reasonableness commends certain internal limitations on property rights and liberties. Because the good of practical reasonableness can be realized only if practical reason is exercised freely, property's features must, wherever possible, empower rather than coerce owners to act for right reasons. But it must rule out some reasons for action.

At least two sets of features within the common law of property cannot be understood apart from their operation on reasons for action. The first is property law's support for charitable choice and action. The second feature is the refusal of many common law courts to enforce abusive exercises of use rights. Charity and abuse of rights represent opposite postures that owners can adopt with respect to what we call "rights." At these extremes one can perceive the advantages of perfectionist jurisprudence over other theories that focus on the material consequences of property use. Without an account of practical reason – its internal operation and its moral implications – these features of mediated dominion might remain mysterious.

Property law's treatment of charity is best understood by considering charity as an action exercised for basic reasons for action, motivations that possess intelligible value as constituent aspects of human flourishing in and of themselves. Many of property law's provisions for charitable action are best explained in this light, and some cannot be explained otherwise. Chapter 5 explores this area of property law.

The idea of abuse of rights, which plays a poorly understood role in common law, originates in an understanding that an owner's reasons for action matter at least as much as the material consequences of his action. It requires judging some reasons for action to be legitimate justifications for the exercise of property rights and others to be illegitimate. One therefore cannot understand the operation of abuse of rights without a robust account of practical reason. Despite its long history of use in private law and substantial scholarly interest in it, the principle of abuse of rights has not been fully developed into a recognized doctrine in common law. Chapter 6 takes up the task of examining abuses of rights and sketching what a workable abuse of rights doctrine might look like.

Chapter 7 takes up a question that Chapter 6 leaves open, namely if use rights can be abused, and on that basis not given juridical force, what sense is there in calling them rights? Use rights stated abstractly are rights in a peripheral sense. They narrow the category of reasons that may be considered against their exercise by establishing categorical exclusionary reasons for action, and they perform other normative work in law. But they are not conclusive and absolute, as inviolable rights are.

So, property norms, like rights and duties generally, vary in force and effect. Chapter 8 classifies different property norms according to their operation on practical deliberations. Absolute norms, such as prohibitions against owning human beings and discriminating on the basis of race, act as fully exclusionary reasons, ruling all primary reasons out of consideration and binding conclusively the deliberations and judgments of moral agents. Other property norms are categorical but not absolute. These norms rule out categories of reasons, even sometimes all but one or two category of reasons. Finally, many property norms are entirely context dependent, and operate only as presumptions, customs, maxims, or other open-ended guides to practical reason.

Most property norms find their way into property through institutions of private ordering, but some are imposed on property by state action. Chapter 9 takes up the vexed question of how duties and rights are specified in property law. Some argue that government should have a free hand to regulate private property where collective action can be expected to produce more benefits for the greatest number of people. Others have argued that any burden that governments place on property rights amounts to a compensable taking. A better approach is to consider property rights as corollaries of duties that are specified first by institutions of private ordering and the development of common law doctrine, and secondarily codified by legislative authorities. Private law can therefore be autonomous from public law without being static.

1

Practical reason and private law

The importance of private property

People have conflicting intuitions about private property. On one hand, many people think private property is important. On the other hand, many people think that private property rights are not always exercised justly. Those intuitions are both reasonable. Reasoned cases are made for and against private property.

The reasoned case *in favor of* private property is grounded in the plans of action that human beings make for their lives using things. This reasoned case affirms a common intuition. Many people believe that domains of ownership should be secure against intrusion by political authorities, such as branches of governments and (perhaps more controversially) publicly traded corporations. Consider, for example, the backlash that followed the US Supreme Court's decision in *Kelo* v. *City of New London.*[1] The Court ruled that state and local governments have the right to take private property by eminent domain for any public purpose, contrary to the clear language of the Fifth Amendment limiting takings to "public use," and to convey it to large corporations that promise to produce jobs and economic prosperity. The decision was publicly condemned by people across the political spectrum; one survey revealed that 95 percent of Americans opposed it. In the ensuing months, all but a few states and the executive branch of the national government enacted legal reforms to restrict the use of eminent domain.[2]

The intuition motivating this response can be stated as a reasoned argument. As private property makes people *feel* better-off, it also enables them to *be* better-off, not only materially but also morally. Whatever other good ends that people realize within domains of private ownership,

[1] 545 US 469 (2005).

[2] Ilya Somin, "The Limits of Backlash: Assessing the Political Response to Kelo" (2009) 93 *Minnesota Law Review* 2100 at 2108–54; President of the United States, Executive Order 13406 (June 23, 2006).

they realize the good of becoming practically reasonable people. Practical reasonableness is a basic human good; it is better to be reasonable than to be unreasonable. Thus, even leaving aside all of the material benefits that private property makes possible, society has a strong moral interest in preserving the domain of freedom that private property creates.

This argument does not depend upon private property freedom being absolute. To the contrary, property owners must not have the right to do purposeful wrongs if property law is to serve the practical reasonableness of those owners. This is the basis of the reasoned argument *against* property rights. Though private property protections generally insulate the practical reasoning of owners from outside scrutiny, abusive exercises of property rights signal a failure of practical reasoning, so exclusion and use must sometimes be scrutinized. Free choice has no value when used for evil ends, and valueless choices can cause harm not only to the victims of the wrongful act but also to the perpetrator. Law should not secure a right to do wrong.

This argument enlists moral norms to shape, limit, or even extinguish property rights, affirming the intuition that condemns unjust harm. An owner has no right to make an unreasonable use that harms his neighbors, and a jury can reasonably conclude that one has no right to operate a copper smelting plant to emit pollutants where they could cause harm.[3] This argument also justifies governments in the exercise of their police powers prohibiting uses that would constitute a nuisance under private law, and which the owner therefore has no common law right to make, such as the operation of a brick kiln in a residential neighborhood.[4]

Conflicting intuitions about private property

These two views of property perform significant normative work in law even where they are not expressly acknowledged. Two cases illustrate their power.

Private property is important

Michael and Chantell Sackett planned to build their dream home in rural Idaho. They purchased an empty lot for $23,000 near a lake in a quiet setting. They researched the permitting history of the lot and inquired

3 *St. Helen's Smelting Co.* v. *Tipping* [1865] 11 HL Cas 642, 11 All ER 1483.
4 *Hadacheck* v. *Sebastian*, 239 US 394 (1915).

about regulatory requirements. According to their counsel, they complied with local laws and received assurances from the US Army Corps of Engineers that no federal permits were required. Having performed their due diligence, the Sacketts began construction by placing fill material on part of the lot.[5]

Then the Environmental Protection Agency (EPA) appeared. The EPA asserted that the construction encroached upon protected wetlands in violation of the Clean Water Act.[6] The EPA ordered the Sacketts to stop construction, to restore the site to its prior condition, and to allow EPA officials unrestricted access to their land, all under the threat of heavy fines. The Sacketts denied that their land was in fact situated on wetlands. Their lot was not adjacent to the lake, and several permanent structures sat between the Sacketts' lot and the lake. The Sacketts' lot had appeared dry enough for the Army Corps of Engineers to clear the project. But EPA asserted that water was found on the land. (A justice of the US Supreme Court later described the collection of water that concerned the EPA as a "little drainage problem."[7])

The disagreement between the two agencies reflected ambiguity and confusion in the positive law. The Supreme Court has never clearly defined which lands count as wetlands and has called the Clean Water Act's use of the term "notoriously unclear."[8] Federal agencies have in many cases claimed wetland protection over lands that appear to be dry. Thus, as the Court has acknowledged, affected landowners "lack guidance"[9] and must "feel their way on a case-by-case basis."[10]

Nevertheless, the Sacketts had no legal recourse to contest the EPA's assessment. The EPA denied their request for a hearing, and two federal courts ruled that federal law provided no mechanism to challenge the EPA's assessment. This left the Sacketts with a Hobson's choice. They could restore the property to its original condition, apply for a permit that they believed they were not required to obtain, pay the associated

5 Pacific Legal Foundation, *Sackett* v. *EPA Fact Sheet* (February 12, 2012) available at file:///C:/Users/ajmac/Downloads/TalkingPoints_2-12-12.pdf.

6 *Sackett* v. *Environmental Protection Agency*, 566 US __, 132 S Ct 1367 (2012).

7 Transcript, *Sackett* v. *Environmental Protection Agency*, US Supreme Court 10-1062 (January 9, 2012), 38, available at www.supremecourt.gov/oral_arguments/argument_transcripts/10-1062.pdf.

8 *Sackett* v. *EPA*, 132 S Ct at 1376. The Clean Water Act prohibits the discharge of pollutants into "navigable waters." The Supreme Court has interpreted this term to include non-navigable wetlands that are adjacent to navigable waters. 132 S Ct at 1370.

9 *Sackett* v. *EPA*, 132 S Ct at 1370.

10 *Rapanos* v. *United States*, 547 US 715 at 758 (2006) (Roberts CJ concurring).

expenses, and risk being denied; or they could expose themselves to an enforcement action by the EPA and the associated fines, which could run up to $75,000 per day. Either way, they would incur expenses far in excess of the value of their house lot. This predicament rendered the EPA the de facto adjudicator – prosecutor, judge, and jury – of the Sacketts' property rights, which the EPA had nullified.

The US Supreme Court granted certiorari, then ruled unanimously in favor of the Sacketts. The Court accepted and decided the case on narrow grounds of statutory construction. It interpreted the Administrative Procedure Act to extend to the Sacketts a right of judicial review and ruled that the Clean Water Act did not preclude such review. The decision produced no dissents even though the Court's interpretation was arguably not the most persuasive reading of the statutes. The Administrative Procedure Act requires hearings only after a final agency action and, as the EPA had not yet moved to enforce its compliance order against the Sacketts, it was not obvious that its action was yet final. Also, the Clean Water Act gives the EPA discretion to choose between issuing a compliance order and bringing a civil action in court to enforce the Act's provisions. The EPA argued that allowing the Sacketts a right of judicial review of the EPA's compliance order would eradicate the distinction between those options.

As a rule, US courts defer to reasonable agency interpretations. And indeed, two lower federal courts had read the same statutes, considered the same arguments, and had discerned no right of review. The US District Court had dismissed the Sacketts' claims without hearing oral argument, finding no reported cases supporting their position, and ample authority supporting the EPA's interpretation of the statutes.[11] This opinion was itself not reported in the Federal Supplement reports, perhaps because it was viewed as unremarkably correct. Similarly, the US Court of Appeals for the Ninth Circuit ruled that the Clean Water Act precludes review.[12]

What then can explain the Supreme Court justices' unanimous ruling for the Sacketts? Though the Sacketts' property rights played no role in the Court's express reasoning, it is not difficult to imagine that the effect of the EPA's action upon the Sacketts' reasoned plans for their property influenced the outcome of the case. The justices were surely mindful of their obligation to construe statutes to avoid constitutional conflict

[11] *Sackett* v. *Environmental Protection Agency*, 2008 WL 3286801 (D. Idaho 2008).
[12] *Sackett* v. *Environmental Protection Agency*, 622 F 3d 1139 (9th Cir 2010).

unless such a construction is plainly contrary to Congress' intent.[13] It seems that the Sacketts' private rights silently directed the Court's analysis of their public rights and duties. The case generated a strong sense that if the Sacketts were not granted a hearing then property rights in general could be in jeopardy.[14] The Sacketts were David facing Goliath. Trying to build a simple life for themselves in a modest setting, they found themselves trammeled by the regulatory state. As Justice Alito exclaimed in concurrence, it seemed "unthinkable" that a nation that values private property "would have put the property rights of ordinary Americans at the mercy of [EPA] employees."[15]

The law cannot tolerate unreasonable exercises of property rights

Francis Palmer made a will, in which he left the bulk of his estate to his grandson, Elmer Palmer. Francis was a widower at the time of the will, and Elmer appears to have been the logical person to receive Francis' farm and "considerable personal property." But when Francis later remarried, he intimated to Elmer that he might amend the will. Elmer decided to prevent this from happening by the surest means possible. He "willfully murdered [Francis] by poisoning him." He then initiated a claim to enforce Francis' devise and bequest.[16]

Elmer argued that the will should be given "effect according to the letter of the law." Francis had lawfully executed the will. He was now dead, and his will had been admitted in probate. Elmer had satisfied all statutory requirements. The courts of New York could find no reason in posited law to deny Elmer title to the residue of Francis' estate. Yet the Court of Appeals of New York refused to recognize Elmer's title. The court insisted that it could never have been the lawmakers' intention that "a donee who murdered the testator to make the will operative should have a benefit under it." If the law were literally construed, the court conceded, Elmer would have a property right in the residue of the estate. But the court was sure that, had the legislators of New York anticipated a

13 *Solid Waste Agency of Northern Cook County* v. *U.S. Army Corps of Engineers*, 531 US 159 at 172–73 (2001).

14 It is interesting to note that thirteen amicus briefs were filed in support of the Sacketts and only one was filed in support of the EPA. See page for *Sackett* v. *Environmental Protection Agency*, Scotusblog, available at www.scotusblog.com/case-files/cases/sackett-et-vir-v-environmental-protection-agency-et-al/?wpmp_switcher=desktop (last visited March 5, 2013).

15 *Sackett* v. *EPA*, 132 S Ct at 1375.

16 *Riggs* v. *Palmer*, 22 NE 188 at 189 (New York 1889).

case such as this, they would have enacted a law to prevent Elmer from taking title. Then the court set out to identify the reason to reject Elmer's claim.

The court first turned to canons of construction, stating that a proposition "which is within the intention of the makers of a statute is as much within the statute as if it were within the letter; and a thing which is within the letter of the statute is not within the statute unless it be within the intention of the makers."[17] But the point of a canon of construction is to help the court to construe something, namely the language of the statute, in such a way as to give effect to the legislature's intent. It is not a license to add content to the law. Furthermore, the canon would not produce the court's desired result on its own logic. The premise of the court's argument was that the legislature had not contemplated a case like this and therefore had *not* intended to provide for such a case. So, the court was not using the canon to discern what the legislature intended but rather what it manifestly did not intend, but should have intended consistent with "common reason."

The court next turned to equity. It quoted Bacon: "By an equitable construction a case not within the letter of a statute is sometimes holden to be within the meaning, because it is within the mischief for which a remedy is provided." Because lawmakers cannot anticipate every case in express terms, the job of a court is to "suppose the law-maker present, and that you have asked him this question: Did you intend to comprehend this case? Then you must give yourself such answer as you imagine he, being an upright and reasonable man, would have given." If a reasonable legislator would have intended for the statute to reach the case then the court is to hold the case "within the equity of the statute."[18]

This also misses the mark. The court did not bring the case within the statute. It excluded the case from the reach of the statute, which unambiguously vested title in Elmer. The court asserted, "In some cases the letter of a legislative act is restrained by an equitable construction; in others, it is enlarged; in others, the construction is contrary to the letter." But it did no more than assert this, and made no attempt to demonstrate that this was a faithful reading of Bacon's equitable canon or that the canon required judgment against Elmer Palmer.

Apparently recognizing that these arguments were unavailing, the court finally made an appeal to the unwritten law of reason. The court considered itself bound to render void any "absurd consequences" of the

[17] *Riggs* v. *Palmer*, 22 NE at 189.

[18] *Riggs* v. *Palmer*, 22 NE at 189.

statute's literal application that would be "manifestly contradictory to common reason." What could be more unreasonable than to attribute to the legislature an intention to allow its succession laws to "have operation in favor of one who murdered his ancestor that he might speedily come into the possession of his estate[.] Such an intention is inconceivable." "We need not," the court concluded, "be much troubled by the general language contained in the laws." It was enough to note a general maxim of the common law, "No one shall be permitted to . . . acquire property by his own crime."[19]

The requirements of reason could be found embedded in the common law whether or not any jurist had before articulated them, and quite apart from the contents of the state's posited enactments. Elmer Palmer's claim was contrary to the "general principles of natural law and justice." To find an *articulation* of the norm, the court reached outside the common law. "Under the civil law, evolved from the general principles of natural law and justice by many generations of jurisconsults, philosophers, and statesmen, one cannot take property by inheritance or will from an ancestor or benefactor whom he has murdered," the court declaimed. The court conceded that no such doctrine had ever been discovered in the common law. But this was not exclusion by omission, the court insisted. It was simply failure to state the obvious. "It was evidently supposed that the maxims of the common law were sufficient to regulate such a case, and that a specific enactment for that purpose was not needed." Though no lawmaker or jurist had ever before articulated a doctrine of abuse of rights, the doctrine was nevertheless latent in the common law maxims. Those maxims "have their foundation in universal law administered in all civilized countries."[20]

Ronald Dworkin fruitfully employed *Riggs* v. *Palmer* to critique the legal positivists' claim that a set of legal rules is exhaustive of the law. For Dworkin, the case illustrated his thesis that when lawyers reason about hard cases, "they make use of standards that do not function as rules, but operate differently as principles, policies, and other sorts of standards."[21] Rules are reasons that operate conclusively; they operate normatively in an "all-or-nothing fashion," obligating judges to reach a particular judgment. Principles, by contrast, identify "a reason that argues in one direction, but does not necessitate a particular decision."[22]

19 *Riggs* v. *Palmer*, 22 NE at 190. 20 *Riggs* v. *Palmer*, 22 NE at 190.

21 Ronald Dworkin, *Taking Rights Seriously* (Cambridge: Harvard University Press 1978), 22.

22 Dworkin, *Taking Rights Seriously*, 24–26.

Dworkin's discussion of rules echoes Blackstone's. Among the characteristics of a rule that Blackstone thought important was a rule's conclusive force upon one's deliberations about what to do and what not to do. One reason to call law a rule of civil conduct was "to distinguish it from advice or counsel, which we are at liberty to follow or not, as we see proper; and to judge upon the reasonableness or unreasonableness of the thing advised."[23] Rules, unlike advice, are conclusive. They bind a person to a particular answer to practical questions. This is how law operates as a reason for action, commanding what is right and prohibiting what is wrong.

An important question that arises is whether property rights are more like rules or principles. Put more precisely, are property rights premises that come at the beginning of a deliberation, from which legal judgments are derived, or are they conclusive reasons for action that come at the end of the deliberation? Unlike inviolable rights, such as the rights not to be killed or enslaved, property rights (and their corresponding duties) rule certain categories of reasons out of consideration, but not all reasons. Francis' will and the statutes of New York together supplied a categorical reason to conclude that Francis had intended to vest a private right in Elmer, and not someone else. But that was not an absolute or conclusive reason for the court to recognize ownership in Elmer. Other, countervailing reasons – the intrinsic unreasonableness of Elmer's action, the interest of the court in not ratifying Elmer's conduct – required the court to refuse to give his private rights the force of law. *Those* reasons were both categorical and conclusive.[24] So, did Elmer have a right to take title, which was countervailed by other reasons, or did he not enjoy the right because the court did not vest title in him? Chapters 6–8 take up this question.

Most of the balance of the book is concerned with two related questions: whether reasons outside the positive rules can count as law and, if so, which ones? Commentary on *Riggs* v. *Palmer* has generally advanced the idea that an otherwise-valid will can be set aside when required by conscience, religion, or some other vaguely stated notion. But this overlooks the New York court's extensive consideration of the *objective* unreasonableness of Elmer Palmer's action. No mandate of individual conscience overcame the property right, nor any mere intuition, emotion, or sentiment. Instead, the very existence of the right depended upon the objective reasonableness of the plan of action through which the

[23] William Blackstone, *Commentaries on the Laws of England* (1769), vol. 1, *44.

[24] Chapters 6–8 take up the task of explaining how property rights can be less-than-conclusive and yet still sensibly be called "rights."

right was secured. The court quoted Aristotle, and cited Blackstone, in support of the supremacy of "common reason" over positive law that produced any irrational results.[25] On this view, some objective standard of reasonableness is inherent within the right itself.

Practical reason and property law

The law allows owners to carry out their plans unless unreasonable. But the whole point of in rem property rights is to allow owners to exercise their rights without justifying their actions as reasonable. And we think that those property protections are important. How do we explain this apparent paradox?

Perfectionism in law

The explanation begins with the observation that property law does its best work in service not merely to whatever owners happen to prefer but rather to ends that are objectively good both for owners and for those with whom owners are in community. These irreducible aspects of the common good both justify and limit rights. They do this by justifying and limiting the duties out of which rights arise, and with which they correlate. This account is not consequentialist, but it is perfectionist. Rights and duties are conclusions of practical deliberations about what is good and bad, right and wrong, to choose and do.

Because perfectionist jurisprudence is not universally known within academic discourse about law, a brief sketch might help some readers. Perfectionist accounts of moral and legal reasoning hold that the good is prior to the right. More fully, rights and duties are derived from reasoned deliberation about the pressing practical question in all normative inquiry – including both morality and law – what should I (not) do? So, reasoning about rights first takes the perspective of the person who owes a duty (or not) to the right holder. That person's reasoning should be directed toward the common good, conceived not as some all-things-considered greatest good for the greatest number but rather as the ensemble of conditions that conduces to the development of individuals and the communities in which they collaborate.[26]

[25] *Riggs* v. *Palmer*, 22 NE at 190.

[26] John Finnis, *Natural Law and Natural Rights* (2nd edn, Oxford: Oxford University Press 2011) [hereinafter NLNR], 147–50.

The priority of justification begins with basic human goods, then moves to moral norms, then to duties, and only finally to rights. Thus, perfectionist theories hold that the law can and should take into consideration accounts of good and bad and the requirements of practical reasonableness that enable us to realize the common good and avoid bad choices. As Joseph Raz explains the most general sense of it, "'Perfectionism' is merely a term used to indicate that there is no fundamental principled inhibition on governments acting for any valid moral reason, though there are many strategic inhibitions on doing so in certain classes of cases."[27]

So property law, like law generally, is best understood as promoting plural and incommensurable human goods and ruling bad choices out of the consideration of private and public actors. This project requires both expansive domains of freedom to pursue plural and incommensurable plans of action and some limits on choice to deflect unreasonable and harmful plans of action. Because basic human goods are not reducible to a single scale of measurement, moral agents must be free to choose which goods to pursue with their resources. But because not all human motivations are good, there are moral constraints that law must respect and safeguard, for example the prohibition against owning human beings.

One must be more precise in order to avoid a prevalent caricature of perfectionist thought. Contemporary perfectionists do not favor coercing morally upright conduct for the sake of building a virtuous character. Rather, in the words of Bradley Miller, "Typically, they hold that there is a *range* of morally valuable choices and a *range* of morally valueless choices, and an individual's autonomy is not threatened but advanced by state action that rightly identifies, discourages, and (in a limited class of cases) prohibits the morally valueless."[28] In contrast to the paternalistic perfectionism associated with Plato and Aristotle, the argument in this book draws upon the non-paternalistic tradition of perfectionist jurisprudence begun by Aquinas and today associated with liberals such as Raz and so-called New Natural Lawyers, such as John Finnis. This non-paternalistic perfectionism eschews criminal punishment and other forms of legal coercion except where an "act

[27] Joseph Raz, "Facing Up: A Reply" (1989) 62 *Southern California Law Review* 1153 at 1230.

[28] Bradley W. Miller, "Proportionality's Blind Spot: 'Neutrality' and Political Philosophy" in Grant Huscroft, Bradley W. Miller, and Grégoire Webber (eds.), *Proportionality and the Rule of Law: Rights, Justification, Reasoning* (New York: Cambridge University Press 2014), 391.

has a public character and jeopardizes public order or public morality or the rights of others."[29]

A perfectionist account of law requires a prior account of reasons for action, which enables us to evaluate reasons as valuable and valueless. To obtain this, we need to adopt the internal point of view of the practically reasonable person, i.e., a person who chooses and acts for good reasons.[30] If at any point any one of us asks, Why am I doing this?, and our present action is not irrational, then there must at bottom be a reason for it. To get all the way to that reason, one might need to interrogate oneself at some length. Why do I go to work? To earn money. Why do I earn money? To feed my family and pay the mortgage. Why do I feed my family and pay the mortgage? Because I love my family and want them to be safe and healthy. Why do I want those things? Because I just do. The state of affairs in which my family is safe and healthy is good, in itself. It is immeasurably better than the state of affairs in which my family is famished and in jeopardy. I've gotten to the bottom, found one or more bases for my efforts at work that are reasons (of course, there are also other reasons) valuable in themselves, without reference to anything more basic.

So, by looking along our reasons for choice and action we see that at least some reasons are transparent for more fundamental, or basic,

29 John Finnis, *Collected Essays of John Finnis, vol. IV: Philosophy of Law* (Oxford: Oxford University Press 2012), 270. See the discussions in Miller, "Proportionality's Blind Spot," 388–94; Joseph Raz, *The Morality of Freedom* (Oxford: Oxford University Press 1986) [hereinafter MOF]; and Robert P. George, *Making Men Moral: Civil Liberties and Public Morality* (New York: Oxford University Press 1993).

30 In the middle of the twentieth century, C. S. Lewis and H. L. A. Hart both exhorted philosophers to bring into their accounts of normativity the ways in which people explain their own behavior. C. S. Lewis, "Meditation in a Toolshed" in *God in the Dock* (Grand Rapids: Eerdmans Publishing 1970), 212–15 (originally published 1945); H. L. A. Hart, *The Concept of Law* (2nd edn, Oxford: Oxford University Press 1994), 90. Since Lewis and Hart recalled attention to the internal point of view, the literature on reasons for action has grown quite rich. The account offered in this book owes much to MOF; Joseph Raz, *Practical Reason and Norms* (Oxford: Oxford University Press 1999); Jeremy Waldron, *The Right to Private Property* (Oxford: Clarendon Press 1988); Neil MacCormick, *Practical Reason in Law and Morality* (Oxford: Oxford University Press 2008). It draws most heavily upon the work of natural law philosophers who work in the non-paternalistic stream of perfectionism, especially NLNR; Thomas Aquinas, *Commentary on Aristotle's Nicomachean Ethics*, C. J. Litzinger (trans.) (Notre Dame: Dumb Ox 1993); Germain Grisez, "The First Principle of Practical Reason" in Anthony Kenny (ed.), *Aquinas: A Collection of Critical Essays* (Notre Dame: University of Notre Dame Press 1969), 340; George, *Making Men Moral*; Robert P. George, *In Defense of Natural Law* (New York: Oxford University Press 1999).

reasons for action. To discern the foundational rationality of a choice, we need to keep looking until we find the most basic reasons, the goods that supply the ultimate, intelligible value of all those intermediate ends, which are ultimately mere means to their realization. This is not to suggest that all choices are grounded in reasons; some choices are irrational. At the end of each chain of reasoning sits one (or more) foundational motivation(s) for action. If that motivation is rational then it has intelligible value as a reason. But it might not.

The basic goods are aspects of the common good, a term that is widely used but little understood. The basic goods are common in the sense that they are universal. John Finnis has observed that all human societies show concern for these goods, or some forms or instantiations of these goods, and the practical principles that guide their realization.[31] Though no value is recognized at all times, in all places, and in the same way, anthropologists find with "striking unanimity" that the basic goods are known to all societies in some way.[32] The basic goods are "good for any and every person."[33]

Knowledge is one such basic good.[34] Knowledge is valuable in itself; it is better to be knowledgeable than to be confused or ignorant. If we were to ask why someone is pursuing an education, a sensible answer would be, "To learn." And it would be sensible without any additional explanation. And what can be said of knowledge can be observed of friendship, aesthetic experience, and other goods, including practical reasonableness itself.[35]

This does not entail that everyone must pursue or prefer the same good or goods. Indeed, the basic goods, being all equally and differently basic, are plural and incommensurable with each other. They cannot be reduced to each other, nor to any summum bonum that is more basic than themselves.[36] The intelligible value of all reasons for action is derived from the basic reasons for action; their values are not derived from each other. The value of knowledge is not reducible to friendship, or beauty. Friendship does not contain all of the goodness of knowledge, or vice versa. This is not to deny that basic goods cannot be instrumentally valuable for the realization of other reasons, including other basic reasons. One studies a professional discipline – medicine, law, music – in order to acquire knowledge. One also reasonably studies medicine or

[31] NLNR, 83–84. [32] NLNR, 83. [33] NLNR, 155. [34] See NLNR, chapter 3.
[35] See NLNR, 59–99.
[36] On basic reasons for action generally, see MOF, 145–46, 279–84; NLNR, chapters 3, 4, and 5.

law in order to pursue other goods that those academic disciplines advance, such as health and civic order. But it also remains rational to acquire knowledge for its own sake. The goodness of knowledge is not exhausted by its instrumental usefulness for realizing other ends. Basic goods remain reasons for action even if their instrumental value is not realized.

Because the basic goods are incommensurable, selections from among them are undetermined. Therefore, human agents – both individuals and groups – are able to exercise the radical capacity of free choice, which gives practical reasoning its self-constituting quality. A choice between an act of charity and an act of acquiring knowledge is truly undetermined; because there is no way to compare those possibilities, there is no way to calculate which is more valuable than the other. It is the actor's choice that itself determines the actor's reason for action. Once the actor chooses to spend resources studying rather than relieving the plight of the poor, the actor has new reasons to achieve the chosen goal, that is, not to fail in the realization of the good that he has set before him.

The pluralism of basic reasons, and the derivative pluralism of life plans and less-comprehensive plans of action, supplies at least two justifications for human freedom. First, people should be free to choose between incommensurable plans of action because such choices are undetermined by reason, and therefore there can be no reason for political authorities to choose for them. Just as there is no single basic good, there is no "collective good" or single, all-encompassing reason that could justify overriding undetermined choices by coercion. Coercing people to pursue a single or collective good is irrational and arbitrary, and therefore unjust.

Second, freedom to choose is freedom to make one's own reasons for future action, and thus to constitute oneself into a particular person of one's own self-directed making. Making undetermined choices – making new reasons for oneself where they did not before exist and would not have existed but for the choice – has moral value for the chooser. On this ground Raz has stated, "[A] government aware of its duty to promote the well-being of people is bound, in today's conditions, to be sensitive to the need for people to be free in the sense of being capable of leading successful autonomous lives."[37] This duty entails preserving the plurality of worthwhile options created by individual initiative and

[37] Joseph Raz, "Liberty and Trust" in R. P. George (ed.), *Natural Law, Liberalism, and Morality* (New York: Oxford University Press 1996), 113; and generally, MOF.

the cooperation that takes place within communities. And it requires political powers to refrain from coercing undetermined choices.

This account of human choosing has political implications, especially for property. It is neither individualist nor collectivist. It privileges neither the preferences of atomized individuals nor the interests of the state but instead insists that those communities that reside in the space between the individual and the state have priority in facilitating normative inquiry, in providing the conditions necessary for self-constitution, and in specifying the rights and duties that we owe to each other, all projects in which property law plays an important role. For one irreducible aspect of one's own good is the basic good of community or friendship, which consists of sharing the good of another human being as one's own good. This sharing can be reciprocal, such that members of a friendship or community pursue a good in part because the other members are also pursuing that good. Cooperation among members of a community is mutually dependent. Each member of the community advances the community's plans of action not only for her own sake but also for the good of others, which in turn is for her own good, which in turn is part of the good of others . . . So, if A and B are friends then "what A wants for himself he wants (at least in part) under the description 'that-which-B-wants-for-himself', and vice versa."[38]

The good realized in friendship or community is not reducible to individual preferences, nor is it merely an aggregate of individual goods, nor some collective net good. Rather, it is a truly common good, shared mutually by all of its participants, in mutually beneficial projects of self-constitution. This shared and reciprocal self-constitution is almost never realized by political institutions and authorities, which must choose between competing conceptions of the good, and so must select winners and losers. But it is regularly realized in private and civic communities that stand between the individual and the state, those groups that we can call intermediary.[39] Intermediary communities are reducible neither to their individual members nor to the state. And the goods that they realize are reducible to neither individual preference nor collective net goods.

As should by now be plain, this account is pluralistic. Because the basic goods are incommensurable, there is no one uniquely correct way to

[38] NLNR, 141.

[39] Development of the idea of intermediary institutions owes much to Peter L. Berger and Richard John Neuhaus, *To Empower People: From State to Civil Society* (2nd edn, Washington: AEI Press 1996).

pursue the good. To assert that a lecture on property law is more valuable than a symphony is incoherent, because there is no single scale on which the value of knowledge and beauty can be measured. Thus, there is no uniquely correct answer to the question of whether people should become intellectual property lawyers or composers, disaster relief workers or members of religious orders, scholars or farmers. To evaluate the goodness in an act of charity requires a different standard of measure than evaluation of an act of friendship, or an act of acquiring knowledge. For the same reason, the good of the Kiwanis club cannot be reduced to the good of the family, which cannot be reduced to the good of the university, which cannot be reduced to the good of the symphony orchestra.

On the other hand, the plurality of goods is not infinite. Indeed, the intelligible value of basic good entails that complete moral pluralism is unworkable. Precisely because it makes sense to say that knowledge is intrinsically valuable, it also makes sense to say that knowledge is better than ignorance. One cannot be neutral as between knowledge and ignorance if one is committed to good states of affairs over bad ones. So, though there cannot be a ranking or hierarchy between or among basic goods, good states of affairs are objectively more valuable than impoverished states of affairs.

A full account of the relative moral value of different reasons is beyond the scope of this book.[40] But it should seem uncontroversial to observe at this point that the value of basic goods is not contingent in the way that merely instrumental goods are. Beauty requires no justification, nor does altruism. Acts taken in pursuit of knowledge, beauty, and charity remain valuable without the realization of other goods. By contrast, merely instrumental goods are valuable because, and only insofar as, they allow humans to realize more basic goods. Medicine, for example, is valuable because, and insofar as, it heals a person from illness. Its value derives entirely from its usefulness to humans in realizing the good of health. Money is also merely an instrumental good. It has no value to a shipwreck survivor who is stranded in isolation.

[40] Compare Andrew M. Yuengert, *Approximating Prudence* (New York: Palgrave MacMillan 2012), 51–68 and NLNR, chapters 3 and 4, with the catalogues of lists of basic values in Sabina Alkire, "The Basic Dimensions of Human Flourishing: A Comparison of Accounts" in Nigel Biggar and Rufus Black (eds.), *The Revival of Natural Law: Philosophical, Theological and Ethical Responses to the Finnis-Grisez School* (Burlington: Ashgate 2000), 73–110, and John Finnis, *Collected Essays of John Finnis, vol. I: Reason in Action* (Oxford: Oxford University Press 2012), 9–12.

Finally, there are non-goods, such as ignorance and violence. These are not reasons in the sense that goods are reasons. That people often act on motivations other than goods does not make those motivations rational. A desire to see another person harmed, though sometimes *emotionally* satisfying, does not supply a *reason* for action. To act out of spite is to succumb to the worst tendency in human nature. To make the loss, misfortune, or frustration of another human being one's purpose for acting in a particular way is to will a state of affairs that is inconsistent with the good. Similarly, to discriminate on the basis of race is not to act for a reason but rather for some sub-rational motivation. Avoiding the evils of these choices is a reason why property law prohibits using one's property to cause harm out of spite and discriminating on the basis of race in public accommodations.

The moral significance of non-goods derives from the fact that they are often adopted as means and ends in peoples' plans of action. In other words, people behave unreasonably, immorally, even irrationally. It might be reasonable to accept non-goods and evils as unintended secondary consequences of one's choices; it cannot be reasonable purposefully to bring them about. Nations sometimes find it necessary to go to war in order to defend themselves, and they accept casualties as a necessary consequence. Individuals sometimes find it necessary to resort to violence in order to defend themselves against physical threats. But we do not think that violence has positive moral value. Before going to war, nations issue declarations stating their reasons. Those reasons are not always persuasive. But that nations consider themselves obliged to justify acts of war indicates that war is not valuable in itself. Indeed, that war is widely viewed as a tragedy indicates that it has no positive moral value but rather is reluctantly accepted, where necessary, as the lesser of two possible evils.

So the moral significance of non-goods depends on how the moral agent is accounting for them in her deliberations. Is she deliberately trying to make people ignorant? Or is she accepting the ignorance of some people because her time and resources are limited and she has decided that she cannot educate everyone? It is the agent's deliberation that constitutes a proper subject of moral approbation or disapprobation. We can and should lament the prevalence of ignorance, and celebrate the acquisition of knowledge. But we cannot pass moral judgment until we know who has an obligation to dispense knowledge to this person on this occasion; who is lying and who is deliberately telling the truth; and so on.

The good of practical reasonableness

One basic, human good in particular supplies much of the justification for and many of the limitations on private property ownership. That is the good of practical reasonableness, which is the good of being able to deliberate about, and choose between, valuable possibilities, and to act consistent with the requirements of reason. Practical reasonableness is, in the words of John Finnis, "reasonableness in deciding, in adopting commitments, in choosing and executing projects, and in general in acting."[41] It enables one "to bring one's own intelligence to bear effectively . . . on the problems of choosing one's actions and lifestyle and shaping one's own character."[42] It is architectonic; it orders the other goods and therefore plays a special role in shaping norms of morality and law.

To respect practical reasonableness, law must be both pluralist as to the choice of incommensurable plans and perfectionist as to deflecting morally harmful choices. Property in the common law tradition meets these needs. It provides plural forms of ownership and institutions of ordering in which different human goods are realized, and yet also adopts norms that deflect purposeful harm. Indeed, the moral intuitions at work within property law seem less mysterious when one grasps the role that practical reasonableness plays in shaping it. Property law facilitates good choices and deflects evil choices in part to promote the practical reasonableness of humans who live under the rule of law.

This is not to suggest that practical reasonableness is the only good or requirement of reason that property serves. To the contrary, reduction of the common good to any one good, including practical reasonableness, is contrary to reason for the same reason that rational choice is possible (because basic goods are incommensurable). But time and space constrain this book to consideration of one good or requirement that has shaped property law. Practical reasonableness lies close to the heart of the work that private property law performs. It provides both a strong justification for recognizing and respecting property rights and a justification for limiting rights and powers of ownership to disincentivize practically unreasonable actions. Because practical reasonableness plays an architectonic role – it orders the goods in the deliberations and choices of moral agents – focusing on practical reasonableness will bring in consideration of the other goods as well. Furthermore, practical

[41] NLNR, 12.

[42] NLNR, 88. Compare Raz's account of the ideal of personal autonomy. MOF, 369, 390–95.

reasonableness has largely been overlooked relative to goods of self-preservation, fairness, and efficiency.

The requirements of practical reasonableness

Because some choices are more fully reasonable than others, morality is needed to guide practical deliberation. It is important to ask not only, What may I choose?, but also, What, if anything, must I choose?, and, What should I not choose? To be fully practically reasonable, one must not only choose ends and means that have intelligible value, one must also choose, consistent with the *requirements* of practical reasonableness, what are commonly referred to as moral principles. We humans need objective moral standards because we require guidance for our practical deliberations, and because the reasons that guide us must be impersonal and universal.[43]

Consider Bill, who draws water from a stream that runs through his property in order to operate his car wash business. Suppose he runs his operation in an environmentally responsible manner, so that the negative environmental externalities of washing cars are dramatically reduced if more cars are washed at Bill's facility than at other facilities, or in peoples' driveways. He provides a quality service at a reasonable price and treats customers and competitors honestly. His use of water from the stream thus serves many good ends, in addition to feeding his family. And yet, if Bill uses all the water from the stream, leaving none for downstream users, that he is acting for good ends does not itself render his actions fully reasonable. Let us assume that Bill's motives are untainted by malice. He still needs some guidance about what he should and should not do. And if Bill's use creates a conflict with other owners, the law needs some solution that will appeal to the reason of all parties. The settlement must be fair, account for the contributions and needs of each, not arbitrarily discriminate against any, and meet other requirements of reason.

John Finnis has summarized those requirements that various schools of moral philosophy have identified as basic: having a coherent plan of life; making no arbitrary preferences among basic goods; making no arbitrary preferences among human persons; detachment from one's plans; commitment to one's plans; attention to consequences in the selection of one's means; respect for every basic good in every act; a

[43] Thomas Nagel, *The Possibility of Altruism* (Oxford: Clarendon Press 1970), 90–111.

favoring of the common good of one's communities; and obedience to one's conscience.[44] The product of all of these requirements is what we commonly call morality. Finnis has observed that, by taking into consideration all of the requirements of practical reasonableness,

> we can see why some philosophers have located the essence of "morality" in the reduction of harm, others in the increase of well-being, some in social harmony, some in universalizability of practical judgment, some in the all-round flourishing of the individual, others in the preservation of freedom and authenticity. Each of these has a place in rational choice and commitments, projects, and particular actions.[45]

That one encounters a diversity of opinion about the content of practical reasonableness is therefore not a sufficient reason to deny that practical reasonableness has objective content. Rather, the "diversity has its source in too exclusive attention to some of the basic value(s) and/or some basic requirement(s), and inattention to others."[46] To resolve the confusion and controversy about the requirements of practical reasonableness, one ought to *broaden* one's view of those requirements, not constrain it.

With this in view, we can appreciate the concern expressed by Stephen Munzer that the choice of a particular scheme of property (or economic system generally) over alternative arrangements will necessarily limit the range of property-related virtues.[47] A proper concern for distributive justice and efficiency is important, but so is temperance, and integrity, and fidelity to family, and . . . Our man Bill, the car wash owner, requires guidance as he tries to act reasonably toward his neighbors, his wife and children, his customers, his employees, and his fellow citizens, all in addition to downstream riparian owners.

The moral norms that property institutions ought to take into account are no different from the requirements of practical reasonableness generally. Just as one ought to live one's life according to a coherent plan, rather than allow oneself to be moved by every whim, one ought to adopt plans for one's use and management of things. Just

[44] NLNR, 103–27. [45] NLNR, 126.

[46] NLNR, 127. Therefore, the basic requirements of practical reason cannot be reduced to a single moral rule, such as a requirement for equal distribution or a prohibition against non-consensual harm, without arbitrarily excluding some equally basic requirements. Compare C. S. Lewis, *The Abolition of Man* (San Francisco: Harper Collins 1944), 83–101.

[47] Stephen R. Munzer, *A Theory of Property* (Cambridge: Cambridge University Press 1990), 146.

as one ought to make no arbitrary distinctions between persons generally, one should not arbitrarily prefer some persons to others in the use and distribution of one's things. This does not mean, of course, that one should not establish *any* preferences. There is nothing arbitrary about tending to the material well-being of one's own children rather than someone else's children. But using one's property to effect racial discrimination would certainly count as practically unreasonable conduct. Racial discrimination in the provision of housing is always wrong in part because discrimination on the basis of race is arbitrary. Race is not a *reason* for differential treatment. And it remains unreasonable even if the person discriminated against never knows about it and secures better housing elsewhere at a lower price. Similarly, one ought to use and manage one's assets with detachment, commitment, a favorable posture toward one's community, and so on.

So, the institutions and norms of property must not arbitrarily reduce morality to any of the basic requirements; they must promote choices that are consistent with all of them. Reasonable institutions of private property will incorporate plural norms. But they must adopt norms, and at least some of those norms must be conclusive. The law should privilege some actions over others, and it should rule some gravely unreasonable actions (e.g., racial discrimination in public accommodations) out altogether. In other words, the law ought to be sensitive to context and to the circumstances of various cases, and should allow freedom to deliberate about what is reasonable. But there should be some categorical norms and even absolute norms in law.

The seventh basic requirement – respect for every basic good in every act – is the principle from which absolute norms are derived. The other basic principles are conditional. Not so with the seventh principle. This principle means that it is immoral to purpose the destruction of a basic good. It is wrong to murder because to murder is to choose to destroy life. It is wrong to enslave because (among other reasons) the purpose of that act is to destroy opportunities for the enslaved person to exercise practical reasonableness. This is true even though acts of murder and enslavement might be useful for the realization of rational ends. An owner might have any number of reasons to enslave another human being, yet it remains unreasonable no matter how much good it might bring about. The moral right not to be killed, lied to, or enslaved is the corollary of the absolute moral duty not to perform those actions. Because there exist some exceptionless moral duties, there are some (not many) exceptionless moral absolutes. Because legal institutions must in justice particularize and promulgate at least some exceptionless duties, there are some (not many) absolute legal rights.

The role of private law in promoting practical reason

The precise role that law should play in mediating choices and action remains a matter of controversy. But the idea that law should play *some* role is not as controversial as some suppose. Every account of private law that takes seriously its normativity is to some extent a perfectionist account. And by viewing the role of practical reason within property law one can go a long way toward understanding moral intuitions about property. On one hand, property law secures the conditions necessary for people to develop their moral agency with respect to things, both individually and in private communities. On the other hand, property law disapproves of choices and actions that are unreasonable, such as a choice to spite one's neighbors or to pollute an irreplaceable natural resource. The community is worse off when its citizens act unreasonably because citizens who act unreasonably constitute themselves as practically unreasonable people – people who are at odds with the common good of the community.

After a century of realism, the prevailing skepticism of any enduring principles in the common law has given way to, if not an enthusiastic endorsement of practical reasonableness, a recognition that principles of moral uprightness play a role in private law.[48] In recent years many commentators have observed that objective values and moral norms are operating within property law.[49] They differ on the question what property is, but they agree that property law relies on moral values and norms to promote various aspects of human well-being.

[48] On the circularity of Holmes' attack on the enduring essence of law, see Paul O. Carrese, *The Cloaking of Power: Montesquieu, Blackstone, and the Rise of Judicial Activism* (Chicago: University of Chicago Press 2003), 107–08.

[49] See Thomas W. Merrill and Henry E. Smith, "The Morality of Property" (2007) 48 *William & Mary Law Review* 1849; Gregory S. Alexander, "The Social-Obligation Norm in American Property Law" (2009) 94 *Cornell Law Review* 745; Henry E. Smith, "Mind the Gap: The Indirect Relation Between Ends and Means in American Property Law" (2009) 94 *Cornell Law Review* 959; Eduardo M. Peñalver, "Land Virtues" (2009) 94 *Cornell Law Review* 821; Hanoch Dagan, "The Public Dimension of Private Property" (2013) 24 *King's Law Journal* 260; the contributors to Gregory S. Alexander and Eduardo M. Peñalver (eds.), *Property and Community* (New York: Oxford University Press 2010); and Stephen R. Munzer (ed.), *New Essays in the Legal and Political Theory of Property* (New York: Cambridge University Press 2010).

Despite this return to perfectionism, there remains a real challenge. The effort to translate moral norms into law threatens the very possibility of moral uprightness, practiced either for its own sake or for the goods that practical reason takes as its object, because law's coercive force threatens to distort practical reasoning. If one chooses a good end out of coercion then one has not taken the good end into one's deliberations and will, only a fear of bad consequences. The ideal of practical reasonableness in property law thus demands both attention to the requirements of practical reason and the freedom to choose well. Property as mediated dominion meets both demands.

Freedom: dominion

Private property law protects practical reason by securing domains of private ownership against outside coercion. This enables free moral agents to deliberate and to bring about good states of affairs according to plans of action, sometimes individually but more often in collaboration with other free moral agents. Property law stands guard around a domain of freedom within which owners and their collaborators promote various human goods, insulated from outside scrutiny and incursions. As Charles Reich observed, humans need "sanctuaries or enclaves where no majority can reach."[50] Private property domains are among those sanctuaries and enclaves.

The dominion that owners and their collaborators exercise over things secures for them both the authority and the freedom to exercise practical reason. It carves out a space within which they may and must make meaningful choices, which have both material and moral effects. Volumes have been filled with discussions about the material consequences; much less has been said about the moral benefits of property dominion. Freedom to make uncoerced, undetermined choices is the freedom to make new reasons for one's own actions. It is the freedom to constitute one's identity, to make oneself, as a person, a family, an institution, or a community, which is not some other person, family, institution, or community that others might prefer but rather is constituted by the choices and actions of the persons and groups themselves. It is the freedom to become reasonable by choosing to act for reasons, to shape one's plans and commitments by choosing some possible reasons over others, and to realize one's plans and commitments by pursuing them with commitment and integrity. It is the freedom to achieve good

[50] Charles A. Reich, "The New Property" (1964) 73 *Yale Law Journal* 733 at 778.

states of affairs, apart from the preferences or pressures of outsiders. It is the freedom, in short, to act in a way that is distinctly human.

As we will see, the owner's dominion is neither absolute nor despotic, but it is robust. Property dominion frees religious communities and political movements to choose and act consistent with their convictions, especially when those convictions are not widely shared. The domain of private property has enabled countless inventors, entrepreneurs, artists, scientists, and authors to make the world a more livable, beautiful, and healthy place. Private property was the silent guardian of the meetings that birthed the civil rights movement in the American South and the abolition of the slave trade in the British Empire. Many of the world's great universities exercise their dominion as owners to explore new and controversial ideas. For better or worse, this book was researched and written entirely on private land, using resources owned by the author and by private universities. Many of the books and articles cited in this book also owe their existence to the freedom exercised within property domains, including *private* property owned by state universities. The variety of perspectives, convictions, and conclusions expressed in those sources and the quality of that scholarship are evidence that plural domains of ownership facilitate the virtuous pursuit of knowledge.

Responsible action: mediated dominion

Freedom and authority can be abused. So when it comes to judicial enforcement of the private rights and duties that arise out of property domains, property law pays careful attention to moral distinctions. It is one thing for private actors to create conclusive reasons – rights and duties – to govern their own future conduct where those commitments are morally unjustifiable. But it is quite another thing for them to demand that courts and other civic institutions give those rights and duties the force of law. So, if a group of landowners agree together to impose on their estates covenants forbidding sales to non-whites, and if they all agree to abide by the obligation of the covenants, then they might have freedom to order their affairs contrary to what reason requires. But if they demand that a court of law enforce one of those covenants to deprive homeowners of their lawful title and possession by equitable action, then they force the court to choose between creating an unjust duty and creating a rule prohibiting enforcement of such duties. The court is obliged to choose the latter.[51] So, rules limiting owner dominion are

[51] *Shelley* v. *Kraemer*, 334 US 1 (1948).

often born when private rights and duties are presented to courts for ratification, and ratification would be inconsistent with the demands of reason.

Often the requirements of reason are imposed not by courts but by private ordering itself. Dominion mediates dominion. One owner's right not to suffer unreasonable interference with his use, or to exercise an easement, or to be made whole for reliance on a promise, acts as a limitation on the rights of another owner to use, to exclude, and to sell. The institutions and practices of private ordering that settle rights and duties also specify many of the boundaries of those rights and duties. In private law unreasonable actions often have legal consequences.

Just as there are good reasons to secure to owners freedom to exercise dominion over things for good ends, there are also reasons to allow owners to experience the consequences of being fully responsible for their actions. The fundamental injustice of the doctrine of coverture was to deny married women those opportunities. A "feme covert" could not exercise dominion over property because she could not enjoy or suffer the consequences of exercising the powers of ownership. She had no authority. Her husband was responsible in law for her conduct and choices.[52] Laws that abolished coverture were understood to secure the dignity and autonomy of the married woman both by shielding her assets from her husband's creditors and by making her responsible for her own decisions.[53]

The second point is often misunderstood. Abolition did not merely give married women equal rights to men, it also gave them equal responsibility, and therefore equal authority. While coverture shielded women from liability even when they acted dishonestly or imprudently,[54] abolition respected women by binding them to their failures and deceits; it gave women freedom to fail financially and morally. The Texas high court observed in 1851 that common law coverture deemed the married

[52] William Blackstone, *Commentaries on the Laws of England* (1769), vol. 1, *442–45; James Kent, *Commentaries on American Law* (New York: Halsted 1827), vol. 2, 109; Jesse Dukeminier et al., *Property* (6th edn, New York: Aspen 2006), 312; Richard H. Chused, "Married Women's Property Law: 1800–1850" (1983) 71 *Georgetown Law Journal* 1359 at 1361.

[53] *Sawada* v. *Endo*, 561 P 2d 1291 at 1295 (Hawaii 1977); Dukeminier, "Property," 312.

[54] *Foxworth* v. *Bullock*, 44 Miss 457, 1871 WL 3964 (1870); *Keen* v. *Hartman*, 48 Pa 497 (1865). Married women often hid behind coverture from the consequences of their choices and actions. *Corbett* v. *Poelnitz*, (1785) 99 Eng Rep 940 at 942 (KB); *Strong and Wife* v. *Waddell*, 56 Ala 471 (1876); *Heck* v. *Fisher*, 78 Ky 643 (1880); *Parker* v. *Kane*, 86 Mass 346 (1862); *Eckert* v. *Reuter*, 33 NJL 266 (New Jersey 1869).

woman, as a result of her marriage, "divested of her faculties as a rational being." With abolition of coverture, the married woman's "capacities, reason, and moral being were likewise resuscitated."[55] Abolition exposed married women to the legal consequences of their choices and actions, and thus treated them as fully human beings.

[55] *Jones* v. *Taylor*, 7 Tex 240, 1851 WL 4054 (1851), *5.

2

The architecture of property

Mediated dominion

Does property have an essential shape? If so, what does it look like? Where are its boundaries drawn? These questions are of obvious interest to scholars of law and property theory. But they have been largely neglected by people who think about economics, ethics, jurisprudence, and political philosophy, even though those people have a lot to say about property, or what they think property is. Their pictures of property often bear a resemblance to the real thing. But what those pictures omit is often significant.

For example, Blackstone's reference to property as an owner's "sole and despotic dominion"[1] is often mistaken for his description of property. But taken as a whole, the *Commentaries* reveal a much more sophisticated understanding of property law than this oft-quoted line suggests.[2] On the other extreme, the case *State* v. *Shack*[3] is thought to demonstrate that the right to exclude is not as robust as Blackstone supposes, and that the state has the power and obligation to shape property's dominion by eliminating or rejecting the absolute right claims of owners. But the case does not bear that weight. Two aid workers, Shack and Tejeras, visited a farm to counsel workers who lived there. The farmer initiated a criminal trespass action. The high court of New Jersey reversed the resulting conviction on the ground that the right to exclude does not include the right to exclude trespassers who are delivering government services to workers. Yet as the court and most commentators on the case failed to notice, Shack and Tejeras were not trespassers.

1 William Blackstone, *Commentaries on the Laws of England* (1769), vol. 2, *2.

2 See Carol M. Rose, "Canons of Property Talk, or Blackstone's Anxiety" (1998) 108 *Yale Law Journal* 601 at 603–06.

3 277 A 2d 369 (New Jersey 1971).

The case is often cited for its dictum that property rights "serve human values," are "recognized to that end, and are limited by it." That dictum has misled many into believing that the court justifiably imposed a new limitation on what would otherwise have been an unlimited right to exclude. The court did nothing of the sort, and its insistence that property rights can be reconfigured according to the superior judgment of courts unnecessarily jeopardized the integrity of property. The court neglected to notice that the farmer's right was already limited under existing common law doctrines to serve the human values at stake, i.e., to require admission of the worker's visitors. So limited, the exclusion right was absolute.

Thomas Merrill and Henry Smith have suggested that the workers were tenants who enjoyed a right to receive guests.[4] Adam Mossoff has argued that the employees might be viewed as licensees. Either way, Shack and Tejeras were justified to enter the farm under the delegated authority of the workers whom they were visiting. Property law has long recognized that a license to enter land implies a license for others whose presence is related to the work for which the license is granted. "To grasp this point," Mossoff illustrates, "no one would have given the New Jersey Supreme Court's decision any notice if it dismissed Shack's trespass lawsuit against pizza delivery men bringing lunch to the migrant farm workers toiling away on his farm."[5] It was not necessary to cast doubt on the security of property duties and rights; it would have been enough to understand what those duties and rights were.

The mangled reasoning of *Shack* could have been avoided had the New Jersey justices been as well instructed in property law as judges in Maine. When an egg farmer in Maine prevented aid workers and lawyers from visiting his employees, who resided in a mobile home park on his farm, the courts of Maine recognized that he enjoyed no right to exclude them. The employees were the farmer's tenants and, as part of their common law right of quiet enjoyment, had a right in reason to receive visitors.[6] The Maine courts found it unnecessary to set themselves up as arbiters of which property rights deserve enforcement because they avoided a simplistic caricature of property rights.

[4] Thomas W. Merrill and Henry E. Smith, *The Oxford Introductions to U.S. Law: Property* (New York: Oxford University Press 2010), 67.

[5] Adam Mossoff, "The False Promise of the Right to Exclude" (2011) 8 *Econ Journal Watch* 255 at 260.

[6] *State* v. *DeCoster*, 653 A 2d 891 at 893–94 (Maine 1995).

The core of property

The classical conception and its challengers

In the classical conception as portrayed by many scholars, property is primarily an individual right to a thing. Relations between persons and the practical reasonableness of their choices enter into consideration secondarily, if at all. But Blackstone's general idea of property as a dominion, "which one man claims and exercises over the external things of the world," should be severed from his rhetoric about despotic individualism. The common law institutions and doctrines that Blackstone described are far less individualistic and despotic than many suppose.

The disadvantages of Blackstone's simplistic aphorism were exploited by legal realists in the twentieth century, who found in Hohfeld's scheme of jural relations the tools with which to cast doubt on what they took to be the classical conception of property. Hohfeld described property as clusters or bundles of in personam rights.[7] James Penner points out that it is not proper on the Hohfeldian account to speak of a right or a duty in rem.[8] A right must be individuated and fully specified as a three-term relation involving a right-holder, a duty bearer, and the required action or omission.

In this disaggregation of property into its constituent jural relations, legal realists discovered political possibilities. They denied that property could have any essential nature. In the United States, their view became the standard understanding in the twentieth century.[9] Property rights came to be viewed as various, contingent, mutable, and determined by state action. In recent years, dissatisfaction with the realist bundle has grown. Careful observers have noted that many property norms *are* specified with respect to the thing. In fact the content of many (though

[7] Wesley Newcomb Hohfeld, *Fundamental Legal Conceptions as Applied in Judicial Reasoning* (New Haven: Yale University Press 1919).

[8] James Penner, "On the Very Idea of Transmissible Rights," in James Penner and Henry E. Smith (eds.), *Philosophical Foundations of Property Law* (New York: Oxford University Press 2013), 244 at 246.

[9] For a good history of the controversy, beginning with Blackstone, see Amnon Lehavi, "The Corporation as a Nexus of Property," 9–17, available at http://papers.ssrn.com/sol3/papers.cfm?abstract_id=2239619. See also J. E. Penner, *The Idea of Property in Law* (Oxford: Oxford University Press 1997), 24–26; Thomas W. Merrill and Henry E. Smith, "What Happened to Property in Law and Economics?" (2001) 111 *Yale Law Journal* 357 at 364–65; Adam Mossoff, "What Is Property? Putting the Pieces Back Together" (2003) 45 *Arizona Law Review* 371 at 372–74; Henry E. Smith, "Property Is Not Just a Bundle of Rights" (2011) 8 *Econ Journal Watch* 279 at 279–81.

not all) property norms is not personal in a Hohfeldian sense. A duty to self-exclude remains the same duty even if the ownership of Blackacre changes, and it is the same duty for all those who have no authority or permission to be there. Property rights are transmissible, and an estate or interest survives the act of transmission as a distinct phenomenon.

In short, the idea that the owner's dominion is solitary and despotic proved problematic, but so has the notion that property is merely a bundle of rights, which are contingent and which the state is free to alter at its discretion.[10] It should be noted here that the problem is not necessarily in Hohfeld, but rather in the legal realists' reduction of property to his analytical scheme. Property is more than merely the sum of the Hohfeldian right–duty relationships that give it shape. While Hohfeld's analytical precision is useful for distinguishing the various rights and duties that arise out of private property, it is far less helpful in understanding the phenomenon of property ownership as a whole; by itself it cannot supply an integrated conception of property.[11] Or, as James Penner and Henry Smith put it, "The bundle picture is a tool for analysis and clarification of subsidiary issues such as the difference between a right and a liberty, but as Hohfeld himself probably realized, a theory of pieces needs to be supplemented or embedded within a theory of wholes."[12]

Recently other models have emerged, developed by the so-called new essentialists.[13] Though they differ on the question of whether exclusion or use is property's primary concern,[14] the new essentialists agree that property has an essential nature. Property can be a unitary phenomenon while using different norms to inform different audiences, even as its

[10] See Thomas W. Merrill and Henry E. Smith, "Optimal Standardization in the Law of Property; The Numerus Clausus Principle" (2000) 110 *Yale Law Journal* 1; Eric R. Claeys, "Bundle-of-Sticks Notions in Legal and Economic Scholarship" (2011) 8 *Econ Journal Watch* 205 at 206; J. E. Penner, "Potentiality, Actuality, and 'Stick'-Theory" (2011) 8 *Econ Journal Watch* 274.

[11] J. W. Harris, *Property and Justice* (Oxford: Oxford University Press 1996), 119–38; Laura S. Underkuffler, *The Idea of Property: Its Meaning and Power* (New York: Oxford University Press 2003), 12.

[12] James Penner and Henry E. Smith, "Introduction," in James Penner and Henry E. Smith (eds.), *Philosophical Foundations of Property Law* (New York: Oxford University Press 2013), xv at xvii.

[13] A name given to Penner, Smith, Merrill, Katz, Claeys, and Mossoff by Lehavi, "Corporation as a Nexus," 13–17, perhaps based on Merrill's article, Thomas W. Merrill, "Property and the Right to Exclude" (1998) 77 *Nebraska Law Review* 730.

[14] See, e.g., Penner, *Idea of Property*, 24–26; Merrill and Smith, "What Happened?," 364–65; Mossoff, "Pieces Back Together," 372–74 (2003); Smith, "Not Just a Bundle," 279–81.

constituent jural relations change over time.[15] Property rights can be understood as rights to things, yet still govern relations between people.

The essentialist rehabilitation of property begins with the duty of self-exclusion. The in rem right to exclude correlates with the duty that non-owners have to exclude themselves from things they do not own. And this is settled and specified without any information about the actual owner. Penner has illustrated this by imagining a stroll through a car park, during which one's "practical duty is only capable of being understood as a duty which applies to the cars there, not to a series of owners." It matters not who owns any particular car, nor what the owner plans to do with it. "The content of my duty not to interfere is not structured in any way by the actual ownership relation of the cars' owners to their specific cars."[16]

In this account, the key to understanding property norms is to grasp that rights are conceptually posterior to duties of non-interference and self-exclusion. Property has its essential nature because we are all under the same general duties with respect to things that do not belong to us. Particular rights to prevent others from entering or taking – the right of an owner to erect fences, to enlist the police in ushering away trespassers, etc. – are derived as incidents of the general right of exclusion.

Many scholars continue to doubt that property has any essential structure. One need not embrace the political projects of legal realists to perceive merit in a Hohfeldian critique. There are reasons to deny that two-term right claims, such as A has a right to x, are rights in fact.[17] These are taken up in detail in Chapters 7 and 8, but one of them is particularly important in the present discussion. The essentialists' two-term specification of property rights creates a dilemma. If abstract, two-term property right statements are fully specified then they are absolute without reference to considerations of the common good – all the various reasons that people take into account when resolving questions of use. Exclusion by itself is not fully satisfying to one who seeks an answer to the basic question in practical reasoning, What is (not) to be done? The duty of self-exclusion does not answer this question for everyone or in every case.

[15] Thomas W. Merrill, "The Property Prism" (2011) 8 *Econ Journal Watch* 247; Penner, "Idea of Transmissibility," 251–52.

[16] Penner, *Idea of Property*, 75–76.

[17] See, e.g., the critiques of property in Grégoire C. N. Webber, *The Negotiable Constitution: On the Limitation of Rights* (Cambridge: Cambridge University Press 2009), 128–33, 143–44; and John Oberdiek, "Specifying Rights Out of Necessity" (2008) 28 *Oxford Journal of Legal Studies* 127.

Two-term right statements must be further specified as three-term statements of correlating rights and duties between persons with respect to things – e.g., B has a duty not to interfere with A's construction of x – before they can provide meaningful guidance within practical deliberation. This requires normative judgment to make property rights consistent with what practical reasonableness requires.

Yet this re-raises the possibility that property rights are only whatever lawmakers say they are, a possibility that threatens to disintegrate property and to leave it meaningless as a normative concept. I think that possibility is avoidable. This book ends with the argument that property rights and duties can be, and generally should be, settled and specified by institutions of private ordering. Private law norms need not be static or prematurely reified in order for private law to be autonomous from political action.[18] But, to understand that argument, we must first understand what property norms are and how they operate within practical reason.

The essentialist debate: exclusion or use

If property has an essence, then what is it? The new essentialists diverge on this question into roughly two groups. Penner, Smith, and Thomas Merrill have argued that the right to exclude is the core of property. In Penner's version of this exclusion thesis, "the right to property is a right to exclude others from things which is grounded by the interest we have in the use of things."[19] Merrill and Smith have developed a version of the exclusion thesis grounded in economic analysis of information costs. Property's core function, its exclusion strategy, "defines a chunk of the world – a thing – under the owner's control, and much of the information about the uses, their interactions, and the user are irrelevant to the outside world." People can therefore interact with property without acquiring personal information about the owner of each thing with which they interact. Exclusion is an efficient, first-cut solution to the problem of resolving use conflicts.[20]

[18] So, for example, considerations of public interest are irrelevant to resolution of a claim for trespass, though public law authorities properly consider them when specifying an owner's right. *Monsanto* v. *Tilly* [2000] Env. L.R. 313 at 340.

[19] Penner, *Idea of Property*, 71.

[20] Smith, "Not Just a Bundle," 282; Thomas W. Merrill and Henry E. Smith, "The Morality of Property" (2007) 48 *William & Mary Law Review* 1849.

The exclusion thesis is elegant. The duty to exclude oneself is simple. It is (largely) independent of context, conditions, and qualifications; it requires very little information to understand, assert, or obey; it can be stated abstractly; and it is easily universalizable. Even scholars who have viewed property as a bundle of rights have taken its core or essence to be the right to exclude.[21] And the US Supreme Court, which has often employed the bundle metaphor, has repeatedly asserted that exclusion is the most essential stick in the bundle.[22] Nevertheless, property is not reducible to exclusion. The exclusion thesis supplies a picture of property viewed from outside the owner's domain. But the exclusion strategy is less helpful from the perspectives of those within the domain of ownership, property owners – estate and interest holders, co-tenants, trustees, beneficiaries, licensees, bailees – and all who collaborate with them: family members, donees, business partners, and fellow venturers in other private and civic activities involving things. These people will want to know what they should (and should not) and may (and must not) do with things. The exclusion strategy gives them no guidance.

Other essentialists take the core of property to consist of exclusive use.[23] They observe that most of the work that property performs is done by usufructs and powers of alienability. Adam Mossoff notes that the uses and transactions of property are as varied as the "innovative ways by which people have created value in these assets," and the right to exclude therefore "does not solely define the nature or the scope of entitlements asserted by the parties against each other."[24] Use comes first. Exclusion is defined by the pre-existing entitlements of use.[25] This approach also leaves doubts. That most legal disputes concern use does not entail that use rights constitute the essence of property. For outsiders, exclusion

21 Morris R. Cohen, "Property and Sovereignty" (1928) 13 *Cornell Law Quarterly* 8 at 12.

22 *Kaiser Aetna* v. *United States*, 444 US 164 at 176 (1979); *Loretto* v. *Teleprompter Manhattan CATV Corporation*, 458 US 419 at 433 (1982); *Dolan* v. *City of Tigard*, 512 US 374 at 384 (1994).

23 Like the exclusion thesis, the exclusive use thesis was adumbrated by earlier scholars. "Enjoyment content, use, is the essence and the basis of all title, of all proprietary rights in our law. This brings it very near to the understanding and expectation of the common man, as it ought to be." Francis S. Philbrick, "Changing Conceptions of Property in Law" (1938) 86 *University of Pennsylvania Law Review* 691 at 701.

24 Adam Mossoff, "The False Promise of the Right to Exclude" (2011) 8 *Econ Journal Watch* 255, 259 [hereinafter *False Promise*].

25 Claeys, "Bundle-of-Sticks Notions," 210–11; Mossoff, "Pieces Back Together," 393–95; Larissa Katz, "Exclusion and Exclusivity in Property Law" (2008) 58 *University of Toronto Law Journal* 275; Eric Claeys, "Property 101: Is Property a Thing or a Bundle?" (2009) 32 *Seattle University Law Review* 617 at 631–34.

norms work much more effectively at governing interactions about things. And though most property *disputes* arise among right-holders, the vast majority of *interactions* concerning things occur between things and non-owners of things. Property norms are supposed to direct the reasoning of people who interact with property. The most successful strategies prevent legal disputes from ever occurring.

Nevertheless, use-essentialists are pointing to a function of property that must not be overlooked. Perhaps the exclusion thesis and the use thesis are describing different facets of the same thing. Penner described use and exclusion as opposite sides of the same coin; Smith used the image of a diamond. Property is a bundle of rights in the same way that a diamond is a collection of carbon atoms. Graphite and coal also consist of carbon atoms, but no one would mistake a lump of coal for a diamond.[26] Smith's oft-time collaborator, Thomas Merrill, uses the metaphor of a prism, which "takes on a different color from different angles."[27] Merrill adapts the prism image from scholars – particularly Henry Smith and Carol Rose – who have pointed out that property appears differently to different audiences. Different people are obliged to process different types of information about property, and their access to information about property will differ. Those under a duty to respect rights, those hoping to acquire rights, and those charged with enforcing rights confront different costs of acquiring information about the rights. Property law is attuned to those differences in sophisticated ways.[28]

It might be helpful to view property as a two-sided coin, a four-sided prism, an eighteen-faceted diamond, or something else. The point is that property can be viewed as having an essential structure and yet also be seen differently from the various perspectives of those who have reasons to take information about and norms of property into their deliberations. If so, then property's norms can be examined using the mechanism of a focal meaning or central case.[29] Some norms might seem more or less

[26] Smith, "Not Just a Bundle," 279.

[27] Merrill, "Property Prism," 247–51. Compare Hanoch Dagan, *Property: Values and Institutions* (Oxford: Oxford University Press 2011), which argues that property utilizes various standardized "institutions" to establish default rules for voluntary interactions with respect to things.

[28] Carol M. Rose, "Possession as the Origin of Property" (1985) 52 *University of Chicago Law Review* 73 at 78–80; Henry E. Smith, "The Language of Property: Form, Context, and Audience" (2003) 55 *Stanford Law Review* 1105.

[29] Concerning focal or central case method, see H. L. A. Hart, *The Concept of Law* (3rd edn, Oxford: Clarendon Press 2012), 13–17; John Finnis, *Natural Law and Natural Rights* (2nd edn, Oxford: Oxford University Press 2011) [hereinafter NLNR], 9–19.

central instances of "property" depending on where the observer is standing. It is not incorrect to speak of peripheral instances of property norms as property both for the reason that those norms are not entirely outside the sphere of property and because from a different perspective those norms might appear to be the most significant thing there is to know about property.

From an outside perspective, we might call the duty of self-exclusion the focal instance of a property norm. What makes a right or duty a *property* norm is that it is a right or duty with respect to a thing – in rem. Therefore, the most essential property norm is one that is fully specified with respect to a thing. On this criterion, the exclusion norm of property is the most focal, central, or essential. On either the duty side or the right side the exclusion norm performs all of its normative work when stated simply in two terms as a relation between a person and a thing – B has a duty to exclude himself from resource x; A has a right to exclude unspecified others from resource x. Unlike a liberty or power, which is merely prima facie and contingent until specified as a full and particular, three-term right–action–duty jural relation – A has a right to use this water for irrigation free of B's prior consumption – the right to exclude is most often conclusive in its abstract, two-term formulation – A's right to possess exclusively x (against everyone almost without exception).

This does not entail that exclusion is the most *fundamental* property norm. Property norms are not all reducible to those that are most fully specified in rem, and in rem norms are not fully reducible to each other. Not even the right to exclude and the duty of self-exclusion are fully reducible to each other. The duty instructs outsiders in the morally upright conduct of respecting value in the use and management of things, apart from any distribution or specification of rights. This can be seen through an illustration of Penner's, which eliminates the right to exclude yet leaves the duty of self-exclusion in place. Penner imagines "a bird laboriously constructing a nest over the course of several hours." One encountering this creative act has "a reason . . . to forbear from smashing the nest just for the hell of it. A child who did so would quite properly be scolded."[30] We need not ascribe to birds the status of right-holders, or the human capacity to plan for reasons, in order to see that one has a moral duty to exclude oneself from the nest. It is a moral duty because one acts wrongly by thwarting creative and productive acts for no reason. After all, one can owe moral duties to oneself and to one's community.

[30] Penner, "Idea of Transmissibility," 244–71.

The duty takes on a different dimension when it correlates with the right of a human being, whether that human being is the fee simple owner who enjoys the right of exclusive possession or is a licensee, bailee, or other holder of an interest in the use and management of the thing. In such cases the duty finds independent grounding in equal respect for human beings as agents of practical reason. Human beings are unique beings in our radical capacity to make and execute plans for reasons. This radical capacity gives rise to many prima facie, and some exclusionary, reasons for others not to thwart its exercise. Indeed, some of those reasons are absolute and conclusive, such as the duty not to enslave.

So, from the right side of the right–duty correlation, the norm of exclusion is grounded in respect for human beings who have authority over things (as fee simple owners, co-owners, families of owners, licensees, bailees, and so on) and are agents of practical reason, beings capable of making plans for reasons. This status requires others to respect the plans and potential plans of those agents, which requires the duty of self-exclusion, which in turn gives rise to and correlates with the right to exclude, specified as a claim-right against all who would trespass or take. The duty to exclude oneself can therefore arise out of either of two principles. I owe it to myself and my community to exclude myself from things I do not own. Thus, the duty of self-exclusion pertains even in Communist nations. More profoundly, I owe it to owners to respect their right to exclude me from things that they do own, and for which they have authority to make plans. The source of the duty affects the content of the correlative right.

Because different duties of exclusion are grounded in different reasons, exclusion is not a unitary phenomenon in law. The strength of the duty varies according to the authority of the possessor to make plans for the thing. So a licensee has no right to exclude, even if the license is exclusive.[31] The holder of an artificer's lien (a mechanic's lien in the United States) who performed repair work on a vehicle has a right to exclude everyone, including the owner, but only for a limited purpose.[32] His interest in the vehicle is merely an interest in receiving payment for services performed on it, and his right to possess the vehicle exclusively is terminated upon payment. A bailee who takes custody of the thing for some purpose has a contingent right to exclude, which is categorical as against everyone except the bailor, against whom the bailee has no

[31] *Moore* v. *MacMillan* [1977] 2 NZLR 81; *Hill* v. *Tupper* [1863] 2 H & C 121, 159 All ER 51.
[32] *Tappenden* v. *Artus* [1964] 2 QB 185 [1963] 3 All ER 213.

exclusion right at all, though third parties cannot assert the bailor's rights against the bailee.[33] Co-tenants in a concurrent estate have no right to exclude each other.[34] Only the fee simple owner, who has full authority to make plans for the thing, has an exclusion right good against the world. And even that right is limited by doctrines of private and public necessity, custom, implied easements, and profits.[35]

From the internal perspective of those with some authority to use, the most salient or important norm is one governing use. Use norms are fully specified in particular contexts by agents and institutions that mediate conflicts between domains of ownership. Thus, Mossoff and Eric Claeys have argued that property consists essentially of exclusive use, and that exclusion does not by itself supply property's normative content.[36] Here one must resist the temptation to conflate questions concerning the norms of property – the presumptions and settlements that guide deliberation; their nature, operation, force, and limits – with questions concerning the authority of property, meaning which moral agents and institutions settle and specify property's norms. The importance of authority questions appears in the scholarship of Larissa Katz, who considers property's exclusion strategy as a way of affirming or protecting the authority of the owner to set the agenda for use of the owned thing.[37] From this perspective, authority is the most essential feature of property.

Authority's independent salience is illustrated by the English case *Carter* v. *Thomas*.[38] A fire broke out in a residence and the local fire brigade, constituted by a local board under the authority of the Public Health Act 1875, responded to suppress the blaze. Thomas, a uniformed member of the brigade, was charged with preventing entry to the premises while the brigade fought the fire. Carter was a uniformed member of a private fire brigade supported by volunteer contributions and donations from insurance companies. He tried to gain entry to fight the fire and was thwarted by Thomas, whom he then pushed aside. His conviction for assault on Thomas was affirmed by Queen's Bench

[33] *The Winkfield* [1902] P 42 [1902] All ER 346.

[34] *Soubliere* v. *MacDonald* [2011] NSJ No. 133 at *21–*23 (Nova Scotia); and generally, Thomas W. Merrill and Henry E. Smith, *The Oxford Introductions to U.S. Law: Property* (New York: Oxford University Press 2010), 114–15.

[35] See IV.C.1 and VII.B.1, and VII.C.2 below.

[36] Claeys, "A Thing or a Bundle?"; Mossoff, "Pieces Back Together."

[37] Katz, "Exclusion and Exclusivity."

[38] [1893] Q.B. 673.

Division on the ground that Thomas had authority to exclude him, either under the power of the statute or by consent of the owner.

Whether or not Carter had a right to be on the premises depended entirely on whether Thomas had authority to exclude him. Both Carter and Thomas were attempting to avert the same harms and to promote the same human goods. Both could invoke the doctrine of public necessity as justification for their entry, so that neither would be liable to the owner for trespass. No evidence appeared that the public fire brigade was more effective at fighting fires than the private one. Yet Thomas was right and Carter was wrong because Thomas acted on authority delegated to him by either the owner, who exercises the right to exclude, or the public, for whose benefit entry for public necessity is recognized in law. Carter could claim neither.

Particularly if "owner" is understood in individualistic terms (a presupposition that Chapter 3 challenges) then it is tempting to conflate the owner's authority with the owner's rights or individual interests. It is generally assumed that whoever has authority will act to promote his, her, or its own interests. So accounts that suppose exclusion and governance to be the rivalrous norms in property *tend also* to suppose two, rivalrous domains of authority – the individual owner, who exercises exclusion for self-interested motivations, and the state acting on behalf of the political community, which governs for the public good. The dichotomy between exclusion and governance tends to map over the dichotomy between the individual and the collective.[39]

One objective of this book is to challenge both of those dichotomies. The perfectionist account defended here supposes that the good is a truly common good, potentially shared by all but also various, plural, and incommensurable in its basic forms. The goods that present reasons for action to the agent engaged in practical reasoning about what (not) to do are not merely individual preferences, nor are they collective, net-best-good states of affairs. And the norms of property that arise out of those agents' judgments are irreducibly complex. The prohibition against owning human beings is not reducible to the duty to feed one's children, which is not reducible to the duty not to take a co-worker's nice car without permission, which is not reducible to the duty not to destroy one's neighbor's business out of spite.

It is not accidental that this account of norms supports a pluralist account of authority. Authority rests not only, nor even primarily, in

[39] See the summary of the literature in Underkuffler, *Meaning and Power*, 65–74.

individuals or political institutions but rather in plural and intermediary human communities – the family, the university, religious assemblies and institutions, charitable groups, business and professional associations, etc. – which have unique and irreducible roles to play in promoting truly common goods and personal responsibility. An important implication of this account is that the functions of institutions and agents of property are not reducible to each other. The state cannot do the job of the individual, who cannot do the job of the family, which cannot do the job of the commercial market, which cannot do the job of the religious assembly.

That property has no most-fundamental essence does not entail, as Stephen Munzer supposes, that property norms are entirely historically contingent. The basic values and requirements of reason are universal, though they are specified differently in different cultural contexts. Nor does it entail that property rights are dependent for their existence on the forbearance of the state.[40] Duties, and therefore rights, are settled by, and operate within, the practical reasoning of all moral agents. So, before they arise from governments they arise first out of reasoned judgments. Indeed, governments are themselves subject to duties that impede them from altering property norms at will.

Common law institutions shaping property

Shaping mediated dominion: common law institutions

Property as mediated dominion is consistent with the common law conception of property. Exactly what the common law was or is remains a matter of some controversy.[41] In a narrow, historical sense it is of course the customary law of England. But its spread throughout the reaches of the former British empire has complicated its nature. For

[40] Contrast Stephen R. Munzer, "Property and Disagreement" in James Penner and Henry E. Smith (eds.), *Philosophical Foundations of Property Law* (New York: Oxford University Press 2013), 289–319.

[41] See Walter Ullmann, *Principles of Government and Politics in the Middle Ages* (London: Methuen 1961), 18–26; Paul O. Carrese, "Common Law" in Mark Bevir (ed.), *Sage Encyclopedia of Political Theory* (2010), and the "Further Readings" cited therein. If a working definition is helpful, Arthur Hogue's definition will suffice with one modification: a body of general rules created by customs, prescribing social conduct, enforced by courts, "characterized by the development of its own principles in actual legal controversies, by the procedure of trial by jury, and by the doctrine of the supremacy of law." Arthur R. Hogue, *Origins of the Common Law* (Bloomington: Indiana University Press 1966), 190.

brevity, emphasis is here given to two misunderstood features of common law, one normative and the other institutional.

Normatively, the common law is not merely a body of rules. Unlike code-based systems of law, the common law finds standards of judgment not in posited rules but rather in prior judgments. As Tocqueville noted, "The English or American lawyer seeks out what has been done before, whereas the French lawyer inquires what he ought to do; the former looks for judgments, the latter, reasons."[42] By contrast to codes and regulations, the moral judgments rendered in common law courts are open-ended. They do not foreclose adaptation in future cases or in different local communities to account for circumstances that are unforeseen at the time of judgment. The common law brooks no abstract theory of justice that fails to respect "experience and . . . the complex multiplicity of human goods."[43]

Gerald Postema has explained, "The law, as common lawyers conceived of it, was not a structured set of authoritatively posited, explicit directives, but of rules and ways implicit in a body of practices and patterns of practical thinking 'handed down by tradition, use, and experience'."[44] In particular, that subset of common law concerned with private interactions and disputes is both constrained by moral principles and open-ended as to particular practical judgments. Ernest Weinrib has described private law as "a set of concepts, a distinctive institutional setting, and a characteristic mode of reasoning."[45] Private law is thus "both an object and a mode of understanding."[46]

Many of the rules to be derived from the general principles and maxims of property law are somewhat indeterminate until specified in particular cases. In defining the nature and contours of property rights, the common law has mediated a "tussle" between two maxims: so use your own property as not to injure your neighbor's, and loss befalls a person without any legal wrong being done.[47] These norms, being

[42] Alexis de Tocqueville, *Democracy in America*, Gerald E. Bevan (trans.) (New York: Penguin 2003), 311.

[43] James R. Stoner, *Common-Law Liberty: Rethinking American Constitutionalism* (Lawrence: University Press of Kansas 2003), 6.

[44] Gerald J. Postema, "Classical Common Law Jurisprudence (Part I)" (2002) 2 *Oxford University Commonwealth Law Journal* 155 at 167, quoting Blackstone, *Commentaries*, vol. 1, 68.

[45] Ernest Weinrib, *The Idea of Private Law* (Oxford: Oxford University Press 2012), 5.

[46] Weinrib, *Idea of Private Law*, 14.

[47] Michael Taggart, *Private Property and Abuse of Rights in Victorian England* (Oxford: Oxford University Press 2002), 144.

abstract and often potentially conflicting, require jurists and juries to give them determinacy in particular cases. After the Cromwellian and Glorious Revolutions in England, the common law came to embrace an additional principle of liberty, particularly from state interference, even as it retained its commitment to the norms of reason.[48]

The common law mind is supposed to be grounded in practical reason. As Hogue argued, "The doctrine of *stare decisis* assumes that court decisions have been reasonable, that what was reasonable in one century may be reasonable in another."[49] Reason persists in law even as political institutions rise and fall, technology changes, and social structures and practices are set aside. For Hogue, "The important word here is *reasonable*. Ever since the Roman law spread through the Mediterranean world, European legal systems have made much of the reasonableness of law."[50]

Institutionally, common law doctrines have grown organically within customary practices and plural institutions of private ordering. Many of the reasoned norms of the common law arose out of property relations. Property laws were developed earliest in the common law,[51] and the early common law was largely the law of property rights and services.[52] The common law incorporates the reasoned judgments of the community's members about the best ways to allocate and manage resources. From allocation of water right to development of land, property law has long allowed private actors to take a first cut at specifying the rights and duties that pertain between people with respect to things, subject to the numerus clausus principle,[53] the rule against perpetuities, and other bright-line constraints imposed as determinations of positive law.

Both general and particular customs have given property law much of its shape.[54] The historical importance of custom need not foreclose understanding unwritten common law as law. Customary law can be

48 Richard Pipes, *Property and Freedom* (New York: Vintage Books 1999), 30–38, 146–51. See, generally, Paul O. Carrese, *The Cloaking of Power: Montesquieu, Blackstone, and the Rise of Judicial Activism* (Chicago: University of Chicago Press 2003); Stoner, *Common-Law Liberty*; James R. Stoner, Jr., *Common Law and Liberal Theory: Coke, Hobbes, and the Origins of American Constitutionalism* (Lawrence: University Press of Kansas 1992).

49 Hogue, *Origins*, 9.

50 Hogue, *Origins*, 9.

51 Ullmann, *Principles of Government*, 166–67.

52 Hogue, *Origins*, 112.

53 See Thomas W. Merrill and Henry E. Smith, *The Oxford Introductions to U.S. Law: Property* (New York: Oxford University Press 2010), 108–09.

54 Blackstone, *Commentaries*, vol. 1, 63–92; Hogue, *Origins*, 188–200. "Indeed," Hogue summarized, "the body of English customs, general and particular, which have obtained the force of law is so large that no one would seriously endeavor to prepare an exhaustive collection." Hogue, *Origins*, 195.

conceived as law that is promulgated by actions, analogous to promulgation by language.[55] It is formalized, specified, and declared (or not) as rules in legal disputes between private citizens who hire their own attorneys, determine their own claims and theories, and submit their disputes to juries for resolution. So, the common law is not best (and has not always been) understood to be judge-made law. It was long thought to be declared by those who were knowledgeable of the customs of the place, especially juries, within the boundaries of reason patrolled by judges.[56] In Joseph Story's view the common law's customs, usages, and maxims are actually grounded in "immemorial practice" and only recognized, not made, by judges.[57]

Custom has been a vehicle for practical reason to enter property law because customs are private coordinating devices chosen and shaped by those who have the most knowledge about the affairs that the custom is supposed to govern. So it remains reasonable, at least prima facie, for courts to defer to customs and even to adopt as rules those customs which the parties themselves have adopted, though other reasons might counsel against adoption in particular cases. A custom permitting hunters to enter unenclosed and uncultivated land, universally exercised and never contested from the time of a state's settlement, reflects the settled judgment of the community that hunting the forests as a common resource best serves the common good.[58] A custom under which a whaler obtains legal possession by fixing his lance in a whale can contravene the general rule that requires corporeal possession in order to obtain title because it is the best solution to a particular practical problem – how to secure a fin-back whale, which sinks when lanced but generally floats or washes ashore some days after it dies.[59]

The jury also has played an important institutional role. While the judge holds forth the norm (e.g., against waste), the jury is the instrument of practical judgment, which brings the common sense of the

[55] See David VanDrunen, "Natural Law, Custom, and Common Law in the Theology of Aquinas and Calvin" (2000) 33 *University of British Columbia Law Review* 699; Henry E. Smith, "Community and Custom in Property" (2009) 10 *Theoretical Inquiries in Law* 5 at 8.

[56] Hogue, *Origins*, 9–10.

[57] Stoner, *Common-Law Liberty*, 21–25. The common law judge, in this view, studies the common law as a practical science, "allowing his mind to be formed according to its mold, making its many rules and principles his own, bringing it to life in the exercise of judgment."

[58] *McConico* v. *Singleton*, 2 Mill Const 244 (SC Const Ct 1818).

[59] *Ghen* v. *Rich*, 8 F 159 (D Mass 1881).

community[60] to bear on the question (whether a particular life tenant has committed waste by consuming more than what is reasonably necessary for her enjoyment and the maintenance of her tenancy). Of course, the division of labor is not absolute; each source of judgment influences the other. The jury is instructed by the judge; the judge finds common law norms within precedents, statutes, the verdicts of juries, and local customs.

The normative and institutional features come together in the observation that practical judgment is performed by all members of political communities, not just judges and legislators. James Stoner argues that "both customary law and jury verdict might be said to register the understanding of justice in the common mind." The common law's emphasis on settled agreement reflects what Stoner has called the common law's "presumption of or aspiration to social consensus."[61]

Another important institution is communal ownership. Individual ownership is neither the only, nor even the most common, instance of private property in the common law. Common law institutions of property ownership employ plural domains of private ownership, which allow not only individuals but also families, religious associations, nonprofit ventures, family businesses, and many other associations and institutions to act cooperatively for a common good within property domains, and to constitute themselves as communities by creating new reasons for action free of outside interference. Within domains of private ownership individual members of the group take others' plans of action into their deliberations as reasons for their own choices and action. Of course, authority within those communities can be abused. But then again, so can the powers of the state, with much greater and more far-reaching consequences.

The common law estates had their origins in the communal aspects of civic life in England and preceded the notion of a state. The derivation of the feudal term "estate" from the Latin word *status* "speaks to us of a time when landholding was inseparably connected with a man's political and personal status in the community."[62] As changing economic realities have given rise to new forms of ownership, such as the corporation, the possibility of communal self-constitution is enhanced. Anyone who has worked in a well-functioning family business has experienced the

[60] See Postema, "Classical Common Law," 163–64; Stoner, *Common-Law Liberty*, 93–94.

[61] Stoner, *Common-Law Liberty*, 12.

[62] Sheldon F. Kurtz, *Moynihan's Introduction to the Law of Real Property* (5th edn, St. Paul: West 2011), 33.

reflexive nature of group action coordinated toward a worthwhile, common goal.[63] Members of the business deliberate and choose how to employ the resources available to them in order to produce services and goods that would not have existed but for their coordinated action. The group's standing plan of action, and all of the subplans of which it is constituted, become reasons for the actions of the group's members. The members' practical reasonableness is constituted in varying degrees by the worthwhile plans of the group, which supply meaning to the work and encourage responsibility.

The efficacy of the family business for promoting practical reasonableness suggests why some aspects of capitalist systems of finance have struck thoughtful scholars as parasitic on, rather than natural components of, domains of private ownership.[64] The more fragmented ownership becomes, as for example in a publicly traded company, the less the norms of private property can be understood to stand guard around a project of communal self-constitution. Those interest-holders who contribute to the venture hoping only for a financial return on their investment are making a helpful contribution to the company's plans of action, but they are invested only in its financial success. They do not take the company's plans into their own choices and actions; the plans of the group are of only instrumental value for pecuniary gain. Of course, many investors choose a company based on its values and the consonance of its business plan with their own values and moral convictions. And we might consider those investments as being morally different from investment through, for example, a mutual fund.

Less sympathetic is the short-seller, who pledges to purchase shares (and thus relies on property norms) in the hope that the company's fortunes will falter. The intuition of disapprobation that many people share about this investor can be understood by reference to his practical reason. He is acting on the hope that things will go badly for the company, its employees, and its shareholders, all while profiting from

[63] From age 13 until age 22, the author worked during school breaks as a farmhand for a family (not his own) that grew and sold at retail fruits and vegetables in Cape Elizabeth, Maine.

[64] Richard Weaver argued that "the abstract property of stocks and bonds, the legal ownership of enterprises never seen," is a "violation of the very notion of *proprietas*." Richard M. Weaver, *Ideas Have Consequences* (Chicago: University of Chicago Press 1948), 132. Capital stock finance mechanisms, Weaver argued, "actually destroy the connection between man and his substance, without which metaphysical right becomes meaningless," and destroy the connection between one's products and one's personal reputation and honor. Weaver, *Ideas Have Consequences*, 132–33, 141.

the legal protections accorded to owners. The success of his project depends on both the failure of the company to achieve its goals and the security of title to the shares that he has promised to purchase.

Are common law institutions necessary?

Is mediated dominion the only property scheme capable of meeting the demands of practical reason? Are there alternatives? Communism is theoretically justifiable. But in practice outright communism can be justified only in a community that is sufficiently single-minded to be committed to a unitary goal and means of achieving that goal, where the members of the community form a joint plan of action. In such a community, actions of one member will be actions of the community. And the community will constitute itself by an act of group agency in accordance with the plan.

In such an idyllic community, any resources used by members of that community in acting on the plan will be used by the community itself, for the constitution of the community's agency and goals. This happens often within families. It happens occasionally in voluntary associations and even within some small political communities, such as business or nonprofit corporations. But this state of affairs seldom lasts forever, and it is almost inconceivable that it could be found in a state as a whole.

Another alternative is a scheme of absolute, individual property rights reified at the time of first appropriation. But such a scheme would fail to satisfy the political community's moral obligation to establish reasonable property institutions because it would fail to account for the ways in which owners act unreasonably. A just institution of property ownership must respond to both the demand of freedom to deliberate and choose *and* the need for moral norms to mediate between citizens with respect to the use and management of things. These two demands will often come into conflict with each other. But people tend to intuit that both demands are important.

This book argues that the estates and rights of ownership that arose in the common law tradition meet the basic need that humans have to develop into practically reasonable human beings. The mediated dominions of private ownership in the common law meet the moral needs of human beings better than the known alternatives. And political communities thus have principled reasons for maintaining them.

Specifying the shape of mediated dominion

Shaping property law

The norms of property, like norms generally, are settled and specified in human communities. They can exist apart from political institutions. Neil MacCormick argued "that we humans are norm-users before we are norm-creators, or legislators. If so, it follows that our sense of duty and obligation to each other is and has to be prior to any authoritative imposition of rules upon us. Were it not so, civil institutions could never have developed."[65] Yet given the plurality of human projects, the ambiguities of language, and the intellectual and moral failures of human beings, property norms, like so many other norms, often require authority to specify and enforce. In order to coordinate the actions of the community's members, those in authority over the community must sometimes choose between two or more rational possibilities.[66] Should unvested contingent remainders be permitted to persist for the duration of a life in being at the time of the creation of the interest plus twenty-one years or should they be terminated if not vested within ninety years? The rule against perpetuities could reasonably take either form, and indeed it has taken both forms in different places and at different times. Someone must decide.[67]

Yet authorities must not choose norms arbitrarily. Because different moral agents – different individuals and groups – come to interact with things in different ways – for different reasons, in different positions of authority – the norms of property must vary. Those who interact with property need guidance, and that guidance must meet the requirements of practical reason.

External norms: dominion

Self-exclusion (theft, trespass, necessity)

Property law shows its most forceful, categorical norms to those who have no ongoing relation to the thing and no permission from those who do. The duties of non-owners to exclude themselves shape much of the owner's dominion by insulating the owner's deliberations from outside scrutiny. It rules out of consideration the questions whether the owner is

[65] Neil MacCormick, *Practical Reason in Law and Morality* (Oxford: Oxford University Press 2008), 29.

[66] Webber, *Negotiable Constitution*, 135–38.

[67] NLNR, chapter 9.

making the best use of the thing, and whether someone else might make a better use. That doctrines prohibiting unlawful entry are aimed at the *practical deliberations* of non-owners is illustrated by the common law rule that a non-intentional, non-negligent entry does not give rise to liability.[68] Forbidden is the *knowing* that one has no right and nevertheless choosing to enter.

The owner's rights, which correlate to the duties of outsiders to exclude themselves, do not *require* the owner to exclude anyone. The owner is free to waive his rights, to license entry, even to relinquish his rights altogether for the good of another. Because humans are social creatures, all of these practices are commonplace. Yet in each case, we recognize the social practice by reference to the baseline of self-exclusion. A gift, for example, is generous and admirable precisely because it alters the legal obligations of donee, who would otherwise be under a duty to exclude himself from enjoyment of the thing. In all of these choices and actions, the owner and her collaborators are free to specify rights and duties in the thing because the law stands ready to enforce their right to exclude.

The duty to self-exclude is robust but not absolute. It does not entail that I have a duty not to look at or admire my neighbor's lawn. I might even have no duty of self-exclusion if entering my neighbor's land is the only way – a necessity in legal terms – to save a human life, say of a child drowning in a swimming pool in the owner's yard. Other doctrines further limit the owner's dominion with greater particularity. These are taken up in greater detail in the following chapters.

No unreasonable interference (nuisance, waste)

By contrast to the right to exclude, usufructs are highly contingent norms, which cannot be fully specified as rights except within the context of particular cases. Common law doctrines prohibiting nuisance and waste, among other specifications of the maxim "Sic utere tuo ut alienum non laedas,"[69] perform much of the work in that process of specification. These are sometimes thought to be in tension with the categorical norms of property. The duty not to interfere unreasonably with another's use of property limits an owner's freedom of action and thus, in the abstract, might seem to be inconsistent with the idea of owners' dominion. But this tension is only apparent.

[68] Restatement (Second) of Torts §166 (1965).
[69] "So use your own property as not to injure another's."

The apparent inconsistency dissolves when we note that owners are also non-owners, and that nuisance law generates duties that pertain not to ownership but to *non*-ownership. Nuisance doctrine subjects A, who owns Blackacre but not Whiteacre, to the duty not to interfere unreasonably in the use of Whiteacre by those who are lawfully using it. The common law governs the practical deliberations of A in his capacity as a non-owner of Whiteacre.

Of course, non-owners are in many instances also owners. Though A has a duty not to interfere with the use of Whiteacre, he also has "rights" to use Blackacre, meaning a basic liberty to do so. And by exercising his liberty to use Blackacre, A may generate externalities that adversely affect Whiteacre. But as we will see, A's liberty to use Blackacre is not really a right in the central sense of a conclusive, exclusionary reason for action. Without an authoritative pronouncement that A's particular use of Blackacre is reasonable in the circumstances, we cannot say whether he has a right to make that use.

As later chapters will show, reasonableness in these cases is determined with reference to moral, as well as economic, considerations. Ronald Coase famously portrayed the problem of harm to property as a reciprocal problem that is morally neutral and resolvable on economic grounds. On Coase's view it is a mistake to pre-judge who is causing unreasonable harm to whom. To be restrained from harming B is for A to suffer the harm of not being able to make the use that he would make but for B's objection. The question is therefore not whether A has a right to make his desired use, but rather whether the law will permit A to harm B or instead permit B to harm A by avoiding harm to himself.[70]

Eric Claeys has identified the disquieting element in Coase's portrait. Coase's theorem assumes that "A and B's 'rights' refer to incompatible and reciprocal permissions to engage in two particular conflicting uses." But in practical reasoning the ideas of causation and harm are not reciprocal in this way. Claeys posits, "Assume that B injures A while successfully repelling A's attempt to hold him up. In Coase's framework, the injuries B inflicts on A are reciprocal negative externalities on A's desire for money from B. In common sense, this portrait is grotesque."[71] What makes the portrait grotesque is that it elides a basic moral distinction, which is grounded in requirements of practical reason.[72]

70 Ronald H. Coase, "The Problem of Social Cost" (1960) 3 *Journal of Law & Economics* 1.

71 Claeys, "Bundle-of-Sticks Notions," 208.

72 Richard Epstein argues that the problem lies with interpreters of Coase who have failed to notice how property establishes baseline rights. Richard A. Epstein, *Takings: Private*

The common law nuisance doctrine authorizes judges and juries to specify property rights and duties by reference to the reasonableness of the uses.[73] Other doctrines also employ reasonableness standards, including waste, necessity, and riparian water consumption. Reasonableness tests within these doctrines raise a fact question, which is context-dependent. It takes in all of the factors that owners should take into their practical deliberations about uses of their property consistent with equal concern for the interests and rights of others. In such cases the law is quite transparent for the underlying first-order considerations. This is why these questions are best left to that ancient institution of practical deliberation and moral judgment: the jury.

So, the justificatory priority begins with basic requirements of practical reasonableness, which prohibit: causing harm for no reason, arbitrarily preferring oneself over another human being, arbitrarily disregarding goods that others value more, and failure to favor the common good of one's community. These basic moral norms are summed up in maxims and the jury charge to pick out those uses of property that cause unreasonable harm. A judgment that a use causes unreasonable harm establishes a three-term jural relation between two persons with respect to an action – A has a duty not to operate a brick kiln next to B's residence. That duty simultaneously specifies the limits of A's usufruct and secures B's liberty. The right is the conclusion of practical judgment not its first premise. But it rests on a judgment about what is right or wrong to do.

The American Law Institute missed all this. The drafters of the Restatement would require the adjudicator to balance the "gravity of the harm" against the "utility of the actor's conduct."[74] This rule neither restates nor improves upon the common law approach. For one thing, it makes the reasonableness inquiry unworkable, except where the case boils down to purely economic factors that can be reduced to a common currency. More fundamentally, practical reasonableness drops out. An owner who is making an economically valuable but practically unreasonable use of his property prevails over the harmed owner who is making a

Property and the Power of Eminent Domain (Cambridge: Harvard University Press 1985), 116–21. He has elsewhere defended the idea of baseline rights on consequentialist grounds. Richard A. Epstein, "Causation – In Context: An Afterword" (1987) 63 *Chicago Kent Law Review* 653 at 654.

[73] Thomas W. Merrill, and Henry E. Smith, *The Oxford Introductions to U.S. Law: Property* (New York: Oxford University Press 2010), 192–200; Stoner, *Common-Law Liberty*, 128, 146–47.

[74] Restatement of the Law (Second) Torts §826 (1979).

use that the market does not value as much. Perhaps this is why courts have generally ignored the Restatement rule.[75]

Internal norms

Freedom: liberties

Perhaps the most difficult norm of all to understand is the most important for shaping deliberation and judgment within the domain of property. That is the liberty. The liberty is not a norm of law. It is the absence of law. In fact, it is the absence of binding reasons for action. One is at liberty when one has no relevant duties to others and others have no relevant duties to one. A liberty is a great, wide-open space within legal reasoning. Perhaps that is why it receives so little attention from lawyers and jurisprudents.[76] The lack of attention is regrettable. Liberty is an indispensable aspect of dominion and a necessary precondition to the exercise of self-constituting choice and action.

Though liberties do not themselves correlate with duties, they are bounded by duties of non-interference. The clearest case is the liberty enjoyed within a fee simple absolute, the largest quantum of ownership, which, before duties are imposed on the owner, puts the owner at liberty to make any use she chooses to make. But liberties also arise out of more limited ownership interests. Consider a hypothetical case posited by Eric Claeys. "If A has a right of access to fish, B has a profit to pick apples, and C retains all other general control over and use of a lot of land, a lawyer can predict when each may exclude the others or strangers from interfering with their uses."[77] In this case, A's easement and B's profit authorize A and B to take actions in reliance on C's obligation not to interfere. They confer authority to alter others' rights. But silently and invisibly from the perspective of law, they also *liberate* A, B, and C. They open new possibilities for A and B, enriching their practical deliberations. The rights require nothing of A and B – there is no obligation to exercise an easement or a profit – but rather create new possible worlds; they enable A, B, and C to develop and adhere to plans of action and thereby to make new, binding reasons for themselves.

[75] Merrill and Smith, *Oxford Introductions: Property*, 194.

[76] But see Simon Douglas and Ben McFarlane, "Defining Property Rights" in James Penner and Henry E. Smith (eds.), *Philosophical Foundations of Property Law* (New York: Oxford University Press 2013).

[77] Claeys, "Bundle-of-Sticks Notions," 211.

Powers

As the last example also shows, much of the moral work in property law is done by powers of ownership.[78] Unlike regulations and other rules that impose duties on owners, powers of ownership do not coerce. Rather, in the words of J. E. Penner, powers "guide the choice of the agent by organizing the effects that actions will have so that one may achieve a particular result."[79] Powers are effective both to enable and to constrain the deliberations and choices of owners and those with whom owners cooperate. Powers work together with other use rights both to make freedom of action possible and to delimit the scope of the actor's freedom. And because powers can be severed from the rights to exclude and from each other, they make it possible to include a number of different people within the dominion of ownership without fragmenting control.[80]

In service to pre-moral choosing, powers clarify the scope of an interested party's freedom of action by signaling what outcomes of the considered action will be affirmed by law. By authorizing actions toward which owners have natural inclinations, powers can subtly shape the deliberations and choices of owners. For example, the powers to bequeath and devise reinforce the natural human inclinations to care for one's family, and to give charitable gifts. To devise one's property to a university or to one's orphaned nephew is very much a choice. But it is a choice enabled by law's readiness to enforce it. Powers are thus particularly well-suited to nurture practical reasonableness without destroying it.

Also, by not authorizing certain actions, powers can to some extent deflect unreasonable actions. If an owner knows that he enjoys no power to take an action that he is inclined to take, that awareness will enter his deliberations and can be expected to weigh against his choice of that action. And some decisions will be rendered completely ineffectual if the owner does not enjoy the power to execute them. An unfaithful husband who owns real estate with his wife in a tenancy by the entirety is constrained in his ability to cause his wife material harm. The tenancy by the entirety does not include the power to devise his interest to a third party, or to encumber his wife's right of survivorship. The shape of the estate thus thwarts the husband from subsidizing his mistress at the expense of his wife.

[78] Penner, *Idea of Property*, 30–31; Merrill and Smith, *Oxford Introductions: Property*, 84–94.

[79] Penner, *Idea of Property*, 17.

[80] F. H. Lawson and Bernard Rudden, *The Law of Property* (Oxford: Clarendon Press 1982), 100–01.

Of the mechanisms that the common law developed for promoting practical reasonableness, none is more ingenious than the powers enabling charitable action. As discussed in Chapter 5, the law of donative transfers contains a number of rules designed to enable owners to make the well-being of others their own reasons for action. Some of those rules cannot be explained except as supports for practical reasonableness. For example, if a donor conditions his gift on the donee not getting married then the restriction is invalid, unless the "dominant motive" of the donor was to provide support until marriage.[81] Under this rule, the validity of the gift turns entirely on the interior attitude of the donor. One gift is enforceable and the other is not depending on whether the donor was primarily concerned with the donee's well-being. Property law thus gently guides the donor toward making the well-being of another a reason for his own action.

The efficacy of powers to influence choice and action should make lawmakers circumspect; tuning powers of ownership badly can have far-reaching consequences. But the efficacy of powers is also a sanguine fact. Unlike duties, powers do not coerce. That an owner has a power does not mean that he must exercise it. And if an owner does not enjoy the power to use his property to achieve a desired end, he is not thereby prohibited from pursuing that end; he must simply find another means of pursuing it. When powers of ownership operate within the core of owner sovereignty, law does not determine the choices of owners. Rather, those choices are still recognizable as the choices of the owners themselves, and thus constitutive of the owners' character, integrity, and authenticity.

Contrast the power to design one's own buildings with a land-use regulation promulgated to ensure more attractive designs. If owners enjoy the authority to build on their lands buildings of their own designs, some of the resulting buildings are likely to be more beautiful than others. Some will probably be quite beautiful; some might be hideous. But whatever they choose to build, owners will have reason to take beauty into account, both because beauty is valuable in itself and because any costs of constructing hideous buildings will be internalized within their estates.

By contrast, a landmark designation, such as the one at issue in the case *Penn Central Transportation Company* v. *City of New York*,[82] can do more than merely prevent the exercise of practical reasonableness; it can actually pervert it. In that case, after a somewhat elaborate regulatory

[81] Restatement (Second) of the Law Property §61 (1983). [82] 438 US 104 (1978).

process, the City of New York prohibited Penn Central from altering the Grand Central Terminal, which it owned, to make room for commercial office space above the terminal. (The Supreme Court ruled that New York City was not liable under the Takings Clause for this restriction on Penn Central's development and use of its property.)

The purpose of placing on the use and development of a beautiful building an external restriction, such as an aesthetic landmark designation, is to preserve the beauty of developed real estate. But notice what such a designation does to the practical reasoning of landowners. The next private landowner to consider constructing a public building will note that the City of New York destroyed Penn Central's development rights because the designers of Grand Central Terminal made the building too beautiful. As Justice Rehnquist noted in his Penn Central dissent, "Penn Central is prevented from further developing its property basically because *too good* a job was done in designing and building it." The city's admiration for beauty that it did not create motivated it to force a conveyance of use liberties from Penn Central to "sightseeing New Yorkers and tourists."[83] The next landowner now has a reason to make his building less beautiful, so that he can avoid Penn Central's fate, and preserve his rights to develop his real estate further in the future. An external restriction on property rights that is justified on the ground of preserving a beautiful building has perverted the way in which beauty will enter the practical reasoning of private property owners. Now, the intelligible value of beauty will no longer be an unequivocal reason for making buildings *more* beautiful, it will also be a reason for making them *less* beautiful.

Powers of ownership do not pervert practical reason in this way. The freedom to construct buildings of one's own design will not always result in the construction of beautiful buildings. Beauty will be weighed against competing considerations, such as cost and function. But that the owner is the owner – that he will internalize the costs of his own choices – gives him a powerful incentive to take into account basic goods such as beauty. Even if he personally places little value in beauty, he will note that others grasp the intrinsic value of beauty, that their appreciation for beauty affects their behavior, and thus will prudently consider how, if possible, to make his building more beautiful.

[83] *Penn Central* v. *New York*, 438 US at 146.

3

The possibility of private property

Property for all?

Before we develop the account of property outlined in the first two chapters, it will be helpful to anticipate an objection. Doing so at this point will help to clarify what property is, and refute a prevalent misconception about the nature of property in common law.

My account of property, which is grounded in a perfectionist understanding of law and morality, is adumbrated to some extent by earlier accounts. Many well-known arguments for property are grounded in a conception of positive liberty or personal autonomy. G. W. F. Hegel, T. H. Green, Richard Weaver, Charles Reich, Neil MacCormick and others have argued that private property is valuable in large part because it promotes freedom to author one's own life. Borrowing from Alan Ryan, I will call those arguments "personalist" that ground a justification for private property in property's service to personal development or positive liberty.[1] To be clear, the goal here is not to defend personalist arguments for private ownership; the good of practical reasonableness provides a stronger justification for the institution of private property than personalist accounts, and a stronger basis for limiting property rights in cases of abuse and unreasonable exercise. But I want to consider a prominent objection to personalist accounts in order to clear the ground for the argument from practical reasonableness that follows.

If personalist arguments are understood to justify only individual private ownership, then they are open to a powerful critique. Following Pierre-Joseph Proudhon, some influential scholars have argued that any liberty-based defense of private ownership that is strong enough to succeed also undermines the case for private ownership, at least to the extent of requiring redistribution of things, and possibly requiring collective ownership. Proudhon famously opined that private property

[1] Alan Ryan, *Property* (Minneapolis: University of Minnesota Press 1987), 71.

is theft because, he argued, it is impossible to respect the interests of property owners without respecting the equal interests of non-owners. "[I]f the liberty of man is sacred, it is equally sacred in all individuals and . . . if it needs property for its external action, that is, for its life, then the appropriation of material is equally necessary for all."[2] By these considerations one sees that "every imaginable argument made on behalf of property, no matter what it may be, always and necessarily leads to equality, that is, to the negation of property."[3] And because private property is impossible, it is also unjust.

Refining Proudhon's strategy, Jeremy Waldron has argued that what he calls a general right claim to own private property defeats itself. The general right to own must be universalized, which requires distribution, which undermines private property. Others have made similar arguments, and the Proudhon strategy is now regarded in many circles as a success. Not all Proudhon-type critiques are identical. Stephen Munzer, for example, has claimed that everyone should own property, but that welfare rights might suffice for some people, and different types of property for others.[4] For simplicity, and because of its influence and ambition, I will address Waldron's version.

Waldron's Proudhon strategy

Universalizable claims of ownership

Following Proudhon, Waldron insisted that any moral, general right claim to property that is grounded in liberty must be universalizable because all possess an equal right to liberty. Owners of property, Waldron observed, "are not the only people who have an interest in owning things."[5] More controversially, Waldron also proposed that the interest that people have in private property is an interest in actually owning things, rather than an interest in being eligible to attain ownership. Nor are social safety nets sufficient. If private property must exist in society then "everyone should be a proprietor."[6]

[2] Pierre-Joseph Proudhon, *What Is Property?*, Donald R. Kelley and Bonnie G. Smith (eds. & trans.) (Cambridge: Cambridge University Press 1994), 53–54.
[3] Proudhon, *What Is Property?*, 33.
[4] Stephen R. Munzer, *A Theory of Property* (Cambridge: Cambridge University Press 1990), 142, 182.
[5] Jeremy Waldron, *The Right to Private Property* (Oxford: Clarendon Press 1988), 326.
[6] Waldron, *Right to Property*, 23–24.

Building on Hegel's theory of embodiment of the will, Waldron posited that owning things is necessary for an individual's ethical development "since it is only through owning and controlling property that he can embody his will in external objects and begin to transcend the subjectivity of his immediate existence." Therefore, "Hegel is adamant that property is necessary: unless he can establish himself as an owner, an individual's development in other areas of ethical life will be seriously at risk." A Hegelian must confront "the fact that, from an ethical point of view, propertyless individuals are left stranded in their natural subjective immediacy."[7]

For these reasons, in any dispute between an owner and a non-owner, "a putative general right to property may figure on either side." Personalist interests must be weighed against private ownership, just as they are weighed in favor of private ownership. Indeed, individual interests in self-constitution can weigh more heavily *against* private property than for it. Claims grounded in liberty are actually stronger "in the case of the propertyless than in the case of proprietors faced with expropriation."[8] Property might have already served its purpose in advancing the liberty of proprietors, so they are less likely to need their property in the future. At the same time, while redistribution need not deprive proprietors of all of their property, failure to redistribute leaves the propertyless with no property, and thus no opportunity to develop morally. In short, if anyone has a general right to own things, then everyone does, and the state must therefore expropriate and redistribute accordingly.

Waldron's insistence on universalizability of moral claims has important implications for property law. At the very least, universalizability of claims grounded in material need commends some sort of social safety net, designed to secure the subsistence of citizens who fall on hard times, in those societies that can afford it and where primary institutions such as the family and religious associations have failed to do the job.[9] Below subsistence levels of material well-being, liberty simply is not possible; life itself is not possible. But Waldron claimed that his critique requires more; it requires that all people have sufficient materials with which to realize liberty. This idea has attained the status of conventional wisdom among many property scholars.[10]

[7] Waldron, *Right to Property*, 377–78. [8] Waldron, *Right to Property*, 329, 330.

[9] See Mary Ann Glendon, *The New Family and the New Property* (Toronto: Butterworths 1981), 101–40.

[10] For example, Akhil Reed Amar, "Forty Acres and a Mule: A Republican Theory of Minimal Entitlements" (1990) 13 *Harvard Journal of Law & Public Policy* 37;

Waldron is surely correct that right claims to exercise liberty must be universalizable. Human beings are human beings, whether they own property or not. But Waldron's premise that the development of liberty requires a government-guaranteed claim to own things is highly contestable. And his conclusion does not follow from his premises; he fails to demonstrate that state-enforced redistribution outperforms private ownership. Such a demonstration would be exceedingly difficult because the best evidence shows that mediated dominion outperforms collectivist, socialist, and other redistributivist practices. Most directly to the purposes of this book, Waldron's conception of "property" bears little resemblance to the institutions of property as they are found in many common law countries. Waldron ignores the ways in which mediated dominion naturally distributes both resources and opportunities to exercise liberty, even without state action.

Waldron distinguished four types of pre-political property right claims. Type-one claims, immunities against expropriation, and type-two claims, natural rights to appropriate things, are special right (SR) claims. Type three consists of claims of a general eligibility to hold property (GR3), which are "satisfied so long as there are institutions of private property in [one's] society from which [one] is not as a matter of law a priori excluded." A type-four claim (GR4) is one to a general right to actually have private property.[11]

Waldron was quick to translate abstract GR4 right claims into property rights, threatening to render the "right to property" a meaningless concept. That one has an abstract "right" to receive property does not, in itself, entail that any other, particular person has a duty to give one property or make it available. But leave that weakness of his argument aside at present. Let us assume, for the sake of argument, that if personalist defenses of private property entail a GR4 right claim then political

Joseph William Singer, *Entitlement: The Paradoxes of Property* (New Haven: Yale University Press 2000), 167–71; Hanoch Dagan, "The Social Responsibility of Ownership" (2007) 92 *Cornell Law Review* 1255 at 1259–60; D. Benjamin Barros, "Property and Freedom" (2009) 4 *NYU Journal of Law & Liberty* 36 at 55–57; Joseph William Singer, "Original Acquisition of Property: From Conquest & Possession to Democracy & Equal Opportunity" (2011) 86 *Indiana Law Journal* 763; "Pluralism and Perfectionism in Private Law" (2012) 112 *Columbia Law Review* 1409 at 1417–18. Adumbrating Waldron's argument were C. B. MacPherson, "Liberal Democracy and Property" in MacPherson (ed.), *Property: Mainstream and Critical Positions* (Toronto: University of Toronto Press 1978), 199–207; Morris R. Cohen, "Property and Sovereignty" (1928) 13 *Cornell Law Quarterly* 8 at 18–19.

[11] Waldron, *Right to Property*, 17–24.

powers have some duty to take property from property owners and redistribute it to propertyless people, that property owners have a duty to relinquish their property to the political powers for redistribution, and that these duties can be specified consistent with all the requirements of reason. Granting those propositions, Waldron's Proudhon strategy fails for other reasons.

Guarantee to own or eligibility to own?

Waldron's association of personalist arguments with GR4 claims – right claims to require others to supply one with things – is central to his critique of private property. It enabled him to claim that anyone who has genuine concern for the equal dignity of all must accept redistribution. After examining several "GR-based arguments," including many that I am calling personalist, he insisted, "All of them purport to show that owning property is morally important for individuals," and "that the alleged benefits of private property accrue to the individual only from his actual ownership of some significant resources – that is, from the actual exercise of property rights and from the thinking and planning that is associated with that exercise." So "the mere legal opportunity to own property is not enough. Property only does the work for which, it is argued, it ought to exist if individuals actually have it."[12]

It is not obvious that all personalist arguments do, in fact, purport to show that actual ownership is required to exercise liberty. Of those who defend private property on personalist grounds, Waldron pays the most attention to Hegel. But Thomas Hill Green, whom Waldron lumps in with other "GR-based" advocates, was less clearly in favor of a GR4 claim. Green thought that freedom of appropriation is a necessary condition "of the growth of a free morality." He explained, "Moral freedom is not the same thing as a control over the outward circumstances and appliances of life. It is the end to which such control is a generally necessary means, and which gives it its value." He insisted that the rationale of property "is that everyone should be secured by society in the *power of getting and keeping* the means of realising a will, which in possibility is a will directed to social good."[13]

[12] Waldron, *Right to Property*, 24, 408.

[13] Thomas Hill Green, "The Right of the State in Regard to Property" in MacPherson (ed.), *Property: Mainstream and Critical Positions* (Toronto: University of Toronto Press 1978), 103 at 109–10 (emphasis added).

Furthermore, Green worried that distribution of the materials required for moral development could destroy the possibility of free morality. Different people require different resources for their different life plans.

> Either then the various apparatus needed for various functions must be provided for individuals by society, which would imply a complete regulation of life incompatible with that highest object of human attainment, a free morality; or we must trust for its provision to individual effort, which will imply inequality between the property of different persons.[14]

Others have grounded private property protections (and other economic liberties) in the personal agency that private property serves. Their writings (some of which have come after Waldron's book) have quite clearly called for freedom to acquire. For example, J. E. Penner has argued that the interest in exclusively determining the use of things is satisfied by a "freedom from constraint, not the provision of a means to act." He thus defines the general right to property as "a general contingent right to participate in the practice [of exclusively governing use of a thing] by acquiring special rights to specific items of property."[15] In varying degrees of specificity, F. A. Hayek, Neil MacCormick, Roger Scruton, Charles Murray, John Tomasi, and Arthur Brooks have also made liberty-based arguments for rights to obtain property.[16]

Some of these have argued that a guarantee of ownership actually *jeopardizes* liberty. Brooks argues that, for people of all socioeconomic strata, economic liberty consists in "earned success, the ability to create value with your life or in the lives of others."[17] John Tomasi has argued that "[p]ossessing some particular bundle of material goods . . . is not nearly so important as possessing those goods because of one's own actions and choices." Tomasi observes that "a person's self-respect is diminished if one is not (and so cannot think of oneself as) the central

[14] Green, "Right of the State," 111.

[15] J. E. Penner, *The Idea of Property in Law* (Oxford: Oxford University Press 1997), 49–51.

[16] F. A. Hayek, *The Constitution of Liberty* (Chicago: University of Chicago Press 1960), 208; Neil MacCormick, *Practical Reason in Law and Morality* (Oxford: Oxford University Press 2008), 4; Roger Scruton, *The Meaning of Conservatism* (South Bend: St. Augustine's Press 2002), 87–110; Charles Murray, *The Happiness of the People* (Washington, DC: AEI Press 2009); John Tomasi, *Free Market Fairness* (Princeton: Princeton University Press 2012); Arthur C. Brooks, *The Road to Freedom* (New York: Basic Books 2012), especially chapter 2.

[17] Brooks infers from this that materialism is an epistemic error. Money is an index of success, not success itself. "People mistake what they want for the *measure* of what they want." Brooks, *Road to Freedom*, 26–28.

cause of the life one is leading." The necessary causation includes supplying oneself with the material means for one's actions. Tomasi describes a range of self-authorship in material goods. Below the range, extreme poverty and a lack of education "render people incapable of developing their capacities to live as responsible self-authors."[18] The case for social safety nets proceeds from this fact. But the state also must avoid narrowing the range at the top end, as where it truncates self-authorship by supplying needs that humans reasonably desire to supply for themselves, their families, and others in their private associations.

State-enforced actual ownership is neither sufficient nor necessary for liberty

Liberty outside of property domains

Perhaps Waldron would argue that personalist arguments are defensible only insofar as they lead to a GR4 claim; whether or not they *do* lead to a GR4 claim, they *must* do so. On this view, all personalist arguments depend for their success on the premise that a government-backed guarantee of actual ownership is necessary for people to exercise and develop liberty within domains of private ownership. There are at least two good reasons to doubt this premise. First, humans exercise rational deliberation and choice by participating in numerous institutions and practices, not all of which entail actual ownership by all individual members. Second, government-backed guarantees of distribution perform worse than common-law property institutions at putting assets and opportunities to exercise liberty into the hands of those who can benefit from them. This part takes up the first point; the second point is developed in the rest of the chapter.

Some life plans require for their success a lack of individual ownership. When a nun takes a vow of poverty and chooses to minister to the sick and orphaned in Calcutta, India, she has exercised her liberty in an extremely valuable and admirable way. When it is available, the choice of one from among various possible institutions and practices, including those that require propertylessness, is itself an exercise of liberty. Respect for equal liberty therefore entails respect for the choice not to own property. From the perspective of the poverty vow-taker, poverty is an essential means of realizing some more fundamental reason for action,

[18] Tomasi, *Free Market Fairness*, xi, 83, 94.

such as ordering the will toward an ultimate source of meaning, or empathetic service to the poor.

Waldron seemed to allow that actual ownership of things cannot be universalizable without infringing liberty. He reserved a caveat, that the ownership right claim must be honored only for those who have "the taste for" ownership.[19] To what extent does this caveat qualify the universalizability of the claim? Waldron understandably found uncongenial the idea that the taste for ownership could be determined apart from choice, that some are more fit for true liberty than others. But there is a different way to understand the caveat. The choice whether to own property is itself an exercise of liberty. That people like Mother Teresa decline to own things is no reason to suppose that some people are more fit than others to own things. It suggests only that ownership is not a necessary part of every valuable plan of action.

Notice that this interpretation does not defeat a universalizable claim of eligibility to own. That Mother Teresa exercised liberty in choosing poverty does not cast doubt on the efficacy of private property as an institution for the promotion of others' liberty, and indirectly, her own. It is worth noting here that private property even enables the important work of people like Mother Teresa. The United States, with its strong laws and traditions respecting private property, has generous citizens who privately and publicly finance the actions of those who devote their lives in service to the poor.[20]

In a parenthetical aside, Waldron anticipated something like this criticism. "It is no good saying, by the way, that there may be other means by which a propertyless person can stabilize his will."[21] If that claim is true then personalist arguments cannot provide conclusive reasons for honoring claims of ownership, because the other means will be equally available to all, regardless of ownership.

It is perhaps true that a personalist argument cannot by itself supply *conclusive* reasons for choosing a private property institution over a collectivist system of use and management *in the abstract*. But abstractions do not tell us much about the comparative efficacy of private ownership versus redistribution. Given his insistence that resources *be*

[19] Waldron, *Right to Property*, 326. [20] Brooks, *Road to Freedom*, 82.

[21] Waldron, *Right to Property*, 409. Of course, property might enable liberty in a unique way so that other liberty-enhancing institutions are not fungible for it. That possibility *raises* (does not resolve) the question whether it is actual ownership, the opportunity to own, or some other feature of property that does the job.

provided for the propertyless, it is striking that Waldron does not specify any duty to provide. Instead, he analogizes the right to negative liberties. "If someone were propertyless, then his claim to autonomy and the development of his free agency would not have been satisfied; it would have been undermined and violated just as much as if he had been excluded from the scope of religious or political toleration extended by the state."[22] But the analogies to religious and political toleration tell against his argument. No one supposes that equal concern for all entails that each individual must have a religion, or must have a political commitment, and the rights can be satisfied by general duties of abstention. By contrast, Waldron supposes a right to affirmative provision, and the corresponding duty must require action. Who is supposed to act, what must they do, and how do we know that their actions will work?

Even at Waldron's level of abstraction, that many private property institutions are sufficient and efficacious to promote personal agency is a reason in their favor, even if they are not the only sufficient and efficacious institutions for that end. Indeed, it is a good prima facie reason to choose private property institutions over alternative ways to manage resources. There are also other reasons, such as private property's proven record of promoting the material well-being of the least well-off, within a system of broader economic freedoms, its promotion of initiative, its productivity, and so on.[23] But we can leave those aside. Assuming that some reasons might be found to weigh against private ownership, those should be taken into the balance within cases. But their existence, if they exist, is not a reason to disregard the reasons *in favor of* private ownership. The case for property freedoms is a prima facie case, open to rebuttal in particular instances. That personalist justifications for private ownership are not conclusive in the abstract is beside the point. We must have some way to resolve use and management questions and we have moral reasons to prefer private ownership over the known alternatives.

Private property and cooperation

Waldron's argument also plays on an emaciated definition of the term "property." He portrays private property as atomized into exclusively

[22] Waldron, *Right to Property*, 24. [23] Brooks, *Road to Freedom*, 69–80.

individual forms of ownership. The problem is accentuated by Proudhon's assumption that the sum of things to be owned is fixed.[24] In such a world, gains by proprietors must be had at the expense of non-owners, monopolies and widespread non-ownership naturally result, and non-owners are thwarted in their efforts to develop personal agency.

If private property domains are possible in which people tend to own things together in families and private associations, or in which proprietors and non-owners cooperate together to deliberate and make choices about the uses of things, or in which concentrations and monopolies are controlled, or in which collaboration among owners and between owners and non-owners produces new objects that are available for ownership by non-proprietors, or in which owners regularly exercise their property rights by giving things away and licensing entrance by non-owners, then the foundations of Waldron's Proudhon strategy would erode. If one could conceive of a complex of property institutions that incorporated *all* of those features, then the Proudhon strategy would seem to be in serious jeopardy.

Such a complex is more than possible; it exists, though imperfectly, in jurisdictions that have adopted common law institutions of private ownership. Within the mediated dominion of the common law, use, management, and exploitation of property are collaborative exercises. Individuals co-own with other individuals, associations, and communities of people; owners collaborate with each other; and owners collaborate with non-owners. Individual ownership is thus not the only path to liberty within common law institutions of private property.

[24] Proudhon posited,

> If one hundred thousand men settle in a large country like France with no inhabitants, then each man has a right to 1/100,000 of the land. If the number of possessors increases, each one's portion diminishes through this increase, so that, if the number of inhabitants rises to thirty-four millions, each one will have a right only to 1/34,000,000. Now, organise the police system and the government, labour, exchange, inheritance, etc. so that the means of labour shall be shared by all equally, and that each individual shall be free, and then society will be perfect.

Proudhon, *What Is Property?*, 54. In the modern world, where the most powerful sources of wealth are ideas and creative endeavor, rather than land, and where many complex institutions and practices bring humans into cooperative ventures for the management of resources, Proudhon's hypothetical has lost much of its force.

Waldron was understandably concerned about the condition of non-owners. He wrote,

> A person who owns nothing in society (where everything is privately owned) is not at liberty, in a negative sense, to make use of anything – indeed for everything that he *might* use, someone else has a right that he should refrain from using it, and it is a right which they are entitled to enforce.[25]

The parenthetical qualification here invites two responses, one obvious but not particularly telling, the other latent and more important.

The obvious response is that there is no society in which *everything* is owned privately, in any sense. And Waldron allowed that his "point is mitigated by the existence of some common property even in the most comprehensively capitalistic societies: tramps have the streets to walk in and the bridges to sleep under."[26] But that does not free them to develop personally.

Different forms of private property ownership

The less obvious and more important problem with Waldron's argument is the way that he has constructed his concept of private property. Private property is not synonymous with individual ownership. Private property need not be purely individualist in theory, and it is not in fact. Plural ownership – by families, religious communities, and other private associations – comprises many forms of owner dominion, which are ubiquitous in legal practice. Resources are often owned by communities other than the state – groups of people cooperating together to achieve plural ends, which include both common and individual goals. These groups are secure in their collaborations behind the protections that property law affords.

Waldron did not discuss group or associational ownership. He discussed "common property," but in a way that obscured more than it clarified. "In a system of common property," he wrote, "rules governing access to and control of material resources are organized on the basis that each resource is in principle available for the use of every member alike … and *when allocative decisions are made* they are made on a basis that is in some sense fair to all."[27] The use of the passive voice in the emphasized phrase conceals an elision. There is a world of difference

[25] Waldron, *Right to Property*, 410. [26] Waldron, *Right to Property*, 411.
[27] Waldron, *Right to Property*, 41 (emphasis added).

between a state making allocative decisions through the exercise of its coercive powers and a private community of people making such decisions in acts of self-constitution.

Indeed, the example that Waldron gives of "common property" – public parks – suggests that he was really referring to *collective* property, in which the state controls the resource always subject to its right to exclude. Absent legislation (a grant of a privilege by the state), individuals have no legal rights to use or benefit from resources on which states allow public uses. Governments hold title to public land and private citizens do not enjoy legal claims to the incidents of ownership.[28] If a municipality redesignates public land for a new purpose, no citizen has been deprived of any property, even if the new use interferes with a use that the citizen formerly made of the resource.[29] "The government has, with respect to its own lands, the rights of an ordinary proprietor to maintain its possession and to prosecute trespassers. It may deal with such lands precisely as a private individual may deal with his farming property."[30] Even as to public lands the government has the power, free from judicial interference, to disestablish one use and designate another. Its allowance of a private use, without more, creates no vested right in any citizen to continue engaging in the use after the government disallows it.[31]

Truly open-access common ownership, in which resources are held open to all, free from interference by both individuals and the state, is neither ubiquitous nor unheard-of. Some fugitive resources, such as wild animals and sunlight, are beyond anyone's dominion until captured. Intellectual property that has passed into the public domain is common, but because intellectual property is a non-exclusive resource, it does not give rise to problems of exclusion that concerned Proudhon and Waldron. Some examples can also be found in real property law. There are limitations on what states can do with resources held in public trust, such as navigable servitudes[32] and roads laid out for public use.[33] These limitations arise either out of common law boundaries on the state's powers of ownership, as where the state holds in trust for some public purpose, or out of particular private rights, as where the state takes title

28 *Moore* v. *MacMillan* [1977] 2 NZLR 81.
29 *Sauer* v. *City of New York*, 206 US 536 (1907).
30 *Light* v. *United States*, 220 US 523 at 536 (1911).
31 *Light* v. *United States*, 220 US at 535 at 537.
32 *Illinois Central Railroad Co.* v. *Illinois*, 146 US 387 (1892).
33 *Barney* v. *City of Keokuk*, 94 US 324 at 341–42 (1876).

subject to an easement.[34] In both instances the state is under a duty to which its authority is subordinate.

Quasi-commons, such as common areas in a condominium complex or pastures in a rural village, are part common and part private; those outside the defined community remain under an in rem duty to exclude themselves absent an invitation or license.[35] It is a mistake to extrapolate from those cases to make all communal ownership appear to be merely aggregation of individual property interests. Private property that is owned by a group agent has long been known in the common law. Tenure and estates include many concurrent domains, which do not fit into the categories of individual, common, or collective ownership.[36] Marital and other concurrent estates; easements, covenants, profits, licenses, and servitudes; future interests and leasehold estates; corporate ownership; various trusts; all enable private communities of people to cooperate together in the management of things, free from outside interference. These forms of ownership are therefore truly instances of *private* ownership, not collective or common ownership.[37] They are not merely individual interests, nor aggregations of them. For an individual, even an individual member, to take something from a church without permission would constitute theft against the church. The church is itself the owner, an agent that acts on plans that enrich and enliven the reasoning and intentions of its members.

It is worth noting that Waldron is far from alone in overlooking these forms of common law ownership and the agency of non-state groups. Indeed, many scholars define private property abstractly as a system of purely individual property rights, and then distinguish it from so-called common or community property,[38] which is often a jumble of private

34 *Muhlker* v. *New York & H.R. Co.*, 197 US 544 (1905). Both kinds of rights are found in the famous case *Iveagh* v. *Martin* [1961] 1 Q.B. 232, where the defendant asserted a special right to moor his vessel to a quay as a "man of Bosham" within the meaning of letters patent and statutes excusing such men from paying tolls, and a general common law right to navigation of tidal waters.

35 Robert C. Ellickson, "Property in Land" (1993) 102 *Yale Law Journal* 1315 at 1322–23.

36 Sheldon F. Kurtz, *Moynihan's Introduction to the Law of Real Property* (5th edn, St. Paul: West 2011), 277–97; Charles Harpum et al., *Megarry & Wade: The Law of Real Property* (London: Sweet & Maxwell 2012), 22–93, 495–559.

37 Waldron recognized this. That individuals transfer ownership into the corporate form led Waldron to conclude (correctly) that corporate ownership is a form of private property. Waldron, *Right to Property*, 57–58.

38 C. B. MacPherson defined private property as a set of "exclusive individual rights" and contrasted it with "common property," the examples of which were state-owned resources, such as "public parks, city streets, highways." C. B. MacPherson, "The

property, truly common property, and state-controlled collective property. When attention is given to the concept of the community ownership, plural and intermediary forms of ownership are sometimes lumped in as subdivisions of the state. For example, two influential property scholars, Gregory Alexander and Eduardo Peñalver, associate property ownership with "all manner of communities, but especially the state."[39]

Elsewhere, Waldron has differentiated between different communities, "nations, municipalities, neighborhoods, or clusters of condominiums." But this recognition is blunted by his insistence that the formation of such communities involves "the repudiation of any responsibility for deprived people in their vicinity,"[40] as if the differentiation entailed in a community's acts of identity-constitution and corporate responsibility somehow entail corporate selfishness or lack of altruistic motivation.

The collapse of community into the state drives a wholly imagined wedge between the individual and her various non-political communities. It obscures the distinction between private property and collective property and has the potential to subsume all intermediary institutions within the power of the state and to elide the most fruitful zones of freedom, such that all property norms become part of a collective "regulatory scheme."[41] What's more, it gets the order of authority exactly backwards (as explained in later chapters). The family, university, business, nonprofit organization, and other intermediary institutions do not exist to serve the state; rather, vice versa.

To understand the work that private property does in promoting liberty, one must not arbitrarily exclude non-individual private ownership from one's conception of private property. Private property is best

Meaning of Property" in MacPherson (ed.), *Property: Mainstream and Critical Positions* (Toronto: University of Toronto Press 1978), 1 at 4. See also "Takings and Distributive Justice" (1999) 85 *Virginia Law Review* 741; Gregory S. Alexander, "The Social-Obligation Norm in American Property Law" (2009) 94 *Cornell Law Review* 745; Eduardo M. Peñalver, "Land Virtues" (2009) 94 *Cornell Law Review* 821. Some defenders of the classical understanding of private ownership do the same, e.g., Richard Epstein, *Design for Liberty* (Cambridge: Harvard University Press 2011), 69–73. Notable exceptions are Joshua Getzler, "Plural Ownership, Funds, and the Aggregation of Wills" (2009) 10 *Theoretical Inquiries in Law* 241; and Amnon Lehavi, *The Construction of Property: Norms, Institutions, Challenges* (Cambridge: Cambridge University Press 2013)

39 Gregory S. Alexander and Eduardo M. Peñalver, "Introduction" in *Property and Community* (New York: Oxford University Press 2010), xvii.

40 Jeremy Waldron, "Community and Property – For Those Who Have Neither" (2009) 10 *Theoretical Inquiries in Law* 161 at 189–90.

41 Waldron, "Community and Property," 162.

understood as a domain of freedom that is insulated from the collective decision-making of the entire political community. This insulation enables within property domains all forms of private ownership – individual, familial, associational. Charles Reich argued that "property guards the troubled boundary between individual man and the state," but also "draws a circle around the activities of each private individual *or organization*," in order to protect "individual *and private* interests."[42] Property guards the boundaries between the family and the state, the local bookstore and the state, the mosque and the state, the crisis pregnancy center and the state, and around many other groups and institutions.

Of the many instances of private, plural property, I will focus here on what I call intermediary property. Intermediary property enables individuals to come together in collaborative projects using common resources, and thus serves as a mechanism of mediation among individual human beings. It also helps primary institutions, such as families and religious associations, to intermediate between individuals and the state. It carves out a sphere of deliberation (and, in many instances, actual physical space) within which private associations and groups can act for mutual benefit, insulated from collective decision-making.

Intermediary private property is at least as ubiquitous as individual private property, especially with respect to land.[43] Its prevalence explains why private property has intuitive appeal despite unequal distribution of title. Intermediary private property enables people to develop liberty with respect to things before and after they become owners, because it enables both cooperative and individualized exercises of moral agency within the borders of private property domains. In various religious orders, small

[42] Charles A. Reich, "The New Property" (1964) 73 *Yale Law Journal* 733 at 771, 772 (emphasis added).

[43] See Ellickson, "Property in Land," 1394–95; J. W. Harris, *Property and Justice* (Oxford: Oxford University Press 1996), 102–04, 115–18. Harris observed that, while a "vast swathe of the private wealth in modern western societies is held in the form of joint, group, or corporate property," other forms of property holding exist in which members of a community enjoy legal protection from trespassory interference by outsiders and freedom to arrange their internal affairs according to their "mutual sense of community." He called these forms "communitarian" property. Harris, *Justice*, 102–03. Harris asserted that communitarian property existed in primitive societies, but became contaminated by law and dropped out of use when it came into contact with the state and systems of private property ownership. Perhaps. But the central case of what I am calling intermediary property – that is, ownership by a family – functions to this day as Harris' "communitarian" property did in primitive societies. About this, Harris noted only the potential for parents, especially husbands, to exercise unjust domination. Harris, *Justice*, 270–75.

businesses, nonprofit enterprises, and most of all in families, property entitlements are unevenly distributed, yet members nevertheless exercise rational deliberation and choice.

Intermediary property helps individuals to constitute themselves consistently with the demands of sociability. Unless one is prepared to live either in isolation or in constant conflict with others, the ordering of one's will according to reasons must necessarily factor in not only those reasons that one adopts for oneself but also reasons for which others act, with whom one is in community. The sharing of resources provides a strong motivation to take others' reasons into one's practical deliberations. This is seen most clearly with family ownership. Conceptions of private property as a non-individualistic institution run back to what Aristotle considered the most foundational of all civic institutions – the family – the very first community, in which all things are held in common.[44] The history of the common law is a history of familial property rights and duties.[45]

T. H. Green thought it was quite natural that private property "should first appear within societies founded on kinship, these being naturally the societies within which the restraining conception of a common well-being is first operative." Members of a family cooperate in the management of resources for their common good within a system that secures to each "the fruit of his labor."[46] In English common law the estates of ownership developed to reflect cooperative management of resources within clans and familial inheritance.[47] Though primogeniture has been abolished, intestate succession continues to track the bonds of kinship. And if industrialization has diminished the force of kinship somewhat, the biological family nevertheless remains the primary center of moral agency and development. John Finnis has described the biological family as the prototypical comprehensive community of

44 Aristotle, *The Politics* I.1 – I.2, I.8 – I.9. See Ryan, *Property*, 15–16.

45 Arthur R. Hogue, *Origins of the Common Law* (Bloomington: Indiana University Press 1966), 227–34; John Stuart Mill, "Of Property" in MacPherson (ed.), *Property: Mainstream and Critical Positions* (Toronto: University of Toronto Press 1978), 88.

46 Green, "Right of the State," 108. See also Epstein, *Design for Liberty*, 15–16. The idea that family is the fount of property has a long and distinguished pedigree. Melville M. Bigelow, *Papers on the Legal History of Government* (Boston: Little, Brown & Co. 1920), 35–70; Rudolph Sohm, *The Institutes: A Textbook of the History and System of Roman Private Law*, James Crawford Ledlie (trans.) (3rd edn, Oxford: Clarendon Press 1907), 501–05.

47 The fee simple absolute, the most comprehensive estate in Anglo-American law, is granted to "A and his heirs," words that were understood to create a general inheritance. Kurtz, *Moynihan's Introduction*, 37.

people, in which each member "is devoted to finding his or her own self-fulfillment (at least in part) in helping the other members to fulfill themselves, by caring for them and helping them to grow in freedom and responsibility and other basic aspects of human flourishing."[48]

Familial ownership continues to play a central role in private property. Private property carves out zones of freedom within which families and their constituent members develop morally, whether that development is perceived in terms of liberty or as a more comprehensive conception of practical reasonableness. Roger Scruton explains, "Home is the place where private property accumulates, and so overreaches itself, becoming transformed into something shared. There is no contract of distribution: sharing is simply the essence of family life. Here everything important is 'ours'. Private property is added to, and reinforces, the primary social relation."[49] The life of the family, which when functioning well accrues to the moral development of all of the family's members, is secured within the legal protections of the family's domain.

Consider how property must be managed in a marital estate at common law. The most robust form of familial ownership known to common law is the tenancy by the entirety, as modified by the abolition of coverture. Many jurisdictions have abolished the tenancy by the entirety along with coverture, on the assumption that the estate can only take one of two forms, either the pre-abolition form, in which husband could sever but wife could not, or complete severability. But there is a third possibility, which a justice of the Supreme Court of New South Wales raised, that Married Women's Property Acts "did not abolish tenancy by entireties" but rather elevated the wife to equal authority with her husband. "Under such a title in fee simple the two spouses constitute a kind of compound owner, resembling an incorporated association of persons." For this reason, "neither can alienate without the other – even as a member of an incorporated company cannot alienate any interest in the company's lands; and there is no interest in the company's lands that can be sold in execution for his debt."[50]

Many American states retain the tenancy by the entirety in this form. Married women's property acts elevated the wife to "equal legal status"

[48] John Finnis, *Natural Law and Natural Rights* (2nd edn, Oxford: Oxford University Press 2011), 138.

[49] Scruton, *Meaning of Conservatism*, 94. Compare Benjamin Barros, "Home as a Legal Concept" (2006) 46 *Santa Clara Law Review* 255.

[50] *The Register-General of New South Wales* v. *Wood* [1926] HCA 43 (New South Wales), Higgins J, dissenting.

and stripped the estate of those "artificial and archaic rules" that placed the wife under a disability.[51] Now neither husband nor wife may sell, sever, or encumber any part of the title without the consent of the other and both enjoy the right of survivorship.[52] Because of these rights, spouses must cooperate. Each must take account of the others' interests. In the United Kingdom, where tenancy by the entirety has been abolished, spouses enjoy matrimonial home rights, which limit the other spouse's powers of alienation by vesting in a deserted spouse an irrevocable license, enforceable against the deserting spouse's creditors.[53] The right reflects the modern status of wife as "partner" of the husband "in all affairs which are their common concern."[54]

Many commentators today seem to find this baffling. Sheldon Kurtz described the tenancy by the entirety as "an anomaly based on an anachronism."[55] But that view overlooks the important work that intermediary property performs in promoting cooperative deliberation and choice, work that it can do only if it maps over and reinforces the more fundamental institution of marriage. As a result of the strong legal boundaries around the marital estate, spouses must deliberate together about the use and management of their resources. The law of marital estates enriches the deliberations and choices of both spouses even as it constrains the independence of one of them.

Thus it is the right of survivorship, not the relatively recent innovation of unilateral, no-fault divorce, which promotes practical reasonableness within marital ownership. The ideal of "free exit," as Hanoch Dagan calls it, is not an ideal at all but rather an aid to atomized individualism. Far from promoting egalitarianism, the right of one spouse to leave the other for no reason elevates whichever spouse has lost interest in the marital project over the interests of the spouse who wants to continue the cooperation, not to mention any children. Free exit undermines the "fusion" that Dagan rightly affirms as foundational to the marital project, and stands in direct contravention of Dagan's "sharing principle."[56] As

51 *Robinson* v. *Trousdale County*, 516 SW 2d 626 at 630, 632 (Tenn 1974).

52 For example, *Losey* v. *Losey*, 221 So 2d 417 at 418 (Fla 1969); *Medeiros* v. *Medeiros*, 308 NE 2d 783 at 785 (Mass App Ct 1974); *Tkachik* v. *Mandeville*, 790 NW 2d 260 at 265 (Michigan 2010); *Re Estate of Blair*, 317 SW 3d 84 at 89 (Mo Ct App 2010); New Jersey Statutes 46:3-17.4, 3-17.5; *Grahl* v. *Davis*, 971 SW 2d 373 at 378 (Tenn 1998).

53 Harpum et al., *Megarry & Wade*, 1450–55.

54 *Bendall* v. *McWhirter* [1952] 2 QB 466 at 475 per Denning, LJ.

55 Kurtz, *Moynihan's Introduction*, 295.

56 Hanoch Dagan, "The Public Dimension of Private Property" (2013) 24 *King's Law Journal* 260. Contrast Glendon, "New Family," 41–46.

Joseph Raz observed, marriage is one of those freedoms that consists in part in a "degree of unfreedom (being married *is*, in part, not having the freedom to seek other partners)."[57]

The liberating function of property can be overstated; law cannot eradicate dependence. Humans are by nature dependent beings. Even the wealthy are dependent on others for expensive goods, such as friendship, art, and learning. And most of us are not independently wealthy; we are dependent on others for our most basic needs. At its best, private property does not free us from others but instead channels dependence away from less healthy dependencies and toward more healthy dependencies. It encourages moral connections between dependent people and other dependent people. It makes us dependent on those people who will take our well-being into their deliberations as reasons for their own actions.

In central cases, those people will be members of our own family. They might also include those people who act charitably toward us. An assignment of property within a family is done for the purpose of benefiting the individual members of the family. The human beings are the reasons for the choice about how to allocate resources. Similarly, one who makes a gift acts for the purpose of improving the well-being of a person. Because the recipient's good is the reason for the donor's action, the donor has taken the well-being of the recipient into his or her deliberations and choice. Sharing within families and by charitable acts thus establishes moral connections between people, and gives both recipients and providers new reasons to act on behalf of the well-being of the other.

By contrast, dependencies met by purely economic institutions do not create very strong moral connections. Purely economic exchanges are grounded in little more than self-interest. Of course, self-interest can be a powerful motivator to take consideration of another's desires or preferences. To complete an arms-length transaction, one must provide something of value to the other person. But the other person's well-being is of merely instrumental value in such cases. Once the transaction is complete, the well-being of the other person does not persist in one's will as a reason for action.

Least beneficial of all are dependencies on entitlements. Entitlements, which Charles Reich termed the "new property"[58] – employment security

[57] Joseph Raz, *The Morality of Freedom* (Oxford: Oxford University Press 1986), 322 (emphasis original).

[58] Reich, "New Property."

and entitlements to government support – produce dependencies without establishing the well-being of recipients as intrinsic reasons for action in the will of the provider. The state's satisfaction of distributive entitlements is motivated not by concern for the well-being of an individual person but rather by legal duty. Furthermore, an entitlement creates no new reason for the recipient to live well, or to take the preferences or goods of others into consideration. The recipient is entitled precisely because he does not owe anything to anyone – morally or legally – but instead has a lawful claim with no continuing obligations. Indeed, the nature of an entitlement is to eradicate obligations in its recipient.

So, there is a spectrum of dependencies, from families and charitable relations to entitlements. We might say that the family, in particular, is the central institution of healthy dependence. Nevertheless, healthy dependencies are possible outside the nuclear family, and the law should account for the ways in which non-familial institutions supply the needs of human beings. Members of many other associations – family businesses, charities, religious assemblies, universities – also cooperate with each other in the care, use, and management of things, although less comprehensively than in the family. In the early nineteenth century, Alexis de Tocqueville observed that Americans developed charitable habits by participating in free institutions, which impress on the individual "that it is duty as well as self-interest to be useful to one's fellows." Participation in these associations calls one's attention "in the first instance, to the common interest out of necessity and later out of choice; what started out as calculation becomes instinct; and by working for the advantage of one's fellow citizens, finally the habit and taste for serving them takes root."[59] These habits are best developed by voluntary acts of cooperation, and thus must be insulated from collective decision-making.

The insulation is sufficient even if only one member of the association, or a corporation designated by the community as a legal person, has title. Authority can of course be abused. But it is possible for authority to be exercised for a common good; in fact, it happens all the time. And many individual members of the community partake of the moral agency made possible by private ownership. A priest or a church treasurer exercises responsibility for assets of the church despite the fact that the church, not he or she, owns the assets and exercises the right to exclude. Stewardship

[59] Alexis de Tocqueville, *Democracy in America*, Gerald E. Bevan (trans.) (New York: Penguin 2003), 595.

enables members and employees of the church to carry on the church's ministries, including ministries to its own people and to others, who are outside the church. Those who receive assistance from the church are to some extent freed from circumstances that prevent them from exercising liberty. None of this would be possible unless the state stands ready to enforce the church's property rights. Thus, it is not true, as Waldron claims, that "if somebody has no private property of his own, then, as far as a [general right]-based argument is concerned, the existence of an institution of private property does him no good."[60]

It is true that members of many intermediary institutions do not always freely choose their respective stations within the institutions. Children do not choose their parents; many employees would prefer to work for themselves. But as long as property rights receive the state's protection, and as long as the state remains committed to conditions of equal eligibility for ownership, each of the members of the institution can nevertheless benefit. The exercise of liberty in the material world is multipolar and incremental, not unipolar and binary. Individuals within cooperative enterprises enjoy it in varying degrees and in various and incommensurable forms, sometimes even with respect to the same resource.

So members of a private community can benefit both morally and materially from cooperative management of resources, even if ownership rights are not equally distributed, or not distributed at all. An employee is given care of the assets of his employer. He is expected to improve or multiply them, and he is compensated (with property) for his efforts. His role within the community does not entitle him to ownership in the first instance, but the existence of property rules creates opportunities for him to develop his powers of agency and to use those powers to acquire his own property. As Mill noted, though a laborer is at a disadvantage when compared with his employer, he is "far better off" than we would be had his employer not saved and invested resources in the venture that supplies the employment.[61]

What Waldron classified as a GR3 right benefits the laborer because of another practice to which he paid little attention, that of promise-making. Contracting is a form of cooperation that is realized between owners of different things, between owners and non-owners, and between non-owners and non-owners, to create and produce new things and (equally important) new states of being. Waldron acknowledged that some basic liberties can be exercised by those who do not own, if those

[60] Waldron, *Right to Property*, 328. [61] Mill, "Of Property," 86.

people are free to enter into contracts. He observed that even propertyless political radicals can exercise their political liberties by borrowing or hiring printing presses and meeting places from proprietors.[62] Yet he failed to see that by hiring these resources, they cease to be propertyless. He insisted that, unless one owns a home one cannot exercise one's right to privacy because one cannot have a place to retreat from public demands. But by obtaining leasehold estates, bailments, easements, those who do not own freehold title can secure property for themselves. In all of these cases, a promissory obligation between a less-propertied person (tenant, licensee, bailee) and a fee simple owner rests on the security of the fee simple owner's rights.

Consider the case of a sculptor who is hired to produce a mythological scene of his choosing. His patron purchases a block of marble and furnishes a studio, complete with tools. The sculptor then exercises his mental and physical faculties to bring out of the stone a Poseidon, emerging from the sea. He begins by formulating a plan of action. It is an incomplete plan; as he executes the plan he will need to make accommodations for flaws in the stone, mistakes, and other unexpected contingencies. As he works, he creates new states of being, new reasons for his choice and action. He constrains himself by his choices to remove certain bits of stone and to leave others in place. Mindful of the expense of the stone, he takes his time and carefully guides each strike with his hammer. When he finishes work each workday, he is careful to sweep away chips and dust, to put away his tools, and to lock the door as he leaves. In all of these ways the sculptor exercises freedom of action to bring about desirable states of being – order, beauty, cleanliness – in the material world.

Note that the sculptor develops in this way even though he is not the fee simple owner of the stone, the studio, and the tools. The artist develops his liberty with delegated authority. This is possible precisely because property dominion has empowered the patron and the artist to cooperate. Our reasons for action permeate the nature of those things that we create or produce, whatever the extent of our dominion over them, but we can create or produce only if we enjoy private rights. Whether or not the material world has come to reflect the employed sculptor's deliberations in a way that Waldron (following Hegel) would credit as mastery of the material world,[63] the project has been conducive to the sculptor's ethical development, and the material world reflects that development.

[62] Waldron, *Right to Property*, 412–13. [63] Waldron, *Right to Property*, 312–13.

What perfects an institution of property rights, from our sculptor's point of view, is a guarantee of a GR3 claim-right. Where the eligibility for property ownership is a background right, even those who do not own things are given opportunities first to manage, and then to own, by cooperating with others for common purposes. Absent unjust coercion within the cooperative venture, such as enslavement or failure to pay a just wage, participation in the institution of private property can accrue to the liberty of all, even those who do not (yet) own (many) things.

There are of course differences between being a business owner and being an employee, and these have important implications for the development of agency.[64] But private property does not itself prevent a laborer from jumping from non-owner to owner (or back again). There are also important differences between helping with one's family's business and working as an employee of a publicly traded corporation. Many large corporations are more like political institutions than other intermediary institutions in the way in which authority over things is exercised within them. But the law has developed to take the agency and contributions of employees into account. Shop rights in intellectual property law is one example of the law assigning entitlements to reward meritorious contributions, without the state engaging in any redistributive activities.

Private law doctrines also take into account the contributions of non-owners. The doctrine of accession places title to an improved object in the hands of the improver where the improver acts on the original owner's materials in good faith. The doctrine of adverse possession does much the same thing where the original owner has neglected the materials for a long period of time and the adverse party has acted like the true owner, which generally entails maintaining and developing the resource.[65] These doctrines strike a careful balance between security of title and rewarding labor.

Finally, there are the practices of stewardship and charity. Most people develop responsibility and learn to exercise liberty with things either entrusted or given to them by others. Children especially possess everything as stewards for, or donees of, their parents. After learning to ride a tricycle, then a bicycle, then to drive a car, the child is eventually entrusted with custody of the parents' car for a night out. Stewardship begets stewardship, and sometimes ownership, as when children use the

[64] Alan Ryan, *Property and Political Theory* (Oxford: Basil Blackwell 1984), 86–87.

[65] Thomas W. Merrill and Henry E. Smith, *Property: Principles and Policies* (2nd edn, St. Paul: Foundation Press 2012), 162–71, 190–220.

car to travel to their first job, exercise practical reason in fulfillment of their duties at that job, and get paid. All of this requires the state to stand ready to enforce property rights that the children do not have, but from which they benefit.

As Penner demonstrated, charitable use is entailed in the idea of private property; property owners, like all human beings, are social creatures and sharing of property is commonplace.[66] So, perhaps it is not surprising to find that charitable action correlates strongly with support for economic liberties generally, and belief in private property specifically. Seventy to eighty per cent of American households donate to charity every year. Their giving amounts to approximately $300 billion annually. Most strikingly, the most generous Americans are those who believe most strongly in private property and economic liberty. They donate the most money, the most volunteer time, and the most blood.[67] Perhaps this is a coincidence. But Proudhon and Waldron have asked what is possible. It is manifestly possible to favor private property and act on a concern for the propertyless.

Inequality and the least well-off

For all of the reasons stated above, it is possible for private ownership to promote liberty. Ownership and the productive activities that it enables are often cooperative practices. Those practices promote the liberty of both owners and aspiring owners, and create new opportunities for ownership. This is not to suggest that intermediary ownership and cooperative practices can or will eliminate propertylessness. And perfectionist defenders of private ownership need not reject social safety nets for the poor. John Finnis has argued that the injustice of wide disparities of ownership is not the inequality in itself but rather that the wealthy have failed to assist others to secure basic goods. Redistribution does not serve the requirements of justice if it "means no more than that more beer is going to be consumed morosely before television sets by the relatively many, and less fine wine consumed by the relatively few." But justice does require redistribution to the extent that it is necessary and sufficient to preserve the poor from "(non-self-inflicted) illness" and to educate them "to the point where genuine self-direction becomes possible for them."[68]

[66] Penner, *Idea of Property*, 87–90, 93–94.
[67] Brooks, *Road to Freedom*, 81–85.
[68] Finnis, *Natural Law*, 173–74.

On the other hand, redistributivist solutions have performed no better at eliminating poverty, relative to economies that are built on robust private property protections. Tomasi notes, "No widely held economic law suggests that a program of strict economic equality benefits the poor."[69] Peter Wehner and Arthur Brooks observe, "Even societies that have committed themselves to the goal of equality have not been able to achieve it."[70] Indeed, government guarantees can tend to make delivery of goods to those in need *less* likely, because they collectivize and externalize responsibility for provision of goods.[71] And state-enforced distribution is not without moral costs to those whom it is intended to benefit. Poverty traps, rent seeking, the breakdown in marriage and family stability are among the well-known corollaries of public welfare programs.[72]

The crux of Waldron's case against private property is really a case against capitalism. Echoing Marx, Waldron worried that "mass propertylessness, is not only 'appropriate to' a capitalist mode of production; it is its inevitable result."[73] Waldron conflates private property with capitalist systems of corporate finance. The former does not entail the latter. Capital markets can have monopolistic tendencies. Those tendencies can hurt the least well-off, and are rightly curtailed. But that is not an argument against private property.

Furthermore, the relative experiences of capitalist and communist nations in the twentieth century suggest that Waldron's fears of mass propertylessness are misdirected.[74] The Soviet experiment with collective control and distribution not only deprived millions of people of basic sustenance, caused millions of deaths, and enabled totalitarian rule, it also destroyed initiative, vitality, and self-directed action. Richard Pipes has concluded that "the elimination of private ownership" by communists "led to the withering of personality."[75]

[69] Tomasi, *Free Market Fairness*, 234.

[70] Peter Wehner and Arthur C. Brooks, *Wealth & Justice: The Morality of Democratic Capitalism* (Washington, DC: AEI Press 2011), 41.

[71] Tomasi, *Free Market Fairness*, 223.

[72] Tomasi, *Free Market Fairness*, 198–201; Gertrude Himmelfarb, "Welfare as a Moral Problem" (1996) 19 *Harvard Journal of Law & Public Policy* 685.

[73] Waldron, *Right to Property*, 426–27. Karl Marx and Friedrich Engels, *Manifesto of the Communist Party*, Engels (ed.) (Chicago: Kerr & Co. 1906), 37.

[74] Paul Johnson, *Modern Times: The World from the Twenties to the Nineties* (New York: HarperCollins 1992), 92–93, 261–72, 724–28; Richard Pipes, "Human Nature and the Fall of Communism" (1996) 49 *Bulletin of the American Academy of Arts & Sciences* 38; Richard Pipes, *Property and Freedom* (New York: Vintage Books 1999), 209–25.

[75] Pipes, *Property and Freedom*, 216.

Meanwhile, mature capitalist economies have liberated the poor. Where strong economic liberties are secured within a culture of virtue and cooperation, institutions of robust economic liberty accrue to the material benefit of the least well-off and promote their moral agency.[76] Peter Wehner and Arthur Brooks note that economic liberties both allow and trust people to choose and act, and thus foster "certain habits, encouraging individuals to make free and informed choices on most of the matters they confront in their daily lives."[77] John Tomasi observes, "With prosperity, the exercise of thick private economic liberty is for many citizens an essential condition of responsible self-authorship."[78] As some capitalist countries have grown far wealthier, the least well-off have come to prize economic freedom more, and have grown far less enthusiastic about expropriation, collective ownership, and redistribution. In its role in enabling citizens to exercise their moral powers of agency, the economic problem "is not a problem to be solved and put aside," but rather it is increasingly viewed as comprising "the stuff of life."[79]

Waldron does not consider the many ways in which mediated dominion outperforms state-enforced redistribution in practice. There might be countervailing reasons that weigh in favor of redistribution in particular circumstances; Waldron did not provide reasons to prefer it generally,[80] and there is strong evidence that that redistribution does not universalize liberty.[81] He did not demonstrate that unearned property has the same effect on personal development as earned property, and there is ample evidence against his undefended assumption that it does.[82] Finally, it seems implausible that any single authority could determine a rule of

[76] Michael Novak, *The Spirit of Democratic Capitalism* (New York: Madison Books 1991), 156–86; Hernando de Soto, *The Mystery of Capital: Why Capitalism Triumphs in the West and Fails Everywhere Else* (New York: Basic Books 2000).

[77] Wehner and Brooks, *Wealth and Justice*, 30.

[78] Tomasi, *Free Market Fairness*, 183.

[79] Tomasi, *Free Market Fairness*, 57–64, 183.

[80] Alexander and Peñalver recognize that communities other than the state can achieve their ends without resorting to coercion. But in a "modern capitalist economy," they doubt the ability of "private, voluntary communities" to supply all individuals with the resources necessary to develop moral agency. Gregory S. Alexander and Eduardo M. Peñalver, "Properties of Community" (2009) 10 *Theoretical Inquiries in Law* 127. Like Waldron, they do not attempt to show that the state is any more competent to supply the requisite resources to all members of society than the voluntary associations of which they are skeptical, much less natural associations, such as the family. Nor do they demonstrate that efforts by the state would have the same beneficial effect on moral agency as private acts of licensing, bailments, contract, sharing, charity, and cooperation.

[81] Tomasi, *Free Market Fairness*, 223; Pipes, *Property and Freedom*; Pipes, "Human Nature."

[82] Brooks, *Road to Freedom*, 20–31.

distribution, or even a scheme of distribution, which would ensure sufficient resources for the development of positive liberty by all. The incommensurability of human preferences, abilities, and projects must frustrate any attempt to meet the requirements of positive liberty by distributing resources from a central political authority.

Neither property owners nor the state can alone promote liberty. The law must support and depend on other institutions and practices to generate resources and to foster a culture of collaborative use and management. Private property is one important institution among several that enable owners to use their assets productively and that promote liberty and extend to the poorest citizens widespread access to property rights.

4

Property from the inside

Beyond property as politics

Some of private property's critics argue that, if private ownership serves only individual interests or preferences then property is at odds with public concerns.[1] Those accounts trade on the prevalent elision of private, intermediary institutions, and the absorption of all public values into the state. As we saw in Chapter 3, common law institutions of private property defy the individualist–collectivist dichotomy. The plural and ubiquitous forms and practices of intermediary ownership create opportunities and incentives for individuals to take into their deliberations and choices the reasons for which others would act without the state action and coercion that jeopardize property's moral efficacy.

Yet the structure of property institutions cannot alone explain how a person or group that exercises freedom and responsibility with respect to things becomes better off. To see *that*, we need to view property domains from the internal perspective of those who own, manage, and use things for reasons. Looking *at* property ownership – from the outside – is not enough. By looking *along* property ownership toward the reasons for which people act with respect to things, one can observe the operation of moral agency within the domains of ownership, and can understand how private property enables human beings to become better human beings as they constitute themselves by adopting and executing plans of action in pursuit of possibilities that are intelligible as *valuable* possibilities – human goods.

The freedom that owners and their collaborators enjoy within private property's mediated dominion is reasonably exercised in pursuit of many goods. Yet one good is particularly important, which, though no more basic or valuable than any other basic human good, is architectonic; it

[1] For example, Gregory S. Alexander, "Property's Ends: The Publicness of Private Law Values" (2014) 99 *Iowa Law Review* 1257; Hanoch Dagan, "The Public Dimension of Private Property" (2013) 24 *King's Law Journal* 260.

helps humans to order the other goods in their own lives. As owners and their collaborators exercise dominion to achieve other good ends, they realize the good of practical reasonableness. Practical reasonableness is a distinct and basic human good that directs deliberation about possible plans of action. It supplies both substance and shape to deliberations and choices about the use of private property. Substantively, the first principles of practical reason direct human agents toward valuable reasons for action by picking out those opportunities that are worthy of consideration as reasons in their own right. In the more complex practice of moral deliberation, the requirements of practical reasonableness guide choices away from harmful and unreasonable commitments, and thus enable human agents to live flourishing lives in community with others. Choices consistent with the basic requirements of practical reasonableness will be those that promote the common good, not considered in a utilitarian sense as the largest amount of good for the greatest number, but rather as an ensemble of conditions that promotes the flourishing of communities of people.

Just as significant for our purposes is that practical reasoning is a reflexive practice, the exercise of which makes one into a different sort of person. Choosing for reasons creates – constitutes – character, and thereby shapes and guides future deliberations and choices. As owners realize the good of practical reasonableness, they become practically reasonable people. Conversely, unreasonable choices and actions render one less fully reasonable. For all of these reasons, any just institution of private property must account for its effect on the practical reasoning of those who live under it.

This moral reality justifies the duties that give rise to property rights. The capacity of each human being to make plans for the use and management of things provides a strong reason to recognize and enforce the duties of others not to interfere with the plans of owners, including the duties of others who are also owners. Those duties secure and specify the owner's dominion.

Property and perfectionism

The mystery of property's operation

Though many thinkers have observed that property allows owners to be despotic and selfish, many others have commented on the tendency of private property to make people free, virtuous, responsible, prudent, and so forth. Indeed, the idea that property ownership is connected with virtue has a distinguished pedigree. A short survey of these reflections should make clear that the connection between property and human excellence is real, but also that it has been little understood.

Aristotle thought private property necessary for a healthy polis, and particularly for the development of the virtues of temperance and liberality.[2] Richard Weaver, who called property the "last metaphysical right," thought that "somehow it is needed to help [man] express his being."[3] In a society of responsible persons, humans enjoy "a range of free choice which is always expressed in relation to substance."[4] More recently, Stephen Munzer, Eric Claeys, Gregory Alexander, Eduardo Peñalver, and Henry Smith are among those who have commented on the relationship between property and virtue.[5] Clearly, something important is going on within the core of the owner's domain, and whatever it is has moral significance both for the owner and for society. Yet the entire thing remains "mysterious,"[6] or a "mystery" that rests in "prerational sentiments."[7] Practical reasoning, which is transparent from the perspective of the one engaging in it, is naturally opaque to outside observers, who must draw inferences about the agent's reasons for action.[8] Watching a man purchase a shotgun, I might infer that he intends to hunt ducks. But for all I know, he might instead intend to rob a bank.

Part of the difficulty is that mediated dominion does its job so well; property law adds an extra layer of opacity to deliberation within the owner's dominion. In personam duties derive their content from what J. E. Penner describes as the "actions, intentions, or personal histories of the beneficiaries who are the correlative right-holders." In terms of practical reasoning, in personam rights and duties are specified according

[2] Aristotle, *The Politics* II.6. Aristotle had little to say about practical reason's *content*; that the right and morally good is what the good man does is of no use to one wondering whether his own view is practically reasonable. John Finnis, *Natural Law and Natural Rights* (2nd edn, Oxford: Oxford University Press 2011) [hereinafter NLNR], 101–02.

[3] Richard M. Weaver, *Ideas Have Consequences* (Chicago: University of Chicago Press 1948), 131, 134.

[4] Weaver, *Ideas*, 146.

[5] Stephen R. Munzer, *A Theory of Property* (Cambridge: Cambridge University Press 1990), 120–47; Eric R. Claeys, "Virtue and Rights in American Property Law" (2009) 94 *Cornell Law Review* 889; Gregory S. Alexander, "The Social-Obligation Norm in American Property Law" (2009) 94 *Cornell Law Review* 745; Eduardo M. Peñalver, "Land Virtues" (2009) 94 *Cornell Law Review* 821; Henry E. Smith, "Mind the Gap: The Indirect Relation Between Ends and Means in American Property Law" (2009) 94 *Cornell Law Review* 959.

[6] Smith, "Mind the Gap," 959. [7] Weaver, *Ideas*, 134, 146.

[8] John Finnis, *Collected Essays of John Finnis, vol. II: Intention & Identity* (Oxford: Oxford University Press 2012), 13.

to the reasons for which they are exercised. By contrast, the duties that we owe owners (including licensees, bailees, beneficiaries, etc.) to exclude ourselves from the things that they own block "any content which has to do with the specific individuality of particular persons from entering into the right–duty relation."[9] Someone who is subject to a duty not to trespass or steal knows what is required of him – has, in Joseph Raz's terminology an exclusionary reason for action – without any need or right to know anything about the owner or the owner's practical deliberations concerning use and management of the land or item. The owner's reasons for action are thus insulated from outside scrutiny. Viewed from the outside, private property looks something like a magician's hat, from which fully formed products of deliberation emerge. Thus, Henry Smith has observed that we "have a clearer sense of what property is supposed to do than how it is supposed to do it."[10]

Property and the internal point of view

Reasons for action

The key to understanding the moral operation of mediated dominion on practical reason is to adopt the point of view of those who interact with owned things. From the internal point of view of people who interact with things, it becomes clear that the operation of property is not really a mystery, though it is irreducibly complex.

This internal point of view of the practically reasoning person is not reducible to the psychological states that correspond with property ownership.[11] This discussion is not about feelings or emotions, nor the mental and behavioral characteristics that psychologists study. Such an approach to the question maintains the external perspective of scientists though it concerns the workings of the brain. This discussion is about rational choice as the human response to reasons – the response of a being that possesses the radical capacity to bring about new moral realities. To get at this reality, one must eschew the bounds of science and instead look along choosing from the internal perspectives of owners, non-owners, adverse possessors, licensees, bailees, and others

[9] J. E. Penner, *The Idea of Property in Law* (Oxford: Oxford University Press 1997), 28–29.

[10] Smith, "Mind the Gap," 959.

[11] Contrast J. A. Blumenthal, "To Be Human: A Psychological Perspective on Property Law" (2009) 83 *Tulane Law Review* 609; Carol M. Rose, "Psychologies of Property" in James Penner and Henry E. Smith (eds.), *Philosophical Foundations of Property Law* (New York: Oxford University Press 2013), 272.

for whom deliberation and choosing is not a matter of speculative inquiry but rather of practical, and therefore pressing moral, concern.

Start with those inside the domain – owners and those who hold by virtue of the owner's authority. Anyone who has ever had the experience of exercising dominion over a thing understands that decisions can be, and often are, made about the uses of property for *reasons*. Because it is possible for human beings to act for reasons and to create new reasons for themselves by free choice, it is possible for humans to constitute themselves as reasonable beings. The uniquely human capacity to act for reasons, and to create new reasons by making and executing plans of action, is the ground of the moral case for private ownership.

Rational choices are made in response to reasons that have intelligible value as possibilities apart from one's choice of them.[12] Property itself cannot supply the reasons for its use. Private property has no intrinsic value. Even non-fungible property, such as an irreplaceable work of art, is used instrumentally to realize some more basic end or ends, such as understanding, or the experience of beauty. Property is used, left alone, managed, sold, given, created, cultivated . . . for reasons that are aspects of plans of action, inchoate-but-hoped-for dreams, respect for others and other moral requirements – all the valuable motivations for human choice and action.

Practical reasoning is the exercise of ordering all possible reasons for action, basic and instrumental, in one's deliberations and choosing. The *way* in which this exercise is conducted is what produces the self-constitution that is so little understood by lawyers. In the act of making an undetermined choice, one takes into oneself the reasons that one adopts for one's actions, and those reasons become reasons for one's future actions. This exercise "is creative of personal character, and thus of a most significant aspect of the reality of each person who is capable of meaningful relations with other persons."[13]

This is possible in part because reasons for action are only sometimes commensurable. Often, the good to be realized in one possible use of property – say, getting an education to learn – is of an entirely different nature than the good to be realized in another possibility – e.g., riding a bicycle for exercise. Knowledge does not derive its value from health, nor

[12] Compare Christine M. Korsgaard, *The Constitution of Agency* (Oxford: Oxford University Press 2008), 26–68, with John Finnis, *Collected Essays of John Finnis, vol. I: Reason in Action* (Oxford: Oxford University Press 2012), 19–40.

[13] John Finnis, *Moral Absolutes: Tradition, Revision, and Truth* (Washington, DC: Catholic University Press 1991), 58.

does health from knowledge; each of those goods is equally basic, equally fundamental. Neither one contains all of the value of the other. So, each of the potential plans of action is grounded in a basic reason for action. Each of them must be evaluated on its own terms. There is no way to generalize about such possibilities to calculate a single measure of total, collective good or total, collective bad.[14]

Where two incommensurable options stand before a moral agent, the choice itself supplies the ultimate rationality to whatever plan of action the agent adopts. I can drive my car to a Spanish language course or to the gym, but I don't have time or money for both. I must choose. And in the act of choosing, I constitute new reasons for my future deliberation, choice, and action. In a sense (but only in one sense, about which more below), I constitute myself.

The irreducible complexity of pre-moral practical deliberation is one reason why practical reasoning can appear so opaque to outside observers. Even observers who have perfect information about the agent's life circumstances, faculties, tastes and preferences, and prior commitments (do any such observers exist, even among spouses or intimate friends?) cannot account for, predict, or fully explain a free choice, the adoption of one plan of action as against an also-fully-reasonable plan that promises to instantiate a different type of good.

The picture is further complicated by motivations other than reasons, which every reflective person also understands. Reasons are not the only motivations that cause humans to act; we also act from fear, to avoid pain, and on the basis of other sub-rational motivations. So, we need to take moral principles and rules into our reasoning, as well. But we need not consider that complication here. (We will consider it in later chapters.)

Practical reason and the owner's dominion

The ordering of reasons in the will is an important practice within the owner's dominion. Consider Stan and Samantha, a married couple. They own a home together as tenants by the entirety. They use their home instrumentally to serve their communal life together as a family. Their life together – their marriage; their friendship – has value in itself. It is

[14] On incommensurability and the incoherence of consequentialist methods of evaluation, see NLNR, 112–18; Joseph Raz, *The Morality of Freedom* (Oxford: Oxford University Press 1986) [hereinafter MOF], chapter 13. On the incommensurability of life plans and how it is consistent with the existence of moral truth, see Neil MacCormick, *Practical Reason in Law and Morality* (Oxford: Oxford University Press 2008), 89–98; and generally, NLNR.

better for them to share life together than to be alienated from each other. The use of their home is instrumentally useful for realization of human goods that require no further justification.

Other uses of their home are grounded in more complex reasons, either because they involve many more links in the chain of instrumental reasons or because they implicate complicating prudential considerations. Let us revise a familiar hypothetical and suppose that Stan and Samantha are leaders of an underground political movement in a nation suffering under the oppression of an aspirationally totalitarian regime, which has, despite its many unjust actions, not abolished private ownership of homes.[15] In addition to living in communal harmony with each other, they also work together toward the good of ending the tyranny. They host meetings in their home, write books and pamphlets exposing the unjust actions of the regime, shelter dissidents, and engage in other risky projects. Each of these actions has intelligible value in a distinct basic good. The meetings instantiate friendship. The writings promote knowledge. These actions are reasonable regardless of any additional instrumental value they might evince. But in addition, all of their actions are coordinated toward the common good of ending the tyranny, which finds its ultimate justification in justice.

Prudential considerations will complicate Stan and Samantha's practical deliberations. Because the regime is oppressive, Stan and Samantha will weigh the risks of their activities against the probability of success. They might decide to press on against seemingly impossible odds. Or they might reasonably decide to lay low and preserve whatever domestic tranquility they can. They must choose. Either choice takes them into a new reality, which would not exist but for their decision. They are faced with one momentous act of self-constitution after another, all made possible by the regime's decision to allow (at least some) people to own.

Freedom: pre-moral exercises of practical reason

The meaning of self-constitution

What does it mean to constitute oneself through the exercise of practical reason? Looking only at material substance and consequences, this must remain a fanciful notion. I did not make my body, or the circumstances of

[15] Compare Milton Friedman, *Capitalism and Freedom* (Chicago: University of Chicago Press 2002), chapter 1; Jeremy Waldron, *The Right to Private Property* (Oxford: Clarendon Press 1988), 412.

my birth, or my talents and abilities. I cannot even constitute many of my own preferences. I discovered that I like cheese and dislike hummus. I did not create these tastes.

Some property theorists have begun their approach to the question by consulting Hegel. Hegel took seriously the idea of orders beyond our immediate, material experiences and was able to construct a role for the will. But Hegel's abstractions, interesting as they are, do not shed much light on the operation of reason within the mind of a typical property owner, who does not share Hegel's perspective of history. To meet our more modest objectives, we can proceed fruitfully by consulting philosophers who made the perspective of the practically reasoning person their primary object of study. Thomas Aquinas is an obvious candidate. The Thomist account of self-constitution in the order of the will is an interesting alternative to Hegel's theory of embodiment of the will, and suits the goals of this book.

Aquinas opened his Commentary on Aristotle's *Ethics* by observing that the material world is one of four orders that interact with reason. And while reason largely takes the natural world as it finds it, it has power to act on and even to shape the other three orders.

> There is one order that reason does not establish but only beholds, such is the order of things in nature. There is a second order that reason establishes in its own act of consideration, for example, when it arranges its concepts among themselves, and the signs of concepts as well, because words express the meanings of the concepts. There is a third order that reason in deliberating establishes in the operation of the will. There is a fourth order that reason in planning establishes in the external things which it causes, such as a chest and a house.[16]

John Finnis has illustrated Aquinas' insight by reference to a lecture, in which a lecturer and his listeners participate. In the first order (which we study in the "natural sciences"), an audience member "hears the sounds made by the lecturer's vocal chords." In the second order, "the listener hears expositions, arguments, and explanations," and acts to understand them (at least to the extent necessary to disagree with them). In the third order, the lecturer chooses to devote part of his life to communicate knowledge to another person, while the listener chooses to acquire knowledge. In the fourth order, the lecturer and listener share in a

[16] Thomas Aquinas, *Commentary on Aristotle's Nicomachean Ethics*, C. J. Litzinger (trans.) (Notre Dame: Dumb Ox 1993), 1–2. Compare MOF, chapter 14; Amartya Sen, *Development as Freedom* (New York: Knopf 1999).

common language and pedagogical practice, while sitting in a common lecture hall, which are all creations of a common culture.[17]

Like basic reasons for action, these orders or realms are irreducible; none is more foundational than any other, and reason interacts with each realm in a radically different way. However, though irreducible to each other, the four orders in which reason operates are inseparable in the unity of a human person. A human being lives in all four orders, and experiences herself as a self by creating order among the four orders. Bodily existence, conscious understanding, character and the possibilities that open and close through one's choices, and the techniques that one employs and to which one contributes; all together are, in Finnis' expression, "interpenetrated" aspects of our being.[18] Each person's deliberation, choice, and action partake of all four orders. Nevertheless, one's choices are not equally effective at shaping reality in all four orders.

While property plays a role in each of the four realms of reason's order, its role is not understood equally well in all four orders. Nearly all commentary on private property has focused on the role of property in the first and fourth orders. In the first order, one encounters material resources, which can be appropriated and consumed. From Locke and Rousseau to the present, these facts have preoccupied both supporters and critics of special property rights. In the fourth order, people use property to create devices and artifacts, practices and institutions, new wealth, and innumerable possibilities for flourishing in the material world. These practices are the focus of the economic study of property.

Less well understood are the roles that property plays in the second and third orders. In the second order, property can transmit meanings for human consideration. These meanings are freighted with first-, fourth-, and third-order significance. Material things can bear the imprints of institutional and individual plans of action, as where a wedding ring reminds one of one's commitment to one's spouse, and of the entire complex of cultural practices that goes into supporting spouses in their marriage. The ring symbolizes marriage generally. It also symbolizes a plan of action that has distinctive significance within a coherent plan of life – a successful marriage to which the ring's bearer has committed. The ring signals to its owner and to the world that the owner has made a commitment, that by failing to honor that commitment the

[17] NLNR, 136–38. See also Finnis, *Intention and Identity*, 36–39, 83–84; Finnis, *Reason in Action*, 237–43.

[18] Finnis, *Intention and Identity*, 67.

owner would fail in a uniquely tragic manner, and that by honoring the commitment the owner can realize a laudable achievement.

This symbolic function of property should not be mistaken for the (third-order) plan of action itself, or the (fourth-order) cultural institution of marriage, much less for the (first-order) person himself. Self-constitution occurs in the third order, through the exercise of the will in practical deliberations and choices. In the first order, the person and the personal property – even an article that bears enormous personal significance – remain separate and distinct beings.

In her work on the implications of Hegel's thought, Margaret Jane Radin argued that non-fungible objects of personal property, such as wedding rings, become "closely bound up with personhood because they are part of the way we constitute ourselves as continuing personal entities in the world." Such an object, in her view, "has become a part of oneself."[19] In what sense can this be? An item of personal property remains distinct from its owner in what we can immediately recognize as reality, that is, the first order of reality. The loss of one's wedding ring is not the same as the loss of something that is physically part of oneself, such as one's arm. We are embodied beings, and our bodies are part of us, not merely things that we inhabit or possess.[20] By contrast, a ring is precisely an object of possession.

Distinguishing between natural constitution in the first order and self-constitution in the third order makes sense of the rules concerning what things count as objects of property. Because one cannot own a human being, one cannot own part of a human being.[21] But one can own a thing that particularizes a central role in the formation of a human being's third-order identity, such as a wedding ring. The wedding ring is a distinct object of ownership in a way that a human being is not, no matter how bound up the wedding ring is in a person's life plan.

Our bodies are like the ring in the sense that both have material existence. But there the similarity ends. The distinction between

[19] Margaret Jane Radin, "Property and Personhood" (1982) 34 *Stanford Law Review* 957 at 959. For a survey of the literature discussing Radin's original article, see Jeffrey Douglas Jones, "Property and Personhood Revisited" (2011) 1 *Wake Forest Journal of Law & Public Policy* 93.

[20] Finnis, *Intention and Identity*, 33–35; Patrick Lee and Robert P. George, *Body–Self Dualism in Contemporary Ethics and Politics* (New York: Cambridge University Press 2008).

[21] *R* v. *Bentham* [2005] 1 WLR 1057. The common law rule has been modified somewhat by legislated rights to direct the use of gametes and organs. Yet human organs remain market alienable. *Moore* v. *Regents of the University of California*, 793 P 2d 479 (Cal 1990).

ourselves and the things that we inhabit or possess is sensible if we consider that we encounter our traits and characteristics, including both our bodies and our wills; we do not make those traits or choose to inhabit them. Our human being-ness, which is distinctly human by virtue of our capacity to will and choose, is, like our bodies, built into our first-order nature, which reason apprehends but is powerless to change. A human being is a human being simply by his or her nature, not by any exercise of reason or the will. By contrast, an object of property becomes property (and in many instances exists) precisely as a result of the willful actions of political communities (establishing and recognizing property laws), non-political communities (organizing for creative purposes), and individuals (laboring, creating, and purchasing).

Radin is right to identify a connection between personal property and personal identity. But it is not the thing itself that is important. All of the willful plans and actions in which personal belongings become tied up involve self-constituting deliberation and choice within the *person*. The acts of self-constitution are the important things, not the objects themselves. One can have a successful marriage even after mistakenly losing one's ring.

It is in the third order – the order of the will – that domains of ownership do their important work in promoting self-constitution through the exercise of practical reason. Careful attention to the operation of reason in the third order reveals why private property has been credited with moral significance. Consider what self-constitution in the third order consists of: making reasons for one's future actions by choice.[22] Free choice is self-creating. One constitutes oneself in the third order through free choices in the only sense that one can constitute oneself, by choosing to pursue ends that one understands as good and desirable, and thus taking into one's deliberations certain reasons for choice and action rather than other possible reasons.[23] Finnis explains:

> One more or less transforms oneself by making the choice, and by carrying it out, and by following it up with other free choices in line with it. One's choice in fact lasts in, and as part of, one's character . . . To choose is not only to set out into a new world; it is already to become a person (or society) more or less different from the person (or society) that deliberated about the goods and bads in the alternative available options.[24]

[22] MOF, chapter 14; Robert P. George, *Making Men Moral: Civil Liberties and Public Morality* (New York: Oxford University Press 1993), 173–82.

[23] Finnis, *Reason in Action*, 33–34, 239.

[24] Finnis, *Reason in Action*, 239–40.

Consider an example of self-constitution that private property makes possible. Sally decides to become a musician, specifically a trumpet player. Suppose that she is equally adept at music as at athletics, but less adept with languages. Thus, because of first-order considerations, her choice of avocation in music is undetermined as against the possibility of becoming a marathon runner, but partly determined as against the possibility of becoming a linguist. Sally *discerns* that it is wiser, for first-order reasons, to forego an avocation in linguistics. She then *chooses* to forego an avocation in athletics, in order to become a musician. Her exercise of practical reason has partly directed her actions and partly determined them.

If Sally can own a trumpet, and thus be secure in her use and possession of it, insulated from collective decision-making, then she can master the instrument and develop the connatural ability to make music on it. If she succeeds, she will become Sally-the-trumpet-player. This Sally is in one sense the same Sally who set out to learn to make music. But in other ways, the new Sally is a different person. In the third order, trumpet playing has become part of Sally's identity because Sally has transformed herself into someone who acts for the reason of making music, and not for other possible reasons. She is able to make music on the trumpet because she committed time and resources to developing the necessary skills, exercised discipline over her sub-rational inclinations, and daily renewed her commitment to her goal.

Sally's plan of action, which comprises a substantial portion of her life plan, has become particularized in an article of personal property – her trumpet. The reasons that Sally has set before herself, which now constrain and guide her deliberations and actions, are tied up in this instrument. As with a wedding ring, the trumpet has not become part of Sally in a first-order sense. But it is an essential component of the identity that she has constructed for herself in the third order. The character of a skilled musician consists largely in the dexterous subjugation and utilization of the instrument, considered both as a means to the more fundamental end of making beautiful music (aesthetic experience) and as an end in itself (skillful play).

Third-order identity is a real aspect of one's being, and it is lasting. Louis Armstrong was recognizable as Louis Armstrong in a first-order sense without his trumpet, but a photograph of Armstrong holding his trumpet is a more complete, more accurate depiction of "him." And the persona that Armstrong created in the third order lives on, charming all who meet him through the wonders of modern technologies, despite the fact that his bodily existence has ceased. There is something to the fact that the items owned by those we love continue to represent them after they have died. One's character is important because it lasts, even beyond one's bodily life. And the things we own can become bound up in that character when employed in our life plans.

Amish communities understand this phenomenon as well as anyone. The Amish distinction between use of a modern technology owned by another, which is permitted, and title ownership of that technology, which is forbidden, would make little sense if exclusive control of a resource did not have a lasting effect on one's character.[25] Using a technological resource – catching a ride in a car or borrowing a phone – is not viewed as a threat to the Amish identity as a people who live simple lives. The right of exclusive use poses such a threat because owners must deliberate about the use and management of resources, and their reasons become part of them.

Choosing for reasons entails ordering the four orders. Sally's execution of her plan of action has exercised her practical reason in all four orders. In the first order, she has developed her inborn capacity to play the trumpet, overcome her initial lack of skill by nurturing connatural abilities, and mastered the art of ordering the physical world to produce beautiful music. In the second order, she has developed habits of responding to the symbolic significance of notes on pages of sheet music, the gestures and signals of other musicians with whom she plays, and the presence of her trumpet, which constantly reminds her of the need to practice. In the third order, she made a plan of action, committed to it, and followed through on her commitment. Along the way, she participated in and partly helped to shape institutions and practices of music-making. By constituting herself in the third order, Sally structured her world in all four orders, with the indispensable assistance of private property.

Sally's plans for the use of her things are entitled to the non-interference of others because Sally is performing her acts of self-constitution in her capacity as a human being. This is why the categorical (though not exceptionless) norm against stealing is expressed in public law as an exceptionless prohibition.[26] Criminal prohibitions against theft

[25] See Donald B. Kraybill, "Opting Out: How the Amish Have Survived in America" (March 7, 2014) 141(5) *Commonweal* 13.

[26] For example, *R* v. *Baxter and Another*, [2012] 263 FLR 160 (Australian Capital Territory); Iowa Code §714.1. Not perhaps an act of trespass, which gives rise to criminal liability if done for an unlawful purpose or knowingly without consent, necessity, or other

are justified by the significant harm that one causes by stealing the personal property of another. To steal is to upset an array of plans of action that are constitutive of the owner's identity. It is to destroy various instantiations of the basic good of practical reasonableness. And it is to fail to respect the owner as an agent of practical reason. In short, it is *wrong*.

Private law and equity account for these realities in more nuanced ways. Sally's life plan does not transform the trumpet, only Sally's third-order identity. Because the thing does not become part of the owner in a first-order sense, the thing is in a sense fungible for a suitable substitution.[27] So, if one could replace Sally's trumpet with one so identical to it that she would not know the difference, and her plan of action would suffer no adverse consequences, then perhaps Sally has not suffered damages. Nevertheless, that action would be wrongful. For another person to substitute his own judgment on the question of whether another trumpet would be sufficient would in itself fail to respect Sally as a reasoned plan-maker. It would be to usurp her status as the being with authority to use and manage the trumpet for reasons, and therefore to violate one's duty toward her.

So the *motivation* for a taking or entry matters. Thus equity might enjoin a deliberate conversion or trespass, or Sally might be entitled to punitive or exemplary damages where the trespass or conversion was intentional and not motivated by necessity.[28] Sally's right to exclude is limited in the common law according to reasons that figure in the deliberations of ostensible duty-bearers. She may not contravene ancient customs of use in her community.[29] She may not extinguish vested easements, profits, or other property rights. And she may not deny someone assistance necessary to save a life. But the justified intruder must limit the intrusion to what is reasonably proportionate to the danger and must repair harm done in the course of the privileged intrusion.[30]

justification. See the discussion in *Wilson* v. *McDonald*, 193 A Crim R 63 (Ct App Western Australia 2009).

27 Michael Moore made this observation in critiquing Radin's account. Michael S. Moore, "Four Reflections on Law and Morality" (2006) 48 *William & Mary Law Review* 1523 at 1565.

28 *Jacque* v. *Steenberg Homes, Inc.*, 563 NW 2d 154 (Wis 1997); *Lester D. Collicutt Lumber and Building Supplies Ltd.* v. *Dorey and Dorey, 42 NSR (2d) 204* (Nova Scotia 1980).

29 *McConico* v. *Singleton*, 9 SCL 244 (SC 1818); *Oregon* v. *Hay*, 462 P 2d 671 (Or 1969).

30 Mark Lunney, "Trespass to Land" in Ken Oliphant (ed.), *The Law of Tort* (2nd edn, London: Butterworths 2007), 506–07; Restatement (Second) of Torts §197 (1965).

Even with the qualifications found in common law, the argument is sometimes advanced that the right to exclude cannot be grounded in an owner's interest in use because exclusion is over-inclusive. For example, Arthur Ripstein argues that use cannot justify exclusion in part because the exclusion right secures the owner's freedom to decide on potential, as well as actual uses. Critiquing Larissa Katz's idea of exclusive use as a right to set the agenda for the owned thing, Ripstein points out that the owner's agenda includes not only an actual, specific plan for use of the thing but also unspecified, possible uses to which the thing might (or might not) be put.[31]

Whether or not Ripstein's criticism is successful against Katz's account,[32] it fails to consider the *capacity* of owners to make plans for the use of things, which grounds the right to exclude by justifying a duty of self-exclusion. One owes a duty not to trespass on others' things because those others are human beings, agents who possess the radical capacity for choice and action according to reasons, whether or not they have yet exercised that capacity on their things in a way that outsiders can recognize. This is why even inchoate and not-yet-executed plans of action for things are entitled to the respect of outsiders to the owner's dominion. It is the capacity, not the actual exercise, that does the normative work.

Ripstein is correct that the right to exclude is not reducible to a greatest-good calculation, a summing-up of the benefits of allowing the owner to use all-things-considered. But the exclusion right is *neither* prior to the good *nor* contingent on utility. The value of the exclusion right need not be reduced to a consequentialist calculation. Exclusion rights serve many different ends, and there is no cause to assume that those ends must be commensurable with each other or reducible to a single measure.

In addition to all of the other ends that self-exclusion serves, it promotes respect for human beings as agents of practical reason. Human beings are capable of exercising practical reason by virtue of our being the kind of beings that we are, namely human. It is our capacity for practical reasonableness that sets us apart from other kinds of beings and provides the justification for our special treatment in morality and law as beings who present basic reasons for action to the practical reasoning of others.

31 Arthur Ripstein, "Possession and Use" in James Penner and Henry E. Smith (eds.), *Philosophical Foundations of Property Law* (New York: Oxford University Press 2013), 156.

32 Lisa Austin has argued that the right of possession should include potential, future uses for reasons internal to legal practice itself. Lisa Austin, "Possession and the Distractions of Philosophy" in James Penner and Henry E. Smith (eds.), *Philosophical Foundations of Property Law* (New York: Oxford University Press 2013), 182 at 196.

That treatment – the duties that each of us owes to other human beings as agents of practical reason – is not reducible to any other good or requirement of reason.

Four preconditions of undetermined choice

Practical reason cannot be exercised in an impoverished moral and material setting. The realization of practical reasonableness through acts of self-constitution is an expensive good.[33] It cannot be realized apart from a whole set of circumstances and conditions, which require extensive individual and cultural commitments. Four conditions are uniquely important here: (1) freedom from coercion, (2) a variety of good options from which to choose, (3) a stability of settled expectations, and (4) incentives for detachment and commitment.

First, to be free a choice must be uncoerced. Practical reasonableness is a reflexive human good. It is therefore vulnerable to coercive influences. If one chooses in response to a threat, rather than in response to the intelligible value of the option chosen, then one's deliberation and choosing have been perverted.[34] In that case, the motivation for one's action is not the value in the chosen option but rather fear of the circumstance that will be forced on one if one chooses otherwise.

Second, in order to make a choice one must have valuable options (at least two). The options must be grounded in goods that are objectively valuable.[35] A choice from among equally bad options, or between a good option and an evil option, is not really a choice.[36] So, any institution that is attuned to the demands of practical reason must allow its participants to pursue a variety of good opportunities. The available options must also be possible. A choice of the possible over the impossible is not a choice. And the options must be plural and incommensurable, one incapable of being reduced to another. If one option contains all of the goods contained in all other options plus something more, then deliberation does not end in free choice; it ends in discernment of the only rational possibility.[37]

Third, one cannot rationally adopt a plan of action without stable expectations and cultural practices. In order to execute complicated, collaborative, and long-term projects, everyone involved must

[33] On the cultural requirements for realization of expensive goods, such as personal autonomy, see MOF, 119.

[34] MOF, 377–78, 407.

[35] MOF, 373–95; George, *Making Men Moral*, 173–82.

[36] MOF, 411–12; George, *Making Men Moral*, 173–82.

[37] Finnis, *Reason in Action*, 225, 243.

understand what is expected of each of them, and must be able to predict what expectations, rights, and resources will pertain in the future, as the project is carried to fruition. To carry out a plan of action requires that what I started working on yesterday will be available tomorrow for my continued efforts on it.

Fourth, one must commit to one's choice, such that it shapes one's character and identity, yet remain sufficiently detached to adapt or even repent of one's plan as new information comes available. To repent of the choice by making a subsequent inconsistent choice is to undo it in the third order, even if vestiges of it remain in the first, second, and fourth orders. In other words, one must have integrity and fidelity in order realize the good of practical reasonableness. One's plans of action must remain open-ended to account for new circumstances, possibilities, and unstable expectations.[38] But a complete lack of commitment to one's chosen plans demonstrates that one has not really adopted those plans. There is a golden mean between fanaticism and apathy. One cannot make the achievement of a goal one's reason for future action unless one is committed to achieving the goal, though one must remain open to making reasonable adjustments and changes.

Mediated dominion supplies the necessary conditions

For individuals

Private ownership is one of the institutions that make practical reasoning possible, and it is a primary servant of practical reasoning about the material world. Private property serves practical reasonableness primarily by securing the conditions necessary to pursue plural instantiations of human goods in acts of pre-moral deliberation and choice. Each of the preconditions of practical reasonableness considered above meets a corresponding supply in well-constructed institutions of private property, such as those found in common law.

Insulation from coercion

First, private ownership insulates owners and their collaborators from coercion. By insulating deliberations and choices about the use of resources from collective decision-making, private property enables private owners and their collaborators to make and execute plans of

[38] Finnis, *Intention and Identity*, 51; Finnis, *Reason in Action*, 239–43.

action in which those resources play a part. As we noted above, Sally is able to become an accomplished musician because she has complete control over her trumpet. If other people made decisions about the best use of her trumpet then she would always be subject to decisions that from her perspective are capricious and could interfere with development of her musical abilities.

Freedom from coercion is especially important when owners choose to pursue good ends that others do not value, or do not value as much. Our political dissidents, Stan and Samantha, would find it exceedingly difficult to carry on their heroic projects if the government seizes title to their home. Equally to the point, they would find much easier their decision whether to continue their political activities; they would have an almost-conclusive reason to desist. Private property enables owners to pursue goods that collective deliberation does not produce, and to internalize the momentous implications of freely made decisions.

Freedom from coercion is indispensable in part because the goods that owners can realize in private ownership are various. Publius located the origin of private property in the "diversity of the faculties of men."[39] This is an important consideration. Some are better suited to make music, others to practice medicine. But more than diversity of faculties accounts for the diversity of uses. Two owners with identical faculties might reasonably choose two radically different life plans. One might choose to practice a musical instrument in her home; the other might encumber her home with a mortgage in order to finance an education in medicine.

Property duties secure the freedom to choose projects and commitments that others would not choose.[40] These duties impose a heavy burden of justification on anyone who would interfere with private deliberations and choices about the use and management of things. In Charles Reich's useful imagery, property creates a zone of freedom around the owner.[41] This zone is secure against outside influence whether the owner is an individual person or a community of people. The owner's domain can encompass the owner's family, beneficiaries, licensees, bailees, and other collaborators and friends. Within the domain of ownership, these people are not answerable to those without the domain. They generally need not explain their reasoning to others; their practical deliberations remain concealed from the outside world. The opacity of mediated dominion facilitates both individual plans of

[39] James Madison, *The Federalist Papers*, No. 10. [40] Penner, *Idea of Property*, 24–28.
[41] Charles A. Reich, "The New Property" (1964) 73 *Yale Law Journal* 733 at 771–72.

action and plans that are self-consciously directed toward the common good of communities.

Amish practices highlight another important benefit of exclusive dominion. Property's exclusion strategy is particularly important to projects of self-constitution in part because it enables individual and communal owners to push out reasons and actions that are inconsistent with their plans of action, and therefore with their identity. One becomes a person or group that acts in pursuit of reason x in part by not acting for not-x, and in part by not acting for reasons y and z. Without the authority to exclude those who would involve the group in acting for reasons not-x, y, and z, the owners and their collaborators could not define their commitments, and therefore could not constitute themselves around those commitments. So a community that is committed to nonviolence constitutes itself as that kind of community by exercising its right to exclude weapons manufacturers.

Plural and incommensurable goods

Second, private property enables the production of a rich variety of human goods, thus increasing the possible objects of choices. There is an obvious way in which private property increases available goods: institutions of private property result in more, and more varied, material production than collectivist economic systems. There is also a less obvious way. The common law model of private ownership, with its various spheres of mediated dominion, opens possibilities for pursuing human goods of all kinds (not just material goods), which are available in neither collectivist systems of ownership nor systems of purely individual appropriation. These possibilities are not products of property rules. It is not the scheme of claim-rights, use-liberties, and powers of ownership – what lawyers identify as property rights – which creates options for deliberation and choice. Rather human beings and their intermediary institutions create those possibilities. By securing from outside influence the freedom of individuals and institutions, mediated dominion enables those individuals and groups to employ material things in their acts of self-constitution.

Plural domains of ownership guide the use and management of resources between the opposite dangers of collectivism on one side and radical individualism on the other. Private ownership in the common law is a complex of plural decision-making. It accommodates simultaneous, often-redundant, collaborative, and sometimes-rivalrous pursuits of incommensurable goods by individuals and groups of various sizes and commitments. This makes it variable and spontaneously responsive to the possible uses of resources, and most fitting to the open-endedness of social life. Those who would reduce the goods served naturally by private ownership in order to achieve collective goals or to secure individual rights to do wrong should bear a heavy burden of persuasion.

Collective decision-making through political institutions is by nature reductionist. To the extent that it performs its function well, it results in conclusive rules, which operate by ruling out many pursuits and plans. Some reasons for action will be chosen over other possible reasons for action for and on behalf of the entire community; uniform rules of general applicability necessarily reduce possible plans of action. By contrast, common law institutions of private property locate decision-making authority over resources in plural and independent realms, and therefore enable some owners to use their resources to pursue knowledge, others to pursue friendship, and others to pursue health, beauty, religious understanding, and so on. Private property harnesses the natural variety in human faculties and preferences to produce a variety of good options, which enrich deliberations and choices.

On the other extreme, if property is only a right to satisfy individual preferences, then it threatens to eradicate expensive goods and undo the self-constitution of groups and associations. If property is merely a right to appropriate and use as an individual, then it will produce only those goods that individuals can produce in isolation, or at best as a result of their commercial transactions. Many of the most valuable goods, such as education, professions, and symphonies, might never be realized in such an atomized world. Fortunately, that picture is a bad caricature of the property institutions that we inhabit.

The common law maintains walls of protection around both individuals and communities, and assists the work of self-constitution that they are already performing, in all its rich variety. With its complex forms of individual, plural, and intermediary estates of ownership, mediated dominion enables the realization of goods that require cooperation. Marital estates and rules of kinship harness the natural altruism and mutual concern that prompt members of a family to care for each other. Trusts and other forms of corporate ownership enable both for-profit and nonprofit collaboration. Religious communities are able to use their property to provide for their own members and for outsiders. Universities advance knowledge and learning within the community. And so on.

Stability of expectations

Third, a domain of ownership frees the owner to employ the thing in her plans of action, especially long-term plans. An owner is secure in her expectation that she can do with her asset what is necessary to bring her plan of action to fruition. In the words of Harold Demsetz, "Property rights . . . derive their significance from the fact that they help a man form those expectations which he can reasonably hold in his dealings with others."[42] Whatever powers and liberties property allows to the owner are those that the owner can count on being permitted to exercise, without fear that others will intermeddle in her projects and commitments. Or viewed from the perspective of duties rather than rights as Carol Rose framed it, property rules signal, "in a clear and distinct language, precisely what our obligations are and how we may take care of our interests."[43]

In order for an asset to be put to productive use, someone must choose a use for it from among many incompatible options. The choice will most commonly be guided by pre-moral considerations. Should a tract of land be developed as a school in order to promote the good of knowledge, or rather as an athletic field in order to promote the goods of play, health, and friendship? If it is not possible to develop both, one must be chosen over the other. Just as there is nothing inherently unreasonable or immoral in choosing to build a school rather than a ball field, there is nothing unreasonable in choosing to build a ball field rather than a school. It is the choice of one option, rather than the other, which determines the reasons for the property owner's action.

Yet things that are owned can come to bear the imprint of plans of action only if property rights are secure. Following Hegel, Jeremy Waldron observed that working on a material to fashion an item of personal property is a concrete way to make reasons for one's future action. It solidifies one's intentions by taking the intended shape. "Once a sculptor begins carving a pieta out of a block of marble he may not be able to change his mind and carve a man on horseback instead."[44] As we saw earlier, the sculptor can exercise practical reason even though he is not the fee simple owner of the materials on which he works, as long as his authority rests on the security of the property rights of the fee simple

[42] Harold Demsetz, "Toward a Theory of Property Rights" in Robert C. Ellickson, Carol M. Rose, and Bruce A. Ackerman (eds.), *Perspectives on Property Law* (3rd edn, New York: Aspen 2002), 135 at 136.

[43] Carol M. Rose, "Crystals and Mud in Property Law" (1988) 40 *Stanford Law Review* 577.

[44] Waldron, *Right to Property*, 312.

owner. The stability that the material imposes on the sculptor's plan of action is "more difficult to achieve if resources are not owned privately."[45] In the absence of property rights, the sculptor is open to interference by those who have no stake in the success of the project.

The more complicated a plan of action becomes, the more significance an owner's security assumes. Suppose Sally wants to expand her musical horizons and decides to join her efforts to those of other musicians. If Sally joins a brass band then she will come into contact with those who are likely to have the greatest interest in using her instrument and other equipment – other trumpet players. The settled expectations that property law establishes as background principles enable communities to develop their own particularized practices and expectations about the use of things. If the members of Sally's trumpet section decide to share mutes, pencils, or even instruments during rehearsals, they can make that arrangement. But if not, everyone is secure in the use of his own stuff. Either way, they can collaborate because they know what is expected of them.

In these ways, mediated dominion enables people to develop a coherent plan of life, a basic requirement of practical reasonableness. A coherent plan of life is constructed not merely with an eye toward the immediate future, or the next year, or the next decade, but also with a vision for what one will want one's life to have looked like upon one's death, even (or especially) if one expects that death to be many years in the future. It is the master plan that gives all of one's shorter-term plans of action sense and meaning. Property performs this work by establishing clear expectations, which make long-term plans for things possible.

Commitment

Fourth, private property encourages commitment to one's projects. Private property performs this task by directing the costs and benefits of choices about things into the deliberation of owners. It is well understood that Sally is most likely to maintain and preserve the economic value of her trumpet if she owns it outright. But the benefits for her moral agency also deserve attention. Private ownership creates both the possibility of, and motivations for, the exercise of responsibility. In particular, private ownership encourages what Richard Weaver called "providence." That my current choices will produce a harvest for the future me to reap requires a certain "play of mind," which is attuned to the personal worth

[45] Waldron, *Right to Property*, 313.

that one derives from planning ahead and following through on one's plans.[46] When this play of mind becomes a habit, a virtue is born.

Recall that commitment is neither fanaticism nor apathy. Private ownership acts like a guardrail around the virtue of commitment, to prevent it from veering off in either direction. Being committed to the management and use of things requires one to be open to change one's course as circumstances demand. It also requires one to attend to what is needed. Consider a farmer. To make one's living growing crops on one's land requires openness and adaptability. A plan of action that entails daily irrigation is no use in a flood. It also requires regular renewal of effort. The farmer, having internalized the consequences of a failed crop, has every incentive to do the work required to get his crop to market.

It is worth pausing here, because the example of the farmer makes it possible to contrast common law institutions of ownership with publicly traded capital ownership on one hand and collectivization on the other. Ownership of the farm by the farmer and/or the farmer's family has become less common as agribusiness has grown. Stockholders who purchase shares in an agribusiness for the purpose of earning dividends and growing wealth have very different kinds of incentives – it would not be unfair to call those incentives instrumentalist – with respect to treatment of the land than the family that owns its own farm. This has consequences for the way that the land is managed and exploited, which Wendell Berry (among others) has fruitfully examined.[47] Even more starkly, the collectivization experiments of the twentieth century destroyed all incentives for farmers to act in practically reasonable ways, and the privation that ensued is well known.[48] Common law institutions of ownership have proven superior to both of those alternatives at promoting the practical reasonableness of those who manage and use the invaluable resource of land.

The mediated dominion of common law ownership contributes to the possibility of order and stability within plans of action, which enables detachment and commitment, two basic requirements of practical reasonableness. It creates strong incentives for owners to take account of future, foreseeable consequences of their present choices, and gives them the authority to make decisions that are likely to bring about the

[46] Weaver, *Ideas*, 138–39.

[47] Wendell Berry, *The Gift of Good Land* (San Francisco: North Point Press 1981).

[48] See Paul Johnson, *Modern Times: The World from the Twenties to the Nineties* (New York: HarperCollins 1992), 724–28; Richard Pipes, *Property and Freedom* (New York: Vintage Books 1999), 211–25.

best consequences.[49] Mediated dominion begets responsibility in using one's property to provide for oneself, one's family, and other dependents. Because owners bear responsibility for the material consequences of their decisions, their deliberations take in many of the considerations that *ought* to inform deliberations about the management of things.

All four conditions

All four of the preconditions of practical reasonableness come together in mediated dominion. Consider what in the United States is perhaps the central case of real property ownership – the residential house. That the state stands ready to enforce one's rights to use, and to exclude others from, one's residence frees one to build a life within one's home that others might not value. Stan and Samantha purchase title to a home, which they hold together in tenancy by the entirety. They can now organize and publish the newsletter to express their minority political views. They can exercise their right to encumber their home with a mortgage in order to obtain a loan, with which they can subsidize their newsletter. And the security of their title means that they can finish what they start; they need not worry about their equipment being coercively turned over to someone else in the middle of publication. Throughout this project, Stan and Samantha are attaining (at least) two significant, human achievements. They are realizing their chosen end – political expression and participation. And they are exercising reason, and so making themselves more fully reasonable. They have thus achieved in some measure practical reasonableness, which is a basic reason for action in its own right.

For groups and communities

Property performs its moral work not only for individual owners but also for communities of individuals, working together for a common good. The common good is realized both within plural ownership, especially intermediary ownership, and by individual owners who collaborate in practices and institutions that private property makes possible, such as

[49] Richard Weaver observed,

> That I reap now the reward of my past industry or sloth, that what I do today will be felt in that future now potential – these require a play of mind . . . [N]o society is healthful which tells its members to take no thought of the morrow because the state underwrites their future.

Weaver, *Ideas*, 138.

the contract. Joint owners in corporate assets and concurrent estates; families and associations of which owners are part; and all those with whom owners cooperate: all of these cooperate for ends that are good for all, and for each.

Joint action and group agency

Groups, like individuals, engage in morally significant acts of self-constitution. Indeed, for voluntary associations (as opposed to natural communities, such as the family), the acts of self-constitution give associations their existence. Such communities as voluntary associations exist as realities almost exclusively in Aquinas' third order, the realm of choice and will.[50] They constitute themselves as individual members act in concert according to the community's plan of action toward shared goals. Without both shared ends and an agreed-upon plan of action for achieving those ends, there would be no association or voluntary community, only a collection of individuals who may or may not happen to be doing the same thing. But the fact that humans can coordinate their actions raises the possibility of communal self-constitution.

Mere coincidence of intention or common knowledge does not form the community. Coordination is necessary. A voluntary community comes into existence when two or more individuals come together to coordinate their activities to a shared objective over some period of time. The members of a community act for at least some of the same reasons in an open-ended commitment according to a shared plan of action. In a community, the goods of individual members are shared, so that the reasons for which one acts are reasons for others to act, in part because they are one's reasons.[51]

Groups and institutions can and do engage in joint action, coordinated by joint intention, which is more than merely the sum of the intentions of individual members.[52] A group's joint intention consists in its plan of action, which coordinates and structures the joint action of the group's members toward a shared goal or goals. Joint intention is formed when at least two people both intend the same plan of action

[50] Finnis, *Intention and Identity*, 84. [51] NLNR, chapter VI.

[52] What follows draws heavily from Richard Ekins, *The Nature of Legislative Intent* (Oxford: Oxford University Press 2012), 47–76; Michael E. Bratman, *Faces of Intention* (Cambridge: Cambridge University Press 1999), 91–162; and to a lesser extent from Peter Morton, *An Institutional Theory of Law: Keeping Law in its Place* (Oxford: Clarendon Press 1998), 26–36.

and the constituent aspects of that plan, and they do so because of their shared intention.[53] One member of the group adopts the plan at least in part because another member has adopted it. Their intentions are said in that instance to interlock. Their intentions are shared and mutually dependent. They are pursuing the same human goods by settled means, and they have constituted the group as an agent around a plan of action.

In this way an association of people can constitute itself as a group, of which its members are part. A group that adopts reasoned, complete, and consistent plans forms an agent.[54] An agent acts in response to reasons and constitutes itself around those reasons. Some of those reasons will be created by the agent, including the plan of action and various subplans that are judged essential to the plan's success. The agent thus creates for itself a new reality with its own language, values, customs, and norms.

By adopting a plan the agent creates new reasons for the actions of its members. It creates, in an important sense, a new reality in the order of the wills of the individuals who comprise the group, who internalize the group's values and commitments.[55] In this way, a group enriches the practical reasoning of its members. It "changes how members of the group should reason," as Richard Ekins puts it, and thus changes their individual identities, often without coercion. Bringing the group's reasons and action into line requires members to "discipline themselves." Each member of the group must consider not only his own reasons for action but also the reasons of other members of the group, and should "attend to the coherence of their joint action."[56]

To the extent that they are committed to success, members of a group dispose themselves to take into their own deliberations and choices the reasons of other members and the plan of action of the group. The success of the group depends on this disposition. And because practical reason is reflexive in nature, by disposing themselves to consider the reasons of other members and the group's plan, the members constitute themselves as people who deliberate and choose for reasons apart from their own preferences. They become less self-focused and they make themselves into communal, civic-minded beings.

[53] Ekins, *Legislative Intent*, 54; Bratman, *Faces of Intention*, 121.

[54] Ekins, *Legislative Intent*, 73. [55] Morton, *Institutional Theory*, 28–29.

[56] Ekins, *Legislative Intent*, 74, 75.

The common good of the community

There are central and peripheral instances of group agency and communal constitution. In central cases, a group chooses and acts not arbitrarily but for ultimate reasons that have intelligible value. Peripheral instances are often defective in some respect. A cult that forms a suicide pact is recognizable as a group with a joint intention because it has unanimously adopted a plan of action. But it has constituted itself by way of a plan of action that we recognize as irrational and destructive. Its attempt at communal self-constitution is a tragic failure. By contrast, a charitable association that forms for the purpose of feeding the homeless has adopted and constituted itself around a plan of action that is grounded in human goods of friendship, health, life, and charity. This is a central case of communal self-constitution.

The intelligible value of certain ultimate reasons explains the attractiveness of the group's shared objective, what we can call, following Finnis and classical philosophers, the community's "common good."[57] Again, the common good is not a collective good; it is not the greatest good for the greatest number. Because basic human goods are incommensurable, no collective good is possible. Rather, the common good is a mutually beneficial good, to which the community is directed through the exercise of practical reason. It subsumes the various and plural goods that are pursued by individual members in their actions, when and to the extent that those actions are undertaken on the basis of the joint intention of the group. Success by a member of a community, as long as it is not achieved at the expense of the common good, is a success for the community as a whole. And vice versa: the common good establishes the conditions that enable individual members of the community to flourish.

John Finnis has explained, "the common good is fundamentally the good of individuals (an aspect of whose good is friendship in community)."[58] When we speak of the good of a community, we mean the common good of members of that community.

> [I]f A and B are friends, then the collaboration of each is for the sake (at least in part) of the other, and there is community between them not only in that there is a common interest in the conditions, and common pursuit of the means, whereby each will get what he want for himself, but also in

[57] NLNR, 150–53; Finnis, *Intention and Identity*, 94–96. See also Tony Honoré, *Making Law Bind* (Oxford: Oxford University Press 1987), 56–58.

[58] NLNR, 168. See also Richard W. Garnett, "The Story of Henry Adams' Soul: Education and the Expression of Associations" (2001) 85 *Minnesota Law Review* 1841.

> that what A wants for himself he wants (at least in part) under the description "that-which-B-wants-for-himself," and vice versa.[59]

Because A and B are in friendship – community – with each other, A has taken B's reasons for action into his own practical reasoning, and B has done likewise with A's reasons for action. The good of B has become part of the good of A, and the good of A has become part of the good of B. The practical reasoning of each of them has been enriched.

This mutual self-constitution finds unique realization within intermediary forms of property ownership. As discussed in Chapter 3, intermediary estates contain mechanisms and incentives for individuals to take into their practical deliberations the reasons of other individuals, with whom they are in community. And because private property enables exchange and promise-making, these zones of freedom often come into contact with each other, sometimes overlapping for a time, sometimes combining. Collaborative property ownership can be (at least aspirationally) permanent, as in a marriage, or temporary, as in a residential leasehold. Notice that the state stands ready to enforce Stan and Samantha's right to exclude others from their residence whether they own their home or lease it, and in many cases will even enforce their right to exclude their landlord. And this right to exclude benefits all who are in their home (both of them, their children, guests and visitors), not just in material ways, but also by enabling them to plan and choose. It enables them to plan and choose together as a family, and thus to realize the good of human community in its most comprehensive form.

It should now be plain that governments and other political authorities are in important respects unlike intermediary institutions; they do not constitute themselves in the same sense. The common good of the political community is a means to an end, the end being the realization of good states of affairs by the community's individual and group members. The common good of a friendship or a family or a religious community is intrinsically valuable; it has intelligible value in and of itself. The good realized in an act of mutual self-constitution is some good that is pursued for its own sake by two (or more) people who are pursuing it in part because of the other person's pursuit of it. The good of both becomes the good of each. By contrast, the formation of a state does not instantiate goods that are good for each because they are good for all; regulation for the sake of regulation is not rational action. Rather, the state *instrumentally* makes possible the realization of basic goods by

59 NLNR, 141

others. Thus, a polity is not self-justifying; its existence is both justified and limited by goods more fundamental than itself.[60] Political bodies, such as states, publicly traded corporations, and trade unions are justifiable to the extent that they enable their members to realize good states of affairs.

A political community engages in self-constitution in the limited sense that it deliberates and chooses means to achieve its instrumental ends. Law-making and enforcement are exercises of group action for a shared purpose.[61] But the constitution of a polity does not create the common good. Rather, it establishes and secures the preconditions – order, peace, national security, the rule of law – that are required for members of the political community to bring about the plural and incommensurable aspects of the common good. Intermediary groups and associations have priority over the state in their claims on individuals because "it is in their membership of Groups, communities, and Organizations, and their engagement as agents in Practices and Activities, that human beings establish their identity." Unless the other forms of social life preceded political society it would be, as Peter Morton colorfully described it, "an association of automatons."[62]

This matters because state action has moral costs. The means available to the state to perform its job – uniform rules, a monopoly on violence, coercion – necessarily foreclose the deliberative self-constitution of others by reducing the full range of options. The state's job is to create, interpret, and enforce exclusionary reasons for the choices and actions of those who are under its authority. Because acts of legislation and regulation necessarily establish exclusionary reasons for the actions of the governed, they foreclose the possibility of joint deliberation, intention, and action by at least some members of the political community on at least some questions. If the political community has the authority to settle not only the preconditions but also the community's plans of action, then there is no room for the self-constituting deliberations and choices of the community's members (individual and intermediary).

The constitution of a political community is also less responsive than other communities to the reasons for its members' actions. It does not provide for its members the way that a family does. And it is not

[60] Robert P. George, "The Common Good: Instrumental but Not Just Contractual" (May 17, 2013) *Public Discourse*.

[61] Ekins, *Legislative Intent*; Finnis, *Reason in Action*, 240–41; Jean Porter, *Ministers of the Law: A Natural Law Theory of Legal Authority* (Grand Rapids: Eerdmans 2010).

[62] Morton, *Institutional Theory*, 249.

responsive to the reasons of its members in the way that a voluntary association is. This is why political authorities have a special duty to respect the freedom of the political community's members to engage in acts of self-constitution. For these reasons, the authority of a political community is limited in principle. Its job is to secure the preconditions that make self-constitution possible. Communal self-constitution occurs within the private communities of civil society. Those communities must be given room to deliberate and choose. The members of the community have a claim in justice to deliberate on and choose the ultimate ends of the community's plural plans of action, even if they do not enjoy authority or the ability to adopt and effectuate all of the necessary instrumental means to achieve those ends.

A similar principle operates one level down; private communities should not do for individuals all things that they can do for themselves. Common use, creation, and exploitation of material resources are performed for the benefit of a community's *members*, including their moral benefit. Because practical reasonableness is directed toward self-constitution, "no common enterprise can itself bring about the all-round flourishing of any individual." The common good consists in large part of individual realizations of practical reasonableness, and therefore "to absorb the individual altogether into common enterprises would thus be disastrous for the common good."[63] Within communal and collective institutions, individuals must be allowed to develop their powers of agency.

In short, the important and intrinsic value of practical reasonableness requires:

> that common enterprises should be regarded, and practically conducted, not as ends in themselves but as means of assistance, as ways of helping individuals to "help themselves" or, more precisely, to constitute themselves. And in all those fields of activity, including economic activity, where individuals, or families, or other relatively small groups, can help themselves by their own private efforts and initiatives without thereby injuring . . . the common good, they are entitled in justice to be allowed to do so, and it is unjust to require them to sacrifice their private initiative by demanding that they participate instead in a public enterprise; it remains unjust even if the material dividend they receive from the public enterprise is as great as or even somewhat greater than the material product of their own private efforts would have been.[64]

[63] NLNR, 168. [64] NLNR, 169.

All of this commends a preference for numerous, localized centers of authority over centralized, collective decision-making. The law should promote plural domains of mediated dominion. Common law institutions of private property, with their mix of individual and intermediary estates, have performed that task reasonably well. The domains within which communities exercise authority over their assets are spheres of self-constitution. The common law establishes boundaries around intermediary estates and secures those boundaries with legal prohibitions against trespassory interference by outsiders. Within those boundaries, the communities that own the property are free to govern their use and management of their assets as they see fit, consistent with the ends for which they are constituted as communities.[65] Within these domains, groups constitute themselves and enable their individual members to realize self-constitution, as well.[66]

Conclusion

In summary, because practical reasonableness is a reflexive basic good, it cannot be coerced. Because it is an expensive good, it requires a rich pluralism, which produces a wide variety of incommensurable and good options. Because it is realized through complex plans of action, practical reasonableness requires stable expectations. And because it requires commitment, practical reasonableness is best realized in institutions that internalize the externalities of human choices. Private property provides all of these conditions.

Yet precisely because it frees owners to take practically reasonable actions, it also frees them to behave unreasonably. Private property would not be controversial if owners acted at all times with the common good in view. So, property rights cannot be absolute. The balance of this book takes up the contours that property law must assume in justice if it is to respect the requirements of practical reasonableness.

[65] See J. W. Harris, *Property and Justice* (Oxford: Oxford University Press 1996), 102–04, his discussion of what he terms "communitarian" forms of ownership.

[66] See Garnett, *Henry Adams' Soul*, 1846, 1852–1856.

5

Property and charity

Property norms and human motivations

The second intuition discussed in Chapter 1 is that unreasonable uses of property are *not* entitled to the law's support. This intuition presupposes that some uses of property are more reasonable than others, that there are limits to the plurality of reasonable exercises of property owner sovereignty. If this intuition is right then there must be some uniquely wrong answers to questions about how to use property. So in order to understand this intuition, we need to examine reasons for action with a more critical eye. If the value of plans of action for things is derived from the reasons for which those plans of action are adopted, and if some plans of action are rightly judged better than others, then we need an account of reasons for action that will enable us to distinguish between good reasons and bad reasons.

We can begin by contrasting two extreme types of plans of action for the use of things, which illustrate the role that reasons for action play in shaping property law. This chapter will consider charity as a reason for owners' actions. Charity will serve as a central instance of a reason for action that requires no more basic justification; it is performed reasonably. In an act of charity the owner relinquishes or abandons his or her property rights without compensation. Charity is the paradigmatic instance of an admirable use of property. Chapter 6 will consider cases in which owners act out of spite, for no reason other than a desire to see a neighbor suffer some harm. The irrationality – and thus immorality – of abuses of rights results from the absence in the actor's practical deliberation of any objectively good reason. Thus, abuses of rights deserve disapprobation and cannot be given legal effect.

First: charity. Any account of private property that aspires to explain its moral implications must confront a striking fact, the coexistence of institutions and norms of private ownership with the lavish generosity of private citizens. Alongside the experience of common law institutions, charity correlates with *belief* in private ownership. Those who give the most are those who believe the most strongly in economic liberties such as property rights.[1] Americans, in particular, share their property in flush times and in lean. In 1996, Americans donated $150.7 billion to charitable organizations.[2] In 2010, in the middle of the Great Recession, Americans donated $291 billion, of which $211.77 billion was donated by individuals.[3] Charitable donations by private Americans exceed the entire gross domestic product of Finland.

This is not a recent phenomenon. More than a century and a half ago Alexis de Tocqueville observed, "I have seen Americans making great and sincere sacrifices for the common good and a hundred times I have noticed that, when needs be, they almost always gave each other faithful support."[4] Furthermore, charitable action has long occupied a prominent and substantial place in the corpus of American property law. Yet most accounts of property today ignore charitable uses of property.

The mechanism of the internal point of view, introduced in Chapter 4, can help remedy this deficiency. One can understand property law's support for charitable action, and particularly its attention to the internal deliberations and intentions of charitable property owners, when one perceives the unique value of charitable action to those who engage in it. Charity is morally valuable when freely and intentionally chosen, but not otherwise. Charity as a moral value cannot be coerced. Anglo-American property law guides and supports charitable intentions. Indeed, many common law rules can be understood only by reference to the basic values that are realized in a transfer made for charitable reasons. These rules are justified not with reference to the consequences of actions but rather by their operation on practical reason, viewed from the internal perspective of those who interact with property.

Explaining charity

The mystery of charity from the external perspective

Something important takes place in an act of charity. The difficulty of course is how to explain it. From the perspective of examining material

[1] Arthur C. Brooks, *The Road to Freedom* (New York: Basic Books 2012), 82.

[2] Lisa Loftin, "Protecting the Charitable Investor: A Rationale for Donor Enforcement of Restricted Gifts" (1998) 8 *Boston University Public Interest Law Journal* 361.

[3] National Center for Charitable Statistics, "Quick Facts About Nonprofits," available at http://nccs.urban.org/statistics/quickfacts.cfm.

[4] Alexis de Tocqueville, *Democracy in America*, Gerald E. Bevan (trans.) (New York: Penguin 2003), 594–95.

consequences, there can be no normative difference between an owner who happens to prefer sharing and one who prefers hoarding unless one is shown to produce superior outcomes on whatever measure – distributive equality, efficiency, prosperity – the examiner cares about. But there is a normative difference. And this difference shows up both in moral deliberation and in law. So, from the external perspective of the social scientist who refrains from evaluating reasons for action, gifts pose a real problem.

In terms of material consequences only, charity might seem wasteful, even irrational. Yet charity is a social fact. No account of private property can satisfactorily assume that property owners exercise sovereignty over their assets only for the purpose of maximizing their individual preferences or satisfying their subjective desires because many owners act charitably. The common law has not operated on that assumption. It has long recognized that property owners at least sometimes exercise dominion over their assets "for the love of God or the love of ... neighbor ... free from the stain or taint of every consideration that is personal, private or selfish."[5]

The potential blindness of external accounts to charitable reasons is not without real consequences. Viewing actions solely in terms of their material consequences without considering the value of charitable *reasons for* action can actually lead one to obscure human goods that people reasonably value. For example, Michael Sandel has demonstrated how some economic thinking obscures the value of gift-giving. From one standpoint, gifts are wasteful because at best they only approximate what will satisfy the recipient's desires, and more often result in a net loss. It is more efficient to give the money that one would have spent on the gift so that the donee can purchase what he or she will find most enjoyable or fulfilling. This view of gifts denies that the "stigma against monetary gifts may reflect norms worth preserving, such as norms of attentiveness bound up with friendship." Sandel concludes, with considerable understatement, that this "case against gift giving is not morally neutral."[6]

Must economic analysis be hostile to charity? Economic analysis is fruitful in evaluating the work that property performs. Economists can

[5] *Garrison* v. *Little*, 75 Ill App 402 at 411 (1897).

[6] Michael J. Sandel, *What Money Can't Buy: The Moral Limits of Markets* (New York: Farrar, Strauss, and Giroux 2012), 98–107.

measure the efficiency of various means to achieve charitable goals.[7] But it is less obvious that economic accounts can explain charity itself. Charitable action is often motivated by non-economic considerations, such as religious duty, moral obligation, and concern for the well-being of another human being.

Scholars of law and economics are not blind to the *existence* of these internal motivations. Some of them have devised a term to capture the motivation of charitable people: "warm glow."[8] But what is it? If conceived as an emotion or feeling, then warm glow is not the *reason* why people act charitably. People give gifts to those whom they love because they want the well-being of those people to be improved. They make donations to the universities from which they graduated because they want to create opportunities for future students to benefit from education, as they did. They do not set out to achieve an emotional state; good feelings are an incidental benefit. Furthermore, charitable action is not always, or even often, attended by a good feeling. Agnes Gonxa Bojaxhiu, also known as Mother Teresa, famously labored among the sick and destitute of Calcutta, India, *in spite of* her inability to derive good feelings from her work.[9]

There are other good reasons to believe that a decision to give is guided by reasons, rather than (merely) good feelings. For example, that donors often place restrictions on gifts to academic institutions suggests that donors consider carefully "the organization's ability to implement their wishes."[10] And the choice of a particular recipient or cause is often the product of careful deliberation. A property owner motivated by no more than diffuse goodwill might donate to the United Way, but is unlikely to donate to a nonprofit organization that provides sustainable drinking water resources to the poor inhabitants of a nation from which that owner emigrated. Yet both types of charitable organizations thrive thanks to the generosity of donors.

Nor can charity be explained solely in terms of social pressure. "Warm glow" is supposed to encompass "social approbation" and "the status of

[7] Jonathan Klick and Robert H. Sitkoff, "Agency Costs, Charitable Trusts, and Corporate Control: Evidence from Hershey's Kiss-Off" (2008) 108 *Columbia Law Review* 749 at 816–22.

[8] James Andreoni, "Impure Altruism and Donations to Public Goods: A Theory of Warm-Glow Giving" (1990) 100 *Economic Journal* 464. See also Brian Galle, "Keep Charity Charitable" (2010) 88 *Texas Law Review* 1213; Susan Rose-Ackerman, "Altruism, Nonprofits, and Economic Theory" (1996) 34 *Journal of Economic Literature* 701.

[9] Mother Teresa, *Come Be My Light* (New York: Doubleday 2007).

[10] Loftin, "Protecting the Investor," 366.

being able to spend generously."[11] But the approval (or envy) of others does not motivate all charitable action. Perhaps approbation and status explain why movie stars and business moguls give, but it cannot explain the motivations of the millions of ordinary people who give anonymously each year.

Perhaps warm glow derives from "moral satisfaction."[12] This gets closer to the thing. When they act for the well-being of another person, humans often experience the satisfaction of a real need to act in a morally upright manner, consistent with norms of practical reasonableness. On the other hand, if charity is a moral duty or obligation then it isn't very charitable. What makes a charitable act admirable and valuable is that it is performed when one had no duty to perform it. So, the value of charitable action cannot consist merely in the satisfaction of a moral duty or obligation.

The challenge for economic accounts of charity in property law is in a sense the same as the challenge for economic accounts of human choice generally.[13] If humans deliberate and choose only about utility in service to unchosen preferences then it is impossible to choose to be charitable. An economic account that treats determination of human goods as prior to human choice cannot account for the moral goodness of admirable acts, such as acts of charity. Yet the moral goodness is a real phenomenon, which one can perceive from the internal perspective of the charitable owner. Owners have the experience of choosing to act charitably, and of being affirmed in the choice by a sense that they have done something good and admirable.

Indeed, the "warm glow" results from having chosen to act in a selfless way when one could just as rationally have chosen to use the asset to secure one's own material comfort. If the donor is not the originator of the choice to give, rather than keep or spend, then the donor has nothing to feel good about. If we are to take seriously the internal perspective of the property owner, then the choice to act charitably rather than uncharitably must be rationally undetermined. The rationality of the charitable action must be determined by the owner's choice, not by some prior duty, biologically determined preference, or unitary utility calculation.

[11] Galle, "Keep Charity," 1222. *See also* Amihai Glazer and Kai A. Konrad, "A Signalling Explanation for Charity" (1996) 86 *American Economic Review* 1019.

[12] Galle, "Keep Charity," 1222.

[13] See Andrew M. Yuengert, *Approximating Prudence* (New York: Palgrave MacMillan 2012), 48–51.

Penner's use theory

Another possible way to understand gifts is to consider them as aspects of the donor's use, which property law protects as a property right. J. E. Penner has defended this view. He observes that human beings are social, that we are better off when those we love are better off, and that we make social uses of our property. Sharing of things is "the norm."[14] (In context, this appears to be a descriptive statement.) Penner is interested in this "mysterious fact about humans," that we take on board the interests of recipients of our gifts as our own interests, by claiming that the recipient's use of the thing is the owner's use as well. "A gift constitutes the ultimate adoption of another's use as one's own."[15]

There is an obvious sense in which a donee's use is not the donor's use. After the donation the recipient is the person who benefits from the gift and controls its use. The donor is no longer using the resource in any recognizable way. Penner brings the recipient's use within the donor's use with an expansive conception of use. "The notion of use," he explains, "must encompass those cases where one excludes others for a purpose without 'using' a thing in a narrow sense." Thus we use our clothes even when we are not wearing them, we use our furniture when we are not sitting on it, and one uses gold even when hoarding it to drive up the price.[16] We continue to engage with the thing, though our engagement is intermittent.

Penner has chosen his examples carefully. His conception of use breaks down if one considers a different example: the neglectful landowner. Someone who hoards land and makes no productive use of it cannot be said to be engaging with the land in any meaningful way. Neglectful absence is non-use. Penner wants the holding of land as a "family seat for oneself and the heirs male of his body" to constitute a meaningful use. But the *mere* holding of title to the land is not use. It is holding for the family that constitutes the action, the purpose of which is a future use by one's male heirs. Penner's solution pushes the concept of use beyond what it will bear. It seems more accurate to say that the domain of ownership protects the owner's rights to use *or not use*, but within certain constraints of reason. Indeed, that seems the best way to understand the justice of the doctrine of adverse possession, which grants title to the adverse possessor against whom the neglectful landowner has taken no action during the statutory period.

[14] J. E. Penner, *The Idea of Property in Law* (Oxford: Oxford University Press 1997), 93.
[15] Penner, *Idea of Property*, 88–89. [16] Penner, *Idea of Property*, 70.

It is not common use that unites donor and donee but rather a common good. Penner understands that owners act in their own interests, and therefore makes no room for shared goods. For Penner, "our goal at the end of the day is to serve our interests." Penner's taxonomy – distinguishing altruistic gifts from charitable gifts, and gifts from transfers for value – relies on the owner's individual interest as the criterion of right. Penner denies that all gifts give rise to an obligation to reciprocate, a view he decries as "plainly cynical."[17] But the only reason Penner can offer why anyone would take into consideration the interests of others is that it is sometimes in one's own interest to do so. But in what sense is this true? Do I have an objective *reason* to act for the well-being of others?

From the perspective of a charitable property owner, we can see that she in fact makes the well-being of another human a reason for her own action. Before making the gift she might very well consider how the gift will affect her tax liabilities, her social stature in the community, and her bank account. But she *also* directs her gift to a person or community of persons for the reason of improving their condition. It might not in all cases be her only or even primary reason for action. But in at least some cases, at least some of the time, people use their property charitably for truly charitable reasons. They buy a sandwich for a homeless person. They give money and artworks to orchestras and museums. They *relinquish* their rights of use without any expectation of in-kind compensation so that their recipients will be enriched. We humans perceive value in acting for those reasons.

Charity and practical reason

Charity performed for basic reasons

When an individual kills another human being, or when a nation goes to war, we demand to know why. We are prepared to accept that some killings and some wars are justified, but some justification must be offered before we are prepared to say that those acts are practically reasonable. Not so with charity. When someone feeds a homeless person, gives blood, contributes labor to disaster relief, or writes a check to the United Way, no one (apart from philosophers and cynics) needs to ask why. Acts of charity require no justification because they are undertaken for ends the value of which is intrinsic to them.

[17] Penner, *Idea of Property*, 208–09.

One of these is human life. Many charitable gifts are made for no other reason than the well-being of the recipient. A charitable act made to benefit a human being directly requires no additional justification because human life is a reason for action in itself. Another basic good motivating charitable action is friendship or community, as where one goes along with a volunteer project because one's friends are participating. Knowledge and community motivate donations to universities. Beauty motivates gifts to museums and orchestras.

This does not necessarily entail that a charitable act is always the most reasonable possible action. Other considerations might come into play to make the act not fully reasonable. A donation to a stranger might prevent one from fulfilling a prior duty to one's children. Some donations are used for immoral causes, such as bribing public officials, and the donor's knowledge of that use might implicate the donor in the immorality of the recipient. But all other moral considerations aside, it makes rational sense to say that one intends to make a gift simply because one wants to make a gift.

It is true that charitable actions are also instrumentally valuable and can be critiqued on prudential grounds in terms of their efficacy. We might ask why Susan volunteered with *this* relief agency, or why Sam gave money to *that* particular university. But those questions invite Susan and Sam to demonstrate the instrumental value of their charitable actions as compared with possible alternative donations. They do not cast doubt on the intelligible value of volunteering for relief agencies and donating to universities. To accept that different acts of charity might yield different instrumental valuations in service to other human goods is not to deny that acts of charity are *also* intrinsically valuable.

Not a basic requirement

That charitable donations have intrinsic worth does not entail that charity is a *requirement* of action. Indeed, it cannot be a requirement of action, either moral or legal, and remain an act of charity. The choice to give is valuable because it is freely made as against another, rational alternative.[18] The donor gives away property that she could have devoted to the pursuit of some other, incommensurable good, such as an education or a bottle of wine. The priority of charity over

[18] Compare Yuengert, *Approximating Prudence*, 65.

learning or aesthetic experience originates in the choice of the donor, not in any duty that the donor was operating under, or any superiority of charity over other goods. That the choice was rationally undetermined at the time that the donor made it is what makes the choice admirable. This is not to suggest that one has no moral duty to help those in need. It is simply to deny that satisfying one's distributive obligations to others is charity. A requirement of charity would destroy charity itself.

Charity is a reflexive practice. It has a transitive effect on the person who chooses it. An act of charity makes the donor a charitable person. By the charitable act the donor makes the well-being of another human being a reason for her own choice and action. She takes the well-being of that person into her deliberations, adopts a plan of relinquishment and self-sacrifice in order to bring the well-being of the other person about, and thus becomes a person who is willing to make sacrifices for the benefit of others. She constitutes herself as a charitable person in the order of the will.

Like practical reasonableness (of which a charitable act might be considered an instance), charity is therefore fragile. To coerce charity is to pervert the practical deliberations of the moral agent. It is to introduce into the agent's deliberations a motivation that can, and in most cases will, supersede the motivation of acting for the well-being of another person. Coercion thus prevents the actor from taking the well-being of another person into her deliberations, and deflects the realization of charity.

Charity is different from what Nagel called "pure altruism," which is "a rational requirement on human conduct."[19] Charity is not merely a matter of universalizing our interests. It is not simply removing our heel from another's gouty toes because we would want him to do the same if roles were reversed.[20] To be sure, we must consider other people's interests in our deliberations, and consider those interests as possible reasons for action, in order to be fully reasonable human beings. To consider only our own individual interests, narrowly conceived, is to fail to act with a will set toward integral human fulfillment. We are morally obligated not to discriminate arbitrarily between persons. Thus, we *must* not discriminate arbitrarily in favor of ourselves against other people if we are to be practically reasonable human beings.

[19] Thomas Nagel, *The Possibility of Altruism* (Oxford: Clarendon Press 1970), 80.
[20] Nagel, *Possibility*, 85.

By contrast, there is no moral obligation to act with charity; there cannot be. To say that one *must* make a donation to another person for that other person's well-being is to destroy the very possibility of the donation being made for that reason. One who gives out of a sense of moral obligation is not giving for the purpose of improving the well-being of that person, and therefore is not realizing the good of charity.

A *legal* requirement of charity would also destroy charity, for the same and additional reasons. Contrary to Waldron, the welfare state is not institutionalized charity.[21] One pays taxes to the welfare state to satisfy one's legal obligation, not to realize the basic good of another human being. The coercive element of coercive taxation alters one's motivations for giving. Even if one pays taxes in part to become more practically reasonable, or to please God, one *also* pays taxes to avoid criminal sanction. And because one is obligated to pay, one cannot choose to undertake an obligation to make the payment. But coercion is not the only problem. That the state stands between the source of the property and the recipient and renders the transaction impersonal prevents the source from taking the recipient's well-being into his or her own deliberations and judgments. The transaction creates no moral connection between the source and recipient (we cannot even call them donor and donee). One has no contact with the recipient of one's taxes, and no way to direct one's taxes to any particular participant.

Legally mandated welfare spending is also inconsistent with the owner's dominion, and therefore with gifts. A gift is a voluntary transfer of the rights of dominion from someone who possesses those rights to someone who does not. If a property owner were under an obligation to give, then he would have no right not to give, and it would be difficult to imagine in what sense he could still be considered an owner. Nor could we make sense of the transfer as a gift. An owner who has an enforceable *legal* obligation to give is not an owner in any real sense, and therefore when he transfers the thing, no legal rights have changed hands. He cannot relinquish his rights to the thing, because he has no right to refuse, and therefore he cannot act charitably. Charity requires private ownership, and it cannot be required without destroying the essential nature of private ownership – the owner's dominion over the thing – the very precondition that it requires.

[21] Jeremy Waldron, "Welfare and the Images of Charity" (1986) 36 *The Philosophical Quarterly* 463.

Charity and law

We can now see why charity is admirable, what makes it so expensive, and in what ways it is fragile. It is admirable because it consists of the owner relinquishing his right not to share. It is expensive because it requires institutions of private ownership that secure to owners the right not to share but empowers them to do so if they so choose. It is fragile because any outside interference in the choice destroys the possibility of charity's realization. Thus, in the realm of charity the law can do more harm than good.

Nevertheless, one should not jump to the conclusion that law has no role to play in promoting charitable uses of property. A command of a sovereign that gives rise to a conclusive obligation, like an act of redistribution by the state, destroys the possibility of charitable choice and action. But private law has ways of promoting charitable action, and even of altering the legal entitlements of those who fail to share, in ways that cause less harm, or no harm at all, to the practical reason of owners. Private law creates powers of ownership, which enable owners to act for charitable reasons. Private law ratifies private trespassory actions taken against hoarding owners through the doctrines of adverse possession and prescription. And private law institutions – especially the jury – are free to soften the right to exclude for moral reasons without jeopardizing practical reasonableness. For example, in a private conversion action brought by a baker against a desperate thief who stole to feed his starving family, the jury can refuse to find for the baker without creating an affirmative legal obligation to share in future cases.

Charity's treatment in private law

Property law

Charitable action receives special consideration in common law property doctrines. Unlike civil law, which considers gifts as species of contract, the common law treats the gift as a distinct phenomenon, with its own logic and rules.[22] More generally, donative transfers in common law are given special respect as acts motivated by concern for the well-being of

[22] Michael Bridge, Louise Gullifer, Gerard McMeel, and Sarah Worthington, *The Law of Personal Property* (London: Sweet & Maxwell 2013), 220–21; Thomas W. Merrill and Henry E. Smith, *The Oxford Introductions to U.S. Law: Property* (New York: Oxford University Press 2010), 92–93. So the American Law Institute treated the subject in the Restatement of the Law (Second) Property (1983), volumes 1–4.

others, and donors' intentions are accorded great weight. A donative transfer or conditions attached to it that cannot reasonably be said to be grounded in intention to improve the well-being of others will not be given juridical enforcement. But otherwise the donor has broad power to determine the rights of those who are interested in his things.

Fixation on donative intent

Property law has long paid careful attention to the internal point of view of the charitable owner. It is easy to miss how radical is the rule of construction of donative transfers, which requires a court to give legal effect to a grantor's intent. The rule requires courts to defer to the authority of donors, and to allow them to supersede the rules of intestate distribution, with all of their inbuilt preferences for familial piety, kinship, and the other supports for the perpetuation of the human race and the political community. The donor is permitted to create new rights and duties that contravene quite foundational policies of the law, so great is the law's respect for, and deference to, the charitable motive.

Many doctrines that originated before the era of legal realism reflect the importance of supporting charitable action. Many of those doctrines persist today. They are in some instances divorced from their original justifications, but the norms they embody continue to exert force by directing legal and political institutions to take seriously charity as a reason for action. The cy pres doctrine authorizes courts to exercise discretion in inferring general donative intent when the donator's expressed intention is not enforceable, impossible to honor, or otherwise defeated, and requires that the alternative use of the trust res be as close as possible to the original intent of the donor.[23] When a charitable trust conveys its assets, it remains bound to use the proceeds for the purpose for which it was founded, even if another use would be more efficient in terms of overall utility.[24]

23 Restatement (Second) of Trusts §399 (1959); Robert A. Lundrigan, "The Cy Pres Doctrine" (1955) 1 *Alberta Law Review* 598.

24 Restatement (Second) of Trusts §372 (1959). So, for example, when a trust is settled to provide health care in a community, and the trust later sells its nonprofit hospital, the proceeds should not be devoted to charitable uses unrelated to health care. "The use of charitable funds for planes, playgrounds and museums, even if well intended, jeopardizes the public's ability to ensure adequate health care services," the end to which the funds were directed by the donors to the trust. Kevin F. Donohue, "Crossroads in Hospital Conversions – A Survey of Nonprofit Hospital Conversion Legislation" (1999) 8 *Annals Health Law* 39 at 62.

Support for charitable intent can be found elsewhere in property law, for example in bailments. Absent an express agreement specifying a bailee's duties, those duties are determined by the reason for which the bailor passed custody to the bailee.[25] Citing the landmark decision in *Coggs* v. *Bernard*,[26] Justice Story summarized the common law rules as requiring slight diligence of a bailee who holds for the sole benefit of the bailor and "great diligence" of one who holds for his own, sole benefit.[27] The scholarly commentary reflects some confusion about the modern rule, with some indicating that the standard of care varies according to the purpose of the bailment and others that the standard depends on the particular circumstances of the case.[28] In the United States, courts generally continue to reward charitable motivation by imposing a low duty of care on the bailee who undertakes the bailment to benefit the bailor, and a high duty of care on a bailee for whose sole benefit the bailor has delivered custody.[29] In the United Kingdom the authorities are more equivocal.[30] A practitioner has offered a plausible explanation for the confusion: "As a practical matter, the test generally applied by many modern authorities is one of reasonable care under the circumstances, with the nature of the bailment being one of the circumstances."[31]

Property law also seeks to protect the integrity of donative intent. Gifts of personal property are enforceable only on evidence of donative intent and some form of delivery, which demonstrates that the donor understood what he was doing.[32] In Philip Mechem's phrase, the donor must have felt the "wrench of delivery ... the little mental twinge at

[25] M. G. Bridge, *Personal Property Law* (Oxford: Oxford University Press 2002), 35–43; Merrill and Smith, *Property*, 87–89.

[26] (1703) 2 Ld Raym 909.

[27] Joseph Story, *Commentaries on the Law of Bailments with Illustrations from the Civil and the Foreign Law* (9th edn, Boston: Little, Brown and Company 1878), sec. 23 at 27.

[28] Bridge et al., *Law of Personal Property*, 87–89; R. H. Helmholz, "Bailment Theories and the Liability of Bailees: The Elusive Uniform Standard of Reasonable Care" (1992) 41 *University of Kansas Law Review* 97.

[29] For example, *Schoenholz* v. *Hinzman*, 289 P 3d 1155 at 1162 (Kan 2012); *Ferrick Excavating and Grading Company* v. *Senger Trucking Company*, 484 A 2d 744 (Pa 1984); *Morris* v. *Hamilton*, 302 SE 2d 51 (Va 1983).

[30] *The Winson* [1982] AC 939; *The Kos* [2012] 2 WLR 976.

[31] Mark S. Dennison, "Bailee's Liability for Damage, Loss, or Theft of Bailed Property"' in 46 *American Jurisprudence Proof of Facts 3d* (New York: West 1998), 361 at 380. Accord, *W.G.H. Nominees Pty. Ltd.* v. *Tomblin*, 39 SASR 117 (South Australia 1985); *McLaughlin* v. *Sears, Roebuck & Co.*, 199 SE 413 (SC 1938).

[32] *Irons* v. *Smallpiece* (1819) 106 ER 467 (KB).

seeing his property pass from his hands into those of another."[33] An owner who understands the personal cost of transfer and makes it anyway sufficiently evinces a present intention to benefit the recipient. Gifts causa mortis are viewed with special scrutiny because courts fear that the person claiming the gift might misconstrue the putative donor's intent for personal gain.[34]

Property law has never honored all intentions equally. Rather, it distinguishes between those intentions that account for the common good and those that evince a narrower self-interest. Charitable gifts, devises, and bequests are given more liberal construction, and subjected to less restrictive constraints, than other dispositions. For example, unlike other trusts, a charitable trust is valid at common law even without a definite beneficiary.[35] This special allowance for charitable trusts raises special problems, such as the question which bequests and devises count as charitable.[36] But that question also is resolved with reference to the interior reasoning of the testator.

Some property law doctrines require courts to contravene grantor intentions that are inconsistent with the well-being of others. Perhaps the most dramatic example of a property doctrine contravening grantor intent is the Rule Against Perpetuities, which prohibits courts from enforcing the wishes of those who would tie assets up indefinitely, preventing their productive use. The Rule Against Perpetuities has long been viewed as an important bulwark against dead-hand control of property, which might prevent the living from providing for human needs. And it supersedes contrary grantor intent. It therefore seems significant that the Rule Against Perpetuities is relaxed or abrogated as to charitable dispositions of property. It yields to the cy pres doctrine in cases where a testator has expressed a general charitable intent.[37] And it applies not at all to a condition that would result in title passing from one charity to another charity.[38]

[33] Philip Mechem, "The Requirement of Delivery in Gifts of Chattels and of Choses in Action Evidenced by Commercial Instruments" (1926) 21 *Illinois Law Review* 341 at 348.

[34] Merrill and Smith, *Property*, 92.

[35] John Chipman Gray, *The Rule Against Perpetuities* (3rd edn, Boston: Little, Brown, and Company 1915), 472.

[36] For many centuries the definition in both England and the United States was derived from the so-called Statute of Elizabeth. Restatement (First) of Trusts §368 (1935), comment a. See *Alden* v. *Lewis*, 182 So 2d 600 at 605 (Miss 1966) and the discussion in "Tudor on Charitable Trusts" (1862) 13 *Law Magazine and Law Review* 311, 316–18. New charitable uses were discerned by analogy to those listed in the statute.

[37] Merrill and Smith, *Property*, 110–11; Lundrigan, "Cy Pres," 598–99, 601–03.

[38] Gray, *Rule Against Perpetuities*, 476; Lundrigan, "Cy Pres," 599.

Property law assumes not the worst of property owners but rather the best. A basic rule in the construction of donative transfers holds, "A gift dictated by a general benevolent purpose is to be liberally construed and, if reasonably possible, upheld as a valid charity."[39] In the words of John Chipman Gray, the law is "very keen-sighted to discover" in a grantor an intention to make an unconditional charitable gift, rather than to allow the gift to fail as a result of a contingency.[40] The common law's eagerness on this point shows up in contrast to the exacting test of charitable intent for tax deduction purposes in the United States. A transfer is not a "gift" under the Internal Revenue Code unless a "detached and disinterested generosity" constituted the transferor's "basic reason for his conduct" – the "dominant reason that explains his action."[41]

This cannot be emphasized enough. Unlike some accounts of property that are influential today, the common law leans toward the presumption that property owners dispose of their assets with an intention to benefit others, to promote the common good. So the First Restatement noted that charitable trusts are valid even where selfish motives are mixed into the settlor's decision to give, such as a desire to acquire fame. "Even if the motive of the testator in disposing of his property is to spite his heirs, the trust is none the less a charitable trust if the purposes are charitable."[42] Recognizing that human beings act for mixed motivations, the law honors the testator's admirable purpose and ignores the rest.

The law privileges donative intent not merely for the material consequences that result from it, but also to incentivize virtuous dispositions. So, an eighteenth-century statute restricting charitable dispositions of land in England was criticized for perpetrating "a double wrong," both because it worked material harm to would-be beneficiaries and because of the "violence done to the manifestation of a just and laudable sentiment on the part of the donor."[43] Another commentator argued that the first reason why the law of England favors charitable bequests is that "they are the free expressions of one of the best human instincts." The second is that "they are enjoined by the system of religious faith whose maxims and commands are incorporated with the municipal law."[44]

39 *Bowditch* v. *Attorney General*, 134 NE 796 at 800 (Mass 1922).
40 Gray, *Rule Against Perpetuities*, 581. See also the cases discussed in Lundrigan, 'Cy Pres', 603–05.
41 *Duberstein* v. *United States*, 363 US 278 at 285–86 (1960).
42 Restatement (First) of Trusts §368 (1935), comment d.
43 "The Law Relating to Charitable Gifts" (1868) 25 *Law Magazine and Law Review* 95 at 104.
44 "Tudor on Charitable Trusts," 312.

The politics exception

As noted above, gifts to charitable enterprises can be upheld even when they are directed to no determined beneficiary, or are unlimited in time in violation of the Rule Against Perpetuities. Courts have long held that this special treatment for charities does not extend to political ventures and activities. That the political exception applies to some apparently political activities and not to others has puzzled recent commentators.[45] At English common law a gift designated for the prevention of cruelty to animals was charitable, while one directed toward the prevention of vivisection was deemed political. These results left the law of England "a bit confused." In the United States, a gift to advance the cause of women's rights has been held not charitable,[46] though a gift to secure suffrage for women was deemed charitable.[47]

The distinction cannot be understood in terms of material consequences. It has been suggested that testamentary gifts to political causes are invalid because "the court has no means of judging whether a proposed change in the law will or will not be for the public benefit, and, therefore, cannot say that a gift to secure the change is a charitable gift."[48] But on this reasoning all charitable gifts should fail. All gifts to charitable enterprises are made in the as-yet unfulfilled hope that the enterprise will redound to someone's benefit. Like for-profit enterprises, charitable ventures are speculative. In no case can a court that is called upon to pass judgment on the validity of the gift guarantee that the recipient of the gift will realize the donor's lofty goals.

The authors of the Restatement thought that political parties cannot be charitable because "[t]here is no social interest in the community in the underwriting of one or another of the political parties."[49] This explanation suffers from at least three flaws. First, it disregards the intention and understanding of the testator, who might have made the gift precisely because he *did* believe that the success of one party would accrue to the public benefit. Second, it is simply not true that competing political

[45] For example, A. S. Klein, "Validity of Charitable Trust to Promote Change in Laws or Systems or Methods of Government" (2011) 22 *American Law Reports 3d* 886; John D. Perovich, "Validity and Construction of Testamentary Gift to Political Party" (1972) 41 *American Law Reports 3d* 833; L. A. Sheridan, "Charity versus Politics" (1973) 2 *Anglo-American Law Review* 47.

[46] *Bowditch* v. *Attorney General*, 134 NE 796 (Mass 1922).

[47] *Garrison* v. *Little*, 75 Ill App 402 (1897).

[48] See the judicial decision quoted in Sheridan, "Charity versus Politics," 56.

[49] Restatement (Second) Trusts §374 (1957), comment j.

parties always serve the public interest equally (well or poorly). To take an obvious example, the public would have benefited immensely had opposition parties successfully thwarted the political goals of the slavery proponents. Third, though it is not always obvious that the underwriting of a particular political party or expression serves the public interest, the underwriting of political discourse generally does serve the public interest in democracies and republics, and political discourse is often conducted, for better or worse, by political parties.

So, when viewed from the external perspective the politics exception to the allowance for charitable gifts might remain enigmatic. But when one considers the distinction between politics and charity through the lens of human choice and action, then the rationale comes more clearly into view. A testator might direct his assets toward political activities in one of two ways. He might view political victory for his cause or party as a condition both necessary and sufficient for the success of his project. He might even view political victory as a form of consolidating or achieving supremacy of his club or cause. Alternatively, he might see politics as a means toward a charitable end, an insufficient aspect of a larger project, the end of which is the betterment of particular human beings in some particular respect.

The efforts of courts to discern whether a testator's political objectives are ultimate ends or rather means to achieve more basic human goods have surely been imperfect, as one would naturally expect. Any attempt to discern the testator's deliberations from fragmentary and cursory written expressions must necessarily involve some speculative inferences. Some of those inferences will be stronger than others. But it does appear that courts are trying, however haltingly, to distinguish between different interior dispositions that testators hold toward their fellow humans, and to discern charitable attitudes whenever possible.[50]

In one case the Supreme Judicial Court of Massachusetts drew a line between two similar bequests contained in the same will. A designation to promote the "cause[] of women's rights" was deemed invalid, while the court upheld dispositions to promote the "cause[] . . . of temperance" and the "best interests of sewing girls in Boston."[51] One commenter found this result "very strange."[52] But the court's reasoning is intelligible if one understands the donor's reasoning, and critically examines the chain of

[50] For example, *Estate of Breeden*, 256 Cal Rptr 813 at 815 (Cal App 1989).

[51] *Bowditch* v. *Attorney General*, 134 NE 796 at 797–99 (Mass 1922).

[52] Sheridan, "Charity versus Politics," 61.

reasons for action between the bequests and their respective goals. The bequest to promote women's rights necessarily required a political outcome for its success. The will was "silent as to the manner and means by which women's rights are to be promoted or secured." But the term "women's rights" had at the time a "definite and well defined meaning," namely the placement of women in equality with men "in a political sense by appropriate legislation." The objective of the bequest could not be achieved without such a political victory.[53]

By contrast, the court deemed the gift for the cause of temperance a charitable bequest because its primary end was the well-being of alcohol abusers and their families. The Eighteenth Amendment had then rendered obsolete any political objectives of the temperance clause. The remaining purpose was "to better the condition of people who suffer from the injurious consequences of intemperance" in the consumption of alcohol. Similarly, the gift for the benefit of "sewing girls in Boston" was directed toward the "welfare and advancement" of a definite class.[54]

The "well-established principle" operating in these and similar cases is that the court should consider an activity to be charitable "despite some subsidiary aspect of it which, viewed alone, would not be charitable."[55] The court is thus obliged whenever possible to construe a charitable bequest clause liberally, to discern in the grantor an intention to improve his fellow human beings and to promote their happiness.[56] Only if political success is "the sole or main object, or a principal object, of the constitution or gift, it will not be charitable."[57] Understood as cases about purpose and intention, these decisions seem less strange.

In Illinois a gift "for the attainment of woman suffrage"[58] was held to be charitable because, the court reasoned, the testatrix "believed it to be for the benefit of women, and for that purpose and because of her interest in their welfare and not from any selfish motive, she made the bequest."[59] The gift thus came within the definition of charity, namely, "Whatever is given for the love of God or the love of your neighbor."[60] Here also one

[53] *Bowditch* v. *Attorney General*, 134 NE at 797–99.
[54] *Bowditch* v. *Attorney General*, 134 NE at 799–800.
[55] Sheridan, "Charity versus Politics," 54.
[56] *Bowditch* v. *Attorney General*, 134 N.E. at 800.
[57] Sheridan, "Charity versus Politics," 59.
[58] *Garrison* v. *Little*, 75 Ill App 402 at 409 (1897).
[59] *Garrison* v. *Little*, 75 Ill App at 412. Similar reasoning is found in other decisions. *Collier* v. *Lindley*, 266 P 526 at 529–30 (Cal 1928); *Taylor* v. *Hoag*, 116 A 826 at 827–28 (Pa 1922).
[60] *Garrison* v. *Little*, 75 Ill App at 411.

observes the tendency of courts to infer the most admirable of intentions, wherever such an inference can reasonably be discerned.[61]

In 1970 a California court refused to enforce a legacy to the Socialist Labor Party of California. The court reasoned that the activities of the party were political, not charitable or benevolent, under California law, because the party was not organized for "religious, scientific, literary, or solely educational or hospital or sanatorium purposes." The court stated, "A political party is not a fraternal organization and bears no resemblance thereto."[62] By contrast, in 1989 a California court held that a testamentary gift to promote the *principles of socialism* was valid as charitable (though not charitable for tax purposes) because the testator was "concerned with societal improvement." It was no impediment that the gift might benefit non-charitable organizations as long as "the *purpose of the gift* remains charitable … and the donor intends no personal benefit to himself."[63]

None of this is to suggest that the rule is desirable, that the law *should* exclude politics from the realm of charitable donative transfers, or that the law *should* include charitable activities that entail political means or effects. It is enough to observe that the line between politics and charity is drawn with reference to the interior intentions and attitudes of donors, and that the law privileges charitable intentions even over very similar intentions.

Gifts causa mortis

The significance of motivation and moral norms is on dramatic display in the common law rule governing gifts made in anticipation of suicide. A gift that would vest rights in a donee on occurrence of a volitional suicide is void.[64] Two explanations for the rule appear in the literature. One is that forfeiture for suicide occurs at the moment just before death, the moment at which the suicidal person acts with an intention to kill herself.[65] On this view, there is no title to pass to the donee the moment

61 Compare *Collier* v. *Lindley*, 266 P at 529–30.

62 *Estate of Carlson*, 88 Cal Rptr 229 at 231–33 (Cal App 1970).

63 *Estate of Breeden*, 256 Cal Rptr 813 at 818 (Cal App 1989) (emphasis in original).

64 *Agnew* v. *Belfast Banking Co.* [1892] 2 IR 204 at 211; *Northwestern Mutual Life Insurance Co.* v. *Collamore*, 62 A 652 at 655 (Me 1905); *In Re Fanning* [1922] 3 DLR 925 at 926 (Ontario); *Ray* v. *Leader Federal Savings & Loan Association*, 292 SW 2d 458 at 467 (Tenn App 1953); *In Re Dudman* [1925] Ch 553 at 555.

65 John B. Minor, *Institutes of Common and Statute Law* (2nd edn, Richmond: Anderson Bros. 1895), vol. 3, 63; William Blackstone, *Commentaries on the Laws of England* (1769), vol. 2, 535.

after death because the donor has already forfeited. But of course, the abolition of forfeiture would have rendered this justification null.

The better account, which explains why the rule has survived abolition of forfeiture and dishonor, is that a gift made in anticipation of suicide is not made in peril of death.[66] An intention to make a gift conditional on an act of self-destruction thus defeats itself for two reasons. First, a court cannot enforce the gift without sanctioning the suicidal act, which the common law forbids as a malum in se offense, even after abolition of forfeiture and dishonour.[67] Though the offense is one after which punishment cannot possibly reach the offender, it remains criminal nonetheless.[68] To borrow terms from Blackstone, the declaration of the common law against suicide persists, though the sanction has been abolished.

Second, enforcing the gift would involve a court in doctrinal incoherence. A volitional suicide is an act within the donor's control. But the condition on the gift – the donor's death – must be contingent, otherwise there can be no reason to ignore the formal requirements for validity of a will. Because a suicidal donor controlled the moment of death, "he escaped from the peril (and so the condition of the gift failed) every moment that he refrained from the act of destruction."[69] In other words, the donor was not a donor; she had no intention to act charitably toward the putative donee.

When the donor did perform the act of self-destruction, she cannot have intended to retain the resource in the event of survival. Thus,

> [T]he motive of a *donatio mortis causa* is to let it take effect only when self-interest is at an end, and the desire to retain the object through the love of life, is still stronger than the desire to give it to the donee. Could words be used more graphically inapplicable to the state of mind of a person intending to commit suicide?[70]

This explains why gifts are enforced when the suicide was non-volitional, as where the donor suffered from mental illness or extreme emotional ill health.[71] In making this distinction, property law follows

[66] *Pikeville Nationall Bank & Trust Co.* v. *Shirley*, 135 SW 2d 426 at 429 (Ky 1940); John R. Rood, *A Treatise on the Law of Wills* (Chicago: Callaghan & Co. 1904), 19.

[67] Thomas J. Marzen et al., "Suicide: A Constitutional Right?" (1985) 24 *Duquesne Law Review* 1 at 79–82.

[68] *State* v. *Carney*, 55 A 44 (NJ Super. 1903); *McMahan* v. *State*, 53 So 89 at 90 (Al 1910); *State* v. *Willis*, 121 SE 2d 854 at 856 (NC 1961).

[69] *Earle* v. *Botsford*, (1883) 23 NBR 407 at 410 (NB).

[70] *Earle* v. *Botsford*, 23 NBR at 410.

[71] *In re van Wormer's Estate*, 238 NW 210 (Mich 1931).

tort. A tortfeasor can be held liable for causing an injury that leads to suicide, but not if the subsequent suicide is performed volitionally.[72] Because suicide is generally presumed to be a deliberate intervening act, it is a superseding cause.[73] But a negligent tortfeasor who causes the victim to lose control of her volition is liable for a resulting suicide.[74]

In short, validity of the gift turns entirely on whether the donor chose to destroy herself while in possession of her rational faculties. If she did then she took into her deliberations, and thus into her character, a reason for action that the law does not countenance, and gave up as valueless that which she owned, and therefore has left nothing that she valued. She has not felt the wrench of delivery. As long as she refrains from destroying herself, she has not intended to benefit the potential donee.

Charity and marriage

The law of donative transfers pays special attention to reasons for action concerning family relations. For example, if a donor conditions his gift on the donee not getting married then the restriction is invalid, unless the "dominant motive" of the donor was to provide support until marriage.[75] As the Second Restatement authors understood it, the rule excuses the transferee from complying with the "socially undesirable attempt of the transferor to use a disposition of property as a means of coercing abstention from marriage. This antisocial character is absent only when the dominant motive of the transferor is found to have been the provision of support until marriage."

When read in light of laws incentivizing marriage, such as criminal penalties for unmarried cohabitation and tax benefits for married couples, this doctrine appears to act as an exclusionary reason on the practical deliberations of potential donors. The law deems marriage an important and valuable practice, and will not permit donors to create private law that disincentivizes it. An Ohio court opined, "In England it was feared that such restraints might promote licentiousness; and in this country the moral factor was considered significant, as well as the social

[72] Victor E. Schwartz, "Civil Liability for Causing Suicide: A Synthesis of Law and Psychiatry" (1971) 24 *Vanderbilt Law Review* 217.

[73] William L. Prosser, *Handbook of the Law of Torts* (2nd edn, St. Paul: West 1955), 273–74.

[74] Restatement (Second) Torts §455 (1965); *Exxon Corp.* v. *Brechen*, 526 SW 2d 519 at 524 (Tex 1975).

[75] Restatement (Second) of the Law Property §6.1 (1983). Compare "Conditions, Conditional Limitations, or Contracts in Restraint of Marriage" (1939) 122 *American Law Reports* 7; Restatement (Third) of the Law Trusts §29 (2003).

benefit to be gained by encouraging and preserving the freedom of choice of a spouse."[76] But these considerations are not to be resolved with reference to the likely effects of the restraint, but rather the "issue to be resolved in each case is the dominant intention of the one imposing the restraint."[77] In other words, an intention to prohibit the donee from marrying freely will never be treated as an intention to improve the donee's well-being.

Other explanations do not work as well. The Restatement authors reported that a restriction on whom the transferee may marry "is valid if, and only if, under the circumstances, the restraint does not unreasonably limit the transferee's opportunity to marry." They explained that freedom to choose one's mate is favored in the law, but "like all freedoms, [it] is subject to qualification." Impediments to marriage generally fail, but "guidance by parents and other donors, with respect to a particular marriage, validly may be exercised by means of partial restraints."[78]

It is not clear that this distinction can be attributed to English common law, as the Ohio court supposed. In one case, the House of Lords invalidated a condition that the beneficiary would forfeit if she were to "contract a marriage with a person who is not of Jewish parentage and of the Jewish faith."[79] The condition was held to be void because it was uncertain.[80] Subsequent decisions have indicated a willingness to enforce more clearly stated conditions of similar effect, such as a proviso that the beneficiaries "shall not marry outside the Jewish faith."[81]

The authors of the Second Restatement thought it obvious that distinctions between different types of marital restrictions "no longer serve any useful function." They opined that it no longer makes sense for parents to influence the marriage decisions of their children.[82] But it would be too hasty to dismiss the common law doctrines as anachronistic. Consider a restraint on marriage until the donee reaches a certain age, such as sixteen years. The Restatement authors acknowledged that restrictions "designed to prevent hasty or imprudent marriages are to be encouraged, and such is the purpose of restraints designed to prevent marriage prior to attainment by the transferee of majority or of some other age when the transferee will have become reasonably fitted for the

76 *Winters* v. *Miller*, 261 NE 2d 205 at 206 (Ohio Common Pleas 1970).

77 *Winters* v. *Miller*, 261 NE 2d at 208.

78 Restatement (Second) of the Law Property §6.2 (1983).

79 *Clayton* v. *Ramsden* [1943] AC 320.

80 *Clayton* v. *Ramsden* [1943] AC at 332.

81 *Donn* v. *Selby*, [1966] 1 WLR 43, 3 All ER 386; *Kramer* v. *Ruda*, [1987] Ch 358 at 359, 377.

82 Restatement (Second) of the Law Property §6.2 (1983).

marital relationship."[83] Whatever else might be said about this sort of restraint, it certainly reflects a reasonable concern of the donor. Would we prefer that parents *not* express concern for their children's age and competency to make such a momentous decision? If that restriction is reasonable then there is no reason in principle to prohibit other limitations.

Other areas of private law

Property law's doctrines governing reasons for action spill over into other areas of private law. The law once prohibited corporations from donating their property to charity. This doctrine was thought to protect the property rights of shareholders, who own shares in a corporation for the purpose of deriving financial benefit, in the forms of dividends and increased share value. The prohibition has been widely abrogated.[84] The new rule, allowing corporations to make charitable gifts that cannot be expected to provide any financial benefit to the corporation, is baffling from an economic perspective. Courts have not been able to articulate why charitable gifts by corporations constitute reasonable business judgments. Commentators also puzzle over a rule "that permits a corporation to take action largely irrespective of corporate benefit."[85]

But what if charitable action is good for the donor? In that case the corporation *would* benefit from taking charitable action. A corporation that gives with no expectation of remuneration constitutes itself a charitable corporation, and thus creates a corporate culture of respect and concern for the well-being of fellow human beings. This is good for the corporation and all of its constituent members and employees, as well as the recipients of the charitable donations.

On this view, the dichotomy between donations that accrue to the benefit of the corporation and those based purely on altruism is false. Because charity, like all instances of practical reasonableness, is a truly common good, it is good for all participants in it, whether or not it directly produces financial benefits for the corporate donor. A charitable gift both recognizes the communal relationships of which the

[83] Restatement (Second) of the Law Property §6.2 (1983).

[84] George D. Ginson, "Corporate Contributions to Charity and Enabling Legislation" (1959) 14 *Business Lawyer* 434; R. Franklin Balotti and James J. Hanks, Jr., "Giving at the Office: A Reappraisal of Charitable Contributions by Corporations" (1999) 54 *Business Lawyer* 965; Nell Minnow, "Corporate Charity: An Oxymoron?" (1999) 54 *Business Lawyer* 997.

[85] See Balotti and Hanks, 'Giving at the Office', 966, 968, 973–78.

corporation is part and creates new relationships, as it forms a moral connection between donor and donee.

In defending a gift to Princeton University, the president of one corporation testified that the gift was reasonably construed as an investment in the corporation's goodwill. "In addition, he expressed the thought that in contributing to liberal arts institutions, corporations were furthering their self-interest in assuring the free flow of properly trained personnel for administrative and other corporate employment."[86] The New Jersey high court found this reasoning persuasive. In affirming the validity of the gift, the court opined that corporations should have authority to act as responsible members "of the communities within which they operate." But it also went farther. Even judged under the common law prohibition against charitable gifts, the donation would stand, because "such expenditures may likewise readily be justified as being for the benefit of the corporation." Gifts to higher education in the long view ensure the "actual survival of the corporation in a free enterprise system." This recognition was consistent with the growth of the common law "for the advancement of the general good." The court also found it "significant" that the state had not imposed on corporations any "compulsory obligations" to give.[87]

None of this is meant to suggest that for-profit corporations should, as a prudential matter, exercise charity at every opportunity. There remain questions of efficiency, efficacy, corporate mission, and fiduciary obligation, which ought to inform the decision whether to donate corporate assets to charitable ventures. Those questions are quite different from the question whether it is good to donate. The basic and reflexive value of charitable action suggests that there is value in charitable actions by corporations, and that such actions are not unreasonable as a matter of principle.

[86] *A.P. Smith Manufacturing Co.* v. *Barlow*, 98 A 2d 581 at 582–83 (NJ 1953).

[87] *Smith Manufacturing* v. *Barlow*, 98 A 2d at 586–89.

6

Abuse of rights

The need for limits

The freedom to exercise practical reason can be used for good or ill. The opportunity to exercise practical reason entails the opportunity to choose, not just one from among many possible good options, but also a bad option. The freedom that enables owners and their families, friends, and neighbors to cooperate and to reason together within communities and intermediary institutions (Chapter 3), and which enables owners to constitute themselves as reasonable people (Chapter 4) and as charitable people (Chapter 5), can also enable them to harm others unreasonably. Freedom to choose can be abused. Property law must account for this possibility.

The law cannot in justice prevent harm simply by eliminating freedom. Private property ownership creates opportunities for owners to behave in unreasonable ways. But this is simply another way of saying that private property creates opportunities for the exercise of practical reason. Without such opportunities, human beings cannot realize the good of practical reasonableness, or adhere to its basic requirements. The very same freedom that makes practical reasoning with respect to things possible also makes it possible to become a practically unreasonable person – a miser, a nuisance, a gambler.

Therefore, use rights must be robust, but they cannot be absolute. That property rights in the common law tradition are robust but not absolute should not surprise us, because the common law developed according to the practical judgments of communities, expressed in conveyances, customs, jury verdicts, legislation, and so on. But the common law continues to develop. So, a challenge for any account of property rights is to discern the boundaries of use rights within the domains of ordering in which rights are continually developing.

One way to understand this challenge is to consider a principled limitation on use rights that has been adopted as law in some common law jurisdictions but not in others – abuse of rights. The principle of abuse of rights lies at the edge of the owner's dominion. Studying abuse of rights is a helpful way to understand the tension between freedom and moral norms.

The idea refers to the use of one's rights out of malice or for motivations that are unintelligible as reasons for action.[1] It is not concerned with actions and their consequences. Instead, it addresses whether an action is undertaken for a good reason or only for spite or malice. A doctrine designed to deflect spiteful or malicious uses of property holds understandable intuitive attraction. As an early commentator put it with considerable understatement, "The possibility that a legal right may be exercised with impunity in a spirit of malevolence or selfishness is one of the unsatisfactory features of [common] law."[2] And at least one court has considered the failure of common law courts to develop a comprehensive remedy for abuses of rights to be a "'reproach to the administration of law,' and an 'omission of duty.'"[3]

Attempts to identify a doctrine of abuse of rights in the common law run into three problems. First, there is the question whether a right can be abused. It appears to be a violation of the principle of non-contradiction to speak of an abuse of rights, "an oxymoron,"[4] or a "juridically improper concept."[5] Abuse of rights seems to suppose that the owner both has and does not have the right. To say that an owner has abused his use right and therefore does not have the right is to speak "nonsense."[6] One scholar has suggested that the term abuse of rights might mean something like "an abusive exercise of an otherwise lawful right."[7] But if an otherwise lawful

[1] In international law the term is used to refer to states exercising their legal rights to cause harm to other states for ends other than those for which their rights are recognized in international law. See Michael Byers, "Abuse of Rights: An Old Principle, A New Age" (2002) 47 *McGill Law Journal* 389. Doctrines of abuse of rights are recognized in civil law jurisdictions. See Joseph M. Perillo, "Abuse of Rights: A Pervasive Legal Concept" (1995) 27 *Pacific Law Journal* 37; A. N. Yiannopoulos, "Civil Liability for Abuse of Right: Something Old, Something New" (1994) 54 *Louisiana Law Review* 1173; *Illinois Central Gulf R. Co.* v. *International Harvester Co.*, 368 So 2d 1009 at 1014 (La 1979). They appear to have originated in France. Michael Taggart, *Private Property and Abuse of Rights in Victorian England* (Oxford: Oxford University Press 2002), 145–49.

[2] H. C. Gutteridge, "Abuse of Rights" (1933) 5 *Cambridge Law Journal* 22.

[3] *Burke* v. *Smith*, 37 NW 838 at 842 (Mich 1888).

[4] Gutteridge, "Abuse of Rights," 47; Taggart, *Victorian England*, 146.

[5] John Finnis, *Collected Essays of John Finnis, vol. IV: Philosophy of Law* (Oxford: Oxford University Press 2012), 387.

[6] Finnis, *Philosophy of Law*, 388.

[7] Anna di Robilant, "Abuse of Rights: The Continental Drug and the Common Law" (2010) 61 *Hastings Law Journal* 687 at 688–89.

right is not a right in fact then it is difficult to imagine what it is. Resolution of this first problem awaits Chapter 7.

When one examines the cases, it becomes apparent that an abuse of rights doctrine must turn on the user's motivations for action. Whoever has the authority to deem some uses abusive must therefore make moral judgments about the user's motivations. This raises a second problem – how to prevent the doctrine from devolving into a "pure piece of sentimentality."[8] If a doctrine of abuse of rights is to operate within the common law, then it must draw on objective standards that help property owners and their neighbors to understand what acts are abusive, and enable juries and courts to render judgment on abusive acts when necessary without making law subjective or redundant of morality.

Third, in most common law jurisdictions courts have not recognized the doctrine as a doctrine, even where they have resorted to the idea of abuse of rights. Some American courts have declined to enforce rights when exercised abusively, but no clear equitable maxim, much less any legal doctrine, has emerged. English courts have expressly rejected abuse of rights as a norm-creating doctrine.[9] There is thus neither express authority for, nor precise definition of, any such doctrine in the common law tradition. This is not an insuperable problem. If a doctrine of abuse of rights can be developed consistent with common law principles, then it can perhaps be shown to be a natural development of those principles. This chapter argues that such a doctrine can be developed from existing case law in common law jurisdictions (including decisions from Louisiana, a civil law state influenced by its common law neighbors) and the last part takes up the task of sketching what such a doctrine might look like.

Abuse of rights in the common law

In order to develop a theory of abuse of rights, we would need some comprehensive story about the nature of rights and their relationships to moral norms. But developing such a story is well beyond the scope of this book. Therefore, in keeping with the common law practice of extrapolating general principles from particular judgments, I will instead try to discern from the cases what has concerned those courts that have grappled with the problem of abusive use-right exercises, and then try to sketch some observations from those cases.

[8] Gutteridge, "Abuse of Rights," 43. [9] Taggart, *Victorian England.*

It is not clear how such a doctrine *could* be justified on the basis of what is often taken to be the common law conception of property, that despotic dominion to which Blackstone made passing reference. Nevertheless, the despotic-dominion conception dissolves under scrutiny. Indeed, two claims about use rights, though provocative, seem unavoidable when one looks at the law closely. First, as developed in at least some jurisdictions, the common law does in fact contain an inherent limitation on use rights, which as a matter of principle constrains courts from giving juridical force to abusive uses of property. In short, judicial officers in common law jurisdictions act as if abuse of rights is not only an intelligible norm but also an imperative.[10] Second, constraint operates not on the basis of actions and consequences but rather on reasons for action. Abuse of rights deems some choices irrational, and therefore lacking moral value, because they are made not for reasons but rather for motivations that are unworthy of the law's sanction.

A review of cases involving abuse of rights reveals that the overriding concern of courts that employ the norm is action motivated by nothing other than a desire to cause harm. All abuse of rights cases turn on the wrongful motivation of the owner who is asserting his right. In these cases courts are not evaluating the all-things-considered costs and benefits of the owner's conduct. Rather, they are looking for an intelligible good end which supplies rationality to the owner's deliberation, absent which they reach the judgment that the owner has acted abusively.

The basic idea in abuse of rights cases is, "The purpose for which a man is using his own property may ... sometimes determine his rights."[11] One might have a right to perform an act with the use of one's things for any reason and yet not have a right to perform that same act for motivation Ø. Building a fence that my neighbor does not like is within my right unless I build the fence because my neighbor does not like it. So in one case it was an abuse of a lessor's rights to evict tenants at the end of a lease term if the purpose of the eviction was to punish the tenants for exercising their voting rights. Bad faith was needed to establish abuse of the right to evict.[12]

[10] For example, *Australian Building and Construction Commissioner Applicant* v. *Construction, Forestry, Mining and Energy Union First Respondent* [2011] ALMD 5098 (Fed Ct Australia 2011); *Rideout* v. *Knox*, 19 NE 390 (Mass 1889).

[11] *Tuttle* v. *Buck*, 119 NW 946 at 947 (Minn 1909).

[12] *United States* v. *Beaty*, 288 F 2d 653 at 657 (6th Cir. 1961); Perillo, "Pervasive Concept," 58–59.

Courts that have declined to recognize any doctrine of abuse of rights take the position that malice and other undue motives are irrelevant to the existence of a property right, if the owner is acting within his right and not infringing some previously recognized legal right of his neighbor.[13] The landmark case among these is *Bradford Corp.* v. *Pickles*, which famously stands for the proposition, "No use of property, which would be legal if due to a proper motive, can become illegal because it is prompted by a motive which is improper or even malicious."[14]

Nevertheless, the common law's treatment of motive is more complicated than the House of Lords acknowledged in *Pickles*. The court was aware of an important abuse of rights case, which helps to illustrate the central importance of human motivation.[15] *Keeble* v. *Hickeringill* is not always recognized as an abuse of rights case because the roles of wrongful and wronged parties appear to be reversed. The issue in that case was whether Hickeringill, the wrongful party, had trespassed against Keeble, the wronged party, by dispersing the ducks that had settled on Keeble's pond.[16] Hickeringill's property rights were therefore not obviously in issue. Further complicating things, as Michael Taggart pointed out, the case lacked "a clear holding as to what legal right was infringed by the unneighborly action."[17]

Yet Hickeringill enjoyed liberties to fire his gun, to draw ducks to his own land, and to scare ducks away. He lost because he exercised his liberties with a malicious intent, that is, an intention to harm Keeble's enterprise rather than to benefit himself. The court reasoned that "where a violent or malicious act is done to a man's occupation, profession, or way of getting a livelihood; there an action lies in all cases." By contrast, for mere competition, "as if Mr. Hickeringill had set up another decoy on his own ground near the plaintiff's, and that had spoiled the custom of the plaintiff, no action would lie." The harm resulting to Keeble – frustration of his efforts to capture the ducks – would have been the same in both cases. Everything turned on the fact that Hickeringill acted with a malicious intent.

One can abuse a right to inherit or to take a devise, as we saw in the discussion of *Riggs* v. *Palmer* [18] in Chapter 1. It is also possible to abuse a

[13] See *Jenkins* v. *Fowler*, 24 Pa 308 (Pa 1855); *Fontainebleau Hotel Corp.* v. *Forty-Five Twenty-Five*, 114 So 2d 357 (Fla App 1959); *44 Plaza, Inc.* v. *Gray-Pac Land Co.*, 845 SW 2d 576 at 579 (Mo App 1992).

[14] 1895 AC 587 at 598.

[15] See Taggart, *Victorian England*, 180–88.

[16] *Keeble* v. *Hickeringill*, 103 ER 1127 (QB 1707).

[17] Taggart, *Victorian England*, 187.

[18] 22 NE 188 (NY 1889).

right of entry.[19] But usufructs are the most often abused. Spite fence cases have produced some of the clearest statements of the justification for curtailing abuses of rights.[20] In one, a landowner could be held liable for nuisance when "from pure unadulterated vengeance and malice" he erected "a very rude, unsightly board fence eight feet, six inches high . . . within four feet of plaintiff's windows," cutting off the sunlight to the plaintiff's house.[21] And liability attached to this action even though the common law recognizes no general right to obtain sunlight on land. Because a fact finder could find that defendant did not benefit from the fence, permitting the action was inconsistent with "good morals."

The unapologetic perfectionism of these decisions is worth dwelling on. One court reasoned, "The ancient maxim of the common law, 'Sic utere tuo ut alienum non laedas',[22] is not founded in any human statute, but in that sentiment expressed by Him who taught good will toward men, and said, 'Love thy neighbor as thyself.' "No one," the court insisted, "ought to have the legal right to make a malicious use of his property for no benefit to himself, but merely to injure his fellow man." The common law placed numerous limitations on property rights, and there appeared no principled reason why the court should not limit an owner's right "to use his land in a particular way with no other purpose than to damage his neighbor."[23]

This was not the end of the court's morality lesson. It went on:

> The right thus to injure one's neighbor with impunity cannot long continue to exist anywhere in an enlightened country where God is acknowledged and the Golden Rule is taught. On this subject, if need be, we will do better to follow the pandects of the heathen Romans, whose jurists have inculcated a doctrine more consistent with the teachings of Him whom they permitted to be crucified, than to be governed by the principles of the common law as expounded by some Christian courts and text writers.[24]

[19] *Re Fair Work Australia*, (2011) 209 IR 135 (Fair Work Australia).

[20] Francis S. Philbrick, "Changing Conceptions of Property in Law" (1938) 86 *University of Pennsylvania Law Review* 691 at 724; *Lord* v. *Langdon*, 39 A 552 (Me 1898); *Rideout* v. *Knox*, 19 NE 390 at 391–92 (Mass 1889); *Burke* v. *Smith*, 37 NW 838 at 842 (Mich 1888); *Flaherty* v. *Moran*, 45 NW 381 at 381–82 (Mich 1890). See also the cases cited in Perillo, "Pervasive Concept," 46 & n 35.

[21] *Barger* v. *Barringer*, 66 SE 439 (NC 1909).

[22] Roughly, "So use your own property as not to injure another's."

[23] *Barger* v. *Barringer*, 66 SE at 439 at 442.

[24] *Barger* v. *Barringer*, 66 SE at 442.

Some of the religious tone has dropped out of more recent decisions, but the language of moral judgment remains. Courts employing the abuse of rights norm speak of "predominant motive[s]";[25] "moral rules, good faith, [and] elementary fairness";[26] "malevolent purpose," "legitimate purpose," and the "moral quality" of deliberate acts.[27] So, in one case, erection of a tower with the "sole purpose" of interfering with airplane overflights constituted an abuse of rights because the tower served no "necessary or incidental use" of the owner's land and intentionally jeopardized the lives of airplane passengers.[28] The court analogized the tower's construction to the setting of a spring gun and quoted an earlier state high court decision's dictum that "'the humanity of the law' prohibits actions done 'purposely to catch and injure even willful trespassers.'"[29] Common human understanding, "guided by the second branch of the great law of love,[30] and the common sense of jurors, must be left, in such a case, to pronounce [judgment] upon the facts."[31]

Significantly, courts decline to employ an abuse of rights norm where the owner has mixed motives, as long as at least one of the owner's motivations is not pure malice. (The significance of this practice is explained in the discussion of the principle of double effect, infra.) So, a landowner may dig a well on his land with the knowledge that his action will diminish the water available to his neighbor "unless in so doing he is actuated by a mere malicious intent to deprive his neighbor of water."[32]

25 *Truschinger* v. *Pak*, 513 So 2d 1151 at 1154 (La 1987).

26 *Truschinger* v. *Pak*, 513 So 2d at 1155; *Illinois Central Gulf R. Co.* v. *International Harvester Co.*, 368 So 2d 1009 at 1014 (La 1979).

27 *Tuttle*, 119 NW at 948.

28 *Commonwealth* v. *VonBestecki*, 30 Pa D & C 137 at 141 (Pa Ct Common Pleas 1937).

29 *Commonwealth* v. *VonBestecki*, 30 Pa D & C at 144.

30 This appears to be a reference to what Christ referred to as the second greatest commandment. The Pharisees asked him to identify the greatest commandment in the Jewish law. He responded, "Love the Lord your God with all your heart and with all your soul and with all your mind. This is the first and greatest commandment. And the second is like it: Love your neighbor as yourself. All the Law and the Prophets hang on these two commandments." Matthew 22:37–40 (New International Version).

31 *Commonwealth* v. *VonBestecki*, 30 Pa D & C at 144.

32 *Greenleaf* v. *Francis*, 35 Mass 117 (1836). Accord *Roath* v. *Driscoll*, 20 Conn 533 (1850) ("It is found, that the defendant is acting from honest motives to advance his interests, without any design unnecessarily to injure the plaintiffs."); *Chesley* v. *King*, 74 Me 164 at 177–78 (1882) ("[T]he testimony is of a character that conclusively negatives the defendant's guilt." Defendant dug the well "to supply the deficiency that he experienced.").

The same applies to spite fences,[33] and to disputes about rights arising under leases.[34]

After conducting a far-reaching survey of the concept of abuse of rights in American and European law, Joseph Perillo identified three types of actions that count as abusive under the doctrine: (1) actions motivated primarily by a desire to cause harm; (2) actions that are unreasonable or are motivated by no cognizable interest of the actor; and (3) exercises of the right that are inconsistent with the purpose for which the right is recognized.[35] Perillo's taxonomy is useful, and we'll return to it below.

A political theory of abuse of rights

Before returning to the thick account of practical reason that this book is developing, it will be helpful to consider an alternative, which many readers will be inclined to find more congenial. This alternative account highlights the unavoidable significance of reasons for action within property law.

Larissa Katz has advanced a political theory of abuse of rights.[36] She recognizes that reasons for action play a central role in the norm's operation, and she affirms the importance of reasons within property law. She even invokes some important principles of practical reason. She grounds her theory in moral obligations to respect the personal autonomy of others. She also refers to the principle of double effect and cites

33 So, one court found,

> In the present case the building [was erected] for a useful purpose; and, while there may have been some malice displayed in putting it so near the complainant's house as to shut off some of the light, that would not be a sufficient reason upon which to found a right in complainant to have the building removed.

Kuzniak v. *Kozminski*, 65 NW 275 at 276 (Mich 1895). See also *Rideout* v. *Knox*, 19 NE at 392 (If the extra height of the fence "is really necessary for any reason, there is no liability, whatever the motives of the owner in erecting it.").

34 *Truschinger* v. *Pak*, 513 So 2d at 1154–55. In this respect, abuse of rights cases differ from retaliatory eviction claims, which often arise under state statutes and rest upon policy judgments concerning incentives and material consequences. See, e.g., *S.P. Growers Association* v. *Rodriguez*, 552 P 2d 721 at 723–28 (Cal 1976).

35 Perillo, "Pervasive Concept," 47. Compare Gutteridge, "Abuse of Rights," 25; di Robilant, "Continental Drug," 691–92. Yiannopoulos identifies an additional category within Louisiana law: "the use of the right in violation of moral rules, good faith or elementary fairness." Yiannopoulos, "Something Old," 1180. See *210 Baronne Street Ltd.* v. *First National Bank of Commerce*, 543 So 2d 502, 507 (La App 1989).

36 Larissa Katz, "Spite and Extortion: A Principle of Abuse of (Property) Right" (2013) 122 *Yale Law Journal* 1444.

John Finnis in her explanation of mixed-motive cases.[37] (The principle of double effect is an important corollary of absolute moral duties, such as the duties not to kill or enslave.)

In spite of all this talk of moral principles, Katz takes a surprising turn. She does not believe that the abuse of rights principle rests on any commitment to "virtue, utility or even social responsibility." Because the use of one's property poses a potential threat "to the autonomy interests of others," property rights "have built-in constraints *on the class of question* that owners may consider." The jurisdiction of a property owner extends only to answering the question "what in their view would be a worthwhile agenda for a thing." Katz calls this "the Basic Question." Owners exceed their authority, and therefore abuse their rights, when they make decisions for reasons that are not responsive to the Basic Question, as where they use their rights with a purpose to pressure others to conform to their wishes.[38]

In support of her account, Katz enlists the authority both of spite cases and of what she calls "leverage" cases. In spite cases, the owner's ultimate end is to cause harm. In leverage cases the owner intends to use her property rights to cause harm in order to achieve a yet more fundamental end, namely the ability to coerce or persuade someone else to accede to her demands. Property rights are legitimately used as leverage only where the owner's decision reflects some person's view (her own or another's) of what constitutes a "worthwhile" use of the asset, and thus is responsive to the Basic Question. By contrast, where an owner employs property rights to inflict harm in order to gain leverage, she is not using her own judgment, or anyone else's, about what use of the asset would be worthwhile.[39]

Katz's theory is attractive because it promises to resolve a tension in property, which the abuse of rights principle highlights. On one hand, reasons for action matter; human virtue is important. On the other hand, property does its job primarily by insulating owners' reasons for action from law. Property is in this sense a political institution. Katz addresses this tension by positing a political theory that avoids rendering judgment on the morality of different reasons for action.

Nevertheless, it is not clear that Katz's political theory is necessary to explain abuse of rights cases. In the cases she discusses, the property owners either evince an intention to cause harm or insist on the

[37] Katz, "Extortion," 1452–69.
[38] Katz, "Extortion," 1444, 1450, 1454, 1458, 1463.
[39] Katz, "Extortion," 1458–68.

enforcement of a right that protects no cognizable interest in their own property – an insistence that results in foreseeable harm. So the traditional explanation for abuse of rights cases, that they are fundamentally about malicious intention or irrational motivations, does the job. For example, in Katz's so-called leverage case, a wood engraver was frustrated by the music produced by his neighbors, musicians who practiced and taught lessons next door. In retaliation, the engraver made noise on makeshift instruments. In a nuisance action filed by the musicians, the court ruled that the engraver's noise could constitute a nuisance because the engraver created the noise with an intent to harm.[40]

More fundamentally, Katz's theory does not fulfill its promise of explaining abuse of rights in political terms. The property owner who enforces her rights to harm or pressure another believes that she *has* in fact answered the Basic Question. She has set an agenda for the thing, which entails using the thing as an instrumental means of influencing another person. She considers this use worthwhile. Katz must have some explanation as to why the right abuser's agenda for the asset is not worthwhile, an explanation that would require some account of good and bad reasons for action. There must be some reason why leverage is *wrongful.*

Katz seems to anticipate this criticism. She asserts that the owner's agenda in a spite case is "contrived,"[41] because the ultimate end of the owner's action is harm to another. By contrivance Katz seems to mean that the owner sets out to harm her neighbor, and only after committing to that end decides to enlist her property rights as means; she would not have decided as she did about the property but for the ulterior motive. But this is true of most uses of property that Katz would presumably find unobjectionable. Parents first commit to send their children to college, and only after committing to that end do they decide to assume a second mortgage on their residence in order to finance the goal. One first decides to visit a friend, then decides to use one's bicycle to make the trek. One needs some evaluative tool for distinguishing the moral difference between the intention to harm and the intention to assist in a child's education or to visit a friend.

So, the work in Katz's Basic Question is done by the word "worthwhile." This word assumes an undefended conception of practical reason, and it is this conception of practical reason that enables Katz to distinguish permissible uses of property rights from abuses. Katz

[40] Katz, "Extortion," 1463–65. [41] Katz, "Extortion," 1456–57.

does not expressly state what conception she is using, but she intimates what she has in mind. For Katz the owner's standing to make decisions about things threatens the autonomy of others because the owner's decisions about use are binding on others. She thinks that property is owned by all collectively until it is appropriated individually. Owners have no unique authority except to the extent that the collective allows them authority to act "in the name of all," and the authority of owners must therefore be limited to the purpose for which it is recognized, namely solving the coordination problem of how to make the best use.[42]

Now Katz's theory has changed from a political theory into a moral theory. Indeed, Katz uses normative language to describe the duty that circumscribes the use right. She states, "I have a moral duty to forbear from imposing my decisions on others because others have an interest in autonomy that I must respect." She believes that "respect for the autonomy of others is a good reason to forbear from imposing even our expert opinions on them."[43]

It is not clear whether Katz is here claiming that autonomy is intrinsically valuable, or rather that autonomy must categorically be respected for some more fundamental reason. She gives indications of both views. Citing the perfectionist liberal Joseph Raz, she asserts that the autonomous self-determination of a social life is "an objectively valuable good," which supplies a categorical reason to refrain from acting. But she also claims that respect for the autonomy of others is "an intrinsic moral duty" because it "expresses the values of tolerance and respect for others, values that give life meaning."[44] Either way, Katz treats personal autonomy as a non-contingent reason, the one reason that performs the normative work in her theory.

As we saw in Chapter 4, freedom from coercion is an important precondition of practical reasonableness, and is for that reason an important value (among other important human goods). And if personal autonomy has some value (as it surely does), it must be valuable not only for property owners but also for non-owners. As the discussion in Chapter 3 affirmed, a just institution of private ownership cannot rest on moral claims unless it is willing to treat those claims as universal. So, owners must have some obligation to consider the personal autonomy of those whom their actions affect.

[42] Katz, "Extortion," 1449–51.
[43] Katz, "Extortion," 1473.
[44] Katz, "Extortion," 1476.

Nevertheless, Katz's theory runs up against another problem: personal autonomy will not bear all of the weight that Katz needs to place on it. If personal autonomy were a categorical reason for action then it would disintegrate moral norms, including the very moral norm that personal autonomy must be respected. If personal autonomy is a categorical reason for action then it supplies non-contingent value to otherwise-unreasonable decisions, including a decision to infringe upon the personal autonomy of another human being. On this premise, every valueless decision becomes valuable if willfully made, and intrinsically evil acts, including the violation of the personal autonomy of another person, are *more* valuable by virtue of having been done autonomously. Alternatively, if respect for personal autonomy is an intrinsic moral duty, it can never be reasonable to infringe anyone's personal autonomy, including one's own. Thus, any value set up against personal autonomy, including personal autonomy, must yield to the intrinsic duty to respect personal autonomy.

Joseph Raz has articulated perhaps the most sophisticated defense of the idea that personal autonomy is intrinsically valuable.[45] The "ruling idea" of personal autonomy, Raz has argued, is "that people should make their own lives" by choice.[46] Personal autonomy is an "ideal of self-creation,"[47] toward which people naturally and rightly direct their wills. In embracing goals and commitments and remaining true to them, one "gives shape to one's life, determines what would count as a successful life and what would be a failure."[48] Resolution changes one's reasons for action, and thus people have some freedom to create values, to generate "reasons which transcend the reasons one had for undertaking one's commitments and pursuits."[49]

Raz claims not merely that people should be free to choose whether to make their own lives, but that people are actually better off if they do so; free choice is an essential ingredient of well-being. Thus, autonomy is valuable even for those who might deny its value. The value of autonomy is on this view a "fact of life," and does not depend on one's choice to value autonomy. Autonomy is, in short, objectively and non-contingently valuable.[50]

Raz embraces the incommensurability thesis, and for that reason rejects consequentialism. So he should not be understood to set

[45] Joseph Raz, *The Morality of Freedom* (Oxford: Oxford University Press 1986) [hereinafter MOF].

[46] MOF, 369. [47] MOF, 370. [48] MOF, 387. [49] MOF, 386–87.

[50] MOF, 7, 390–95.

autonomy up as the summum bonum. Indeed, Raz affirms that the ideal of personal autonomy requires a plurality of available, valuable options. Thus, there must be other basic goods in favor of which personal autonomy can be exercised, and they must be equally basic as autonomy.[51] And Raz hastens to reject the "exaggerated ... doctrine of arbitrary self-creation," which holds that all value derives from choice, which is itself not guided by value.[52] Some values must be objectively valuable, and they cannot be reduced to personal autonomy. So even if autonomy is a basic good, moral evaluation cannot be avoided.

Furthermore, Raz's claim creates a dilemma, which has received attention from very capable thinkers.[53] If personal autonomy were intrinsically valuable, free choice would add something of value to an otherwise-evil act.[54] So, for example, an act of murder should have greater value than an act of negligent homicide. Theft should be a more valuable act than forgetting to return one's library books. But this is backwards. As Raz observes, a "wrongdoing casts a darker shadow on its perpetrator if it is autonomously done by him."[55]

So Raz has acknowledged that the value of personal autonomy must be contingent. Though personal autonomy can be exercised in favor of both good and bad ends, only good choices are valuable. As Raz observes,

> An autonomous life is valuable only to the extent that it is engaged in *valuable* activities and relationships. The loss of an opportunity to murder does nothing to reduce one's chances of having the sort of autonomous life which is of value, hence there is nothing lost in not having the opportunity to murder, and one's autonomy, in the sense of a capacity for valuable autonomous life, is not constrained by the absence of that option.

[51] MOF, 203–06. Raz uses the term "collective goods" to refer to the social conditions that generate valuable options for choice. But the examples that he uses, such as the professions of law and medicine, are products of cooperative plans of action within intermediary institutions, not collective evaluation.

[52] MOF, 387–88.

[53] Donald H. Regan, "Authority and Value: Reflections on Raz's Morality of Freedom" (1989) 62 *Southern California Law Review* 995 at 1075–85; Robert P. George, *Making Men Moral: Civil Liberties and Public Morality* (New York: Oxford University Press 1993), 175–80; Christopher Wolfe, "A Response to Joseph Raz" in R. P. George (ed.), *Natural Law, Liberalism, and Morality* (New York: Oxford University Press 1996), 135.

[54] The only other logical possibility is that evil choices are by definition never autonomous. George, *Making Men Moral*, 175. But this possibility is ruled out by the operation of personal autonomy itself. If the choice to do evil is not truly free, then neither is the choice to abstain from doing evil, i.e., to choose the good. The whole point of personal autonomy of course is to enable people to make good reasons for their own choice and action by free choice.

[55] MOF, 380.

This makes the value of personal autonomy dependent on the way in which it is exercised.[56] The value of personal autonomy is conditional on practically reasonable choice and action, rather than the other way around. So, though freedom from coercion is an important precondition of practically reasonable choice and is therefore an instrumental reason for action, there is nothing *inherently* immoral or unjust in using resources to influence the choices and actions of those under one's authority.

The contingent value of autonomy undermines Katz's moral argument; it weakens her political account too. Katz's theory posits a tension between individual personal autonomy and power, resolved when the law permits owners to exercise dominion over things, or not.[57] Individuals need not be inherently in opposition to each other, or to the collective aggregate of them. Authority is often exercised in order to enable cooperation toward a common good.[58] In order to achieve their common purposes and to promote the common good, communities need to coordinate the actions of their constituent members. Authority is requisite to this coordination. Authority promotes purposes that are central to our being as social creatures, agents of good choosing who act in concert in order to realize ends that are truly good for all, not merely as aggregations or consequentialist maximizations of individual preferences, but truly in the best interests of everyone. Authority is not delegated from some mythical collective, but is instead a natural and necessary predicate for human action in community.

As a political account of the way that authority over property is exercised in non-state communities, Katz's account is thus incomplete. Much authority over things, like most authority generally, is exercised neither as delegated power from collective, political bodies, nor as an exercise of autonomous self-constitution. Much authority over property is exercised in families, churches, neighborhood associations, family businesses, nonprofits, and other intermediary communities and institutions. In these communities, personal autonomy often yields to a truly common good, which is often (though certainly not always) good both

[56] Raz affirms, "Autonomy is valuable only if exercised in pursuit of the good." MOF, 120, 381.

[57] Katz, "Extortion," 1472–82.

[58] John Finnis, *Natural Law and Natural Rights* (2nd edn, Oxford: Oxford University Press 2011) [hereinafter NLNR], 231–32; Jean Porter, *Ministers of the Law: A Natural Law Theory of Legal Authority* (Grand Rapids: Eerdmans 2010), 131–32; George, *Making Men Moral*, 107.

for the community and for the constituent member of the community whose preference is overruled. A parent who withholds a thing from his or her child for the purpose of disciplining the child or teaching the child the virtues of thrift, stewardship, and patience has not acted unjustly. Would Katz allow this?

Leaving all this aside, one cannot find support in law for Katz's ascription of intrinsic value to autonomy. The common law has not treated personal autonomy as a basic reason for action. And where states have enacted laws based on that principle, they have introduced into the law internal contradictions and incoherence.[59] It is beyond the scope of Katz's project to justify the claim that personal autonomy is a categorical good. But the foundational problems with that claim undermine her account, which rests on it. We need a normative account of reasons for action. The abuse of rights norm cannot be understood in purely political terms.

Moral categories

How can law establish standards for judging some uses of property to be abusive? The short answer is that the law condemns as abusive those uses that are inconsistent with the most fundamental, least controversial moral judgments. The abuse of rights norm does not work a wholesale importation of morality into law. It prohibits valueless, intentional harm, but does not incorporate into law the more exacting requirements of a Kantian categorical imperative or the Golden Rule. It is about discerning which reasons for action are wholly incompatible with the rule of law, where law is also conceived as a reason for action. Courts employing the norm are patrolling the outer boundaries of acceptable choice and action, and ruling out only those exercises of rights made with a will that is inconsistent with human well-being, lest those exercises receive the sanction of judicial decree or positive law.

The account I am defending is perfectionist in the way that the common law tradition is perfectionist, though here we are going beyond an explanation of existing common law doctrine to consider whether a new development of the common law might be justified, or even required, on principles that the common law already vindicates. The case law that exists provides some assistance by revealing the primary

[59] Adam J. MacLeod, "The Mystery of Life in the Laboratory of Democracy: Personal Autonomy in State Law" (2012) 59 *Cleveland State Law Review* 589.

importance of reasons for action. The cases show that the courts have been concerned with *moral* considerations: some reasons for action are worthy and others are not. Providing an account of such a doctrine requires making some sense of the moral terms – vengeance and malice, spite, the Golden Rule, even love – that the courts employ to explain their decisions.

This does not mean that economists and consequentialists cannot discern distinctions in the cases. The difficulty from an economic point of view is quarantining abuse of rights within the category of cases in which the only gain to the actor is the harm suffered by others.[60] One approach is to distinguish merely self-interested exercises of rights from so-called opportunistic exercises.[61] As framed by law and economics scholars, equity's anti-opportunism principle takes a "dim view of those who hold back in a way likely to cause unfair surprise to someone else's great detriment."[62] Because property law creates "simple and stable structures as platforms upon which people can coordinate," and to this end insulates much information from the view of duty-holders, it also creates opportunities for right-holders unfairly to benefit from possessing too much information. Equity often operates as a "safety valve" to deter these opportunistic acts.[63]

There appears to be considerable overlap between the anti-opportunism principle in equity and the abuse of rights principle. Henry Smith has observed that the civil law doctrine of abuse of rights resembles his own conception of equity "as an anti-opportunism device." Both combat disproportionate hardship, especially hardship that results from one party "taking unfair advantage of the other."[64] The trick, of course, is to understand what counts as unfair advantage. Smith distinguishes cases of "self-serving, overreaching behavior" from instances of

[60] Richard Epstein, *Design for Liberty* (Cambridge: Harvard University Press 2011), 84–88.

[61] See Restatement (Third) of Restitution and Unjust Enrichment §39 (2011), comment i; Daniel B. Kelly, "Strategic Spillovers" (2011) 111 *Columbia Law Review* 1641 at 1712.

[62] Mark P. Gergen, John M. Golden, and Henry E. Smith, "The Supreme Court's Accidental Revolution? The Test for Permanent Injunctions" (2012) 112 *Columbia Law Review* 203 at 247.

[63] "[E]quity in private law," Henry Smith argues, "is a coherent package of features motivated largely by one overriding goal: preventing opportunism." Henry E. Smith, "An Economic Analysis of Law Versus Equity" (2013), 3, available at www.law.yale.edu/documents/pdf/LEO/Hsmith_LawVersusEquity7.pdf. Those who deliberately attempt to take advantage of an exception to a legal duty "are subject to the full force of the injunctive remedy."

[64] Smith, "Law versus Equity," 33.

merely dire consequences.[65] There remains then the task of defining such moral terms as unfair, self-serving, and overreaching.

Indeed, the challenge for understanding abuse of rights specifically (as opposed to anti-opportunism generally) is grasping the principle's inherent moral content. Not all opportunistic exercises of rights are abusive. The abuse of rights principle operates against a particular type of opportunism, namely the exercise of a right for the wrong reasons. Other doctrines in law and equity are at hand to deal with opportunistic behavior that is not abusive. For example, suppose A sits by and allows B to remove trees from A's land without asserting his right, then B in good faith and by his own effort transforms the wood into something far more valuable, such as furniture. If A waits to assert his claim in the trees until B has dramatically improved their value, then A might lose title to the trees under the doctrine of accession.[66] If a property owner waits too long to assert his rights, and presses his claim only after the other party has possessed the item for some time, or has taken action in detrimental reliance upon the owner's silence, then the owner might lose his rights under the doctrines of adverse possession and estoppel, respectively.[67]

Furthermore, if there is a difference between self-interest and opportunism, it is hard to see how that distinction might inform the practical reasoning of an owner who is self-interested and looking for opportunities to advance his interests. From the internal point of view of the owner, all opportunistic behavior is also self-interested – the opportunistic actor believes that he is acting to attain what is in his interest – and all self-interested action is opportunistic – the actor takes advantage of the opportunities available to him. So Daniel Kelly has concluded, "Although abuse of right may provide courts with a legal justification for examining a party's motivation, the doctrine, by itself, does not provide a functional test for distinguishing self-interested from opportunistic behavior."[68] Smith states, "Perhaps the most salient feature of opportunism is the difficulty in defining it."[69]

[65] Smith, "Law versus Equity," 35. So, for example, Smith divides anti-forfeiture maxims in equity into "broader and narrower versions." Broad versions "rescue people from dire consequences," while narrower versions address extreme consequences that result from "sharp dealing, misleading behavior, and other forms of opportunism." Smith, "Law Versus Equity," 34.

[66] See Thomas W. Merrill and Henry E. Smith, *The Oxford Introductions to U.S. Law: Property* (New York: Oxford University Press 2010), 30–31; *Wetherbee* v. *Green*, 222 Mich 311 (1871).

[67] Merrill and Smith, *Property*, 34–38, 205; Smith, "Law versus Equity," 35.

[68] Kelly, "Strategic Spillovers," 1712.

[69] Smith, "Law versus Equity," 8.

One needs an explanation for courts' focus on internal motivations. We need to understand what abusers of rights are doing (or, to be precise, the reasons for which they are doing what they are doing) to earn the courts' disapprobation.

Abusive exercises of rights

Actions taken with a purpose to cause harm

Returning to Perillo's three categories, one can discern two modest and relatively non-controversial moral principles at work in abuse of rights law. In Perillo's first category of abuses of rights, the wrongfulness of the owner's choice inheres in the deliberate choice to cause harm. The foundational moral principle at work in these cases is the prohibition against causing harm for the purpose of causing harm. Greater than the positive duty to reduce the risk of harm is the "negative duty of not doing willful harm."[70]

When one makes harm to another person one's reason for action, one acts with a will that is inconsistent with the common good. To act with an intention to harm is to set one's will against the well-being of a human being. Less obviously perhaps, it is also to set one's will against one's own well-being. Remember that willful choices are self-constituting; practical reason is a reflexive practice. To make another's misfortunate a reason for one's own action is to make oneself a person who wills misfortune on others.

A deliberate choice to cause harm is thus immoral. In the language of moral philosophy, it violates a basic requirement of practical reasonableness.[71] This basic requirement is not the only principle of practical reasonableness, nor is it the most basic. But it is basic and binding. One way to formulate the requirement is "that one should not choose to do any act which of itself does nothing but damage or impede a realization or participation of any one or more of the basic forms of human good."[72]

The essential logic that makes this first category of abuses abhorrent, and gives rise to the need for a doctrine addressing the practice, is a sort of reverse consequentialism: the means justify the end. *I alone possess a*

[70] *Tuttle* v. *Buck*, 119 NW 946 at 947 (Minn 1909).

[71] NLNR, 118–25, 126–27; Ronald Dworkin, *Justice for Hedgehogs* (Cambridge: Harvard University Press 2011), chapter 13; Robert P. George, *In Defense of Natural Law* (New York: Oxford University Press 1999), 49–54.

[72] NLNR, 118.

legal right to determine the use of this thing, the actor rationalizes, *and I may exercise that right for my own benefit, or for none. Therefore, the law should not be concerned if I exercise it for another's harm.* In this analysis, the right outweighs the purpose for which it is deployed. But a bare assertion of right is not remotely proportionate to the reason that the right-holder has taken into his character, namely harm to his neighbor.

The right abuser's logic fails for the same reason that consequentialist logic fails. The actor cannot justify an unreasonable action on the ground that it was undertaken in furtherance of, or reliance upon, some right or good other than the one being purposefully destroyed. In every choice, in every action, one's chosen end and the means one has chosen to achieve that end each requires its own justification. Each must be justifiably directed toward human goods that provide intelligible reasons for action and must be consistent with the principles of practical reasonableness that guide one toward human flourishing and away from choices that are inconsistent with a will for the well-being of oneself and others.

The abuser's logic fails for another reason. On this logic, legal right is a reason for action that renders all other reasons for action obsolete. By making the right ascendant over all other considerations, the owner perverts the very right that he is invoking. The right exists to serve good ends. But the owner has filled it with evil content by directing it toward evil ends. He has destroyed any reason the community once had for respecting the rights. The owner transforms the right into a wrong, making it ineffectual to perform normative work in the future.

What does this have to do with law? It should not be forgotten that a court gets involved in an abuse of rights case because it is enlisted by the party who is culpably insisting upon the exercise of his putative right. An abusive owner is treating the right as an absolute reason, which trumps all other requirements of practical reason, including the duties that he owes to his neighbors. Worse, the owner is insisting that the court must endorse his reasoning. Were the court to enforce the right, it would sanction the perversion of practical reason and justice that the owner has accomplished. A court has an obligation to preserve its integrity by refusing to sanction immoral acts that would introduce incoherence into the law.[73]

Like the morality of plaintiff's conduct in tort, the morality of an owner's action in property is an extrinsic consideration that comes into the case only when required to preserve the integrity of law and legal

[73] *Hall* v. *Hebert* [1993] 2 SCR 159 (Canada).

institutions.[74] An abusive owner imposes upon the court a Hobson's choice. When a court gives juridical force to a right created by private actors or institutions of private ordering, it is acting, and the result of its action is an endorsement of the private right in law. Either the court must refuse to enforce a private right or it must accept the right along with its abusive exercise and thus import into law, by way of a legal judgment, the owner's perversion of the right. If the court renders judgment against the owner, vagueness is injected into the law with its attendant uncertainty. If, on the other hand, the court renders judgment for the owner in such cases, the right becomes a very different kind of thing altogether. It becomes a license to act with malice toward one's fellow human beings. Neither choice is satisfactory. But it is preferable to limit the right in some principled way than to pervert the right from within. To endorse the abusive exercise would violate the historic common law principle that forbids courts to "permit themselves to be used as instruments of inequity and injustice."[75]

This theory might cause some to worry about the reduction of law to morality. Particularly, if the requirements of practical reasonableness are permitted to trump property rights, then "competing religious, ethnic, or partisan factions find it hard to resist the temptation to use virtue theory as an ideological tool to establish hegemony over rival factions in their common political community,"[76] to impose one controversial conception of morality upon those who disagree.

But law does promote many central goods and virtues, which vary somewhat in their degrees of controversy. It prohibits racial discrimination in housing and pollution of navigable waters, even when those prohibitions are controversial. Indeed, the obligations enforced by such laws are sometimes necessary *because* they are controversial, i.e., because someone does not believe that he or she is bound by such obligations, and will not honor them unless forced to do so. So the question is not whether the law should incorporate principles of practical reason but rather which principles it should incorporate. And it seems that the moral principle prohibiting deliberate harm should be among the least controversial.

Any remaining concerns about legislating moral obligations ought to be assuaged when one considers that the abuse of rights principle

[74] Compare *Hall* v. *Hebert* [1993] 2 SCR at 182.

[75] *Henningsen* v. *Bloomfield Motors, Inc.*, 161 A 2d 69 at 86 (NJ 1960), quoting *United States* v. *Bethehem Steel Corp.*, 315 US 289 at 326 (1942) (Frankfurter J dissenting).

[76] Eric R. Claeys, "Virtue and Rights in American Property Law" (2009) 94 *Cornell Law Review* 889.

operates only when the owner acts with the *sole* motive to cause harm, or without any rational good in mind.[77] Any mixture of motives that includes realization of a human good is sufficient to render the exercise of the right lawful. An important corollary of the moral principle against causing deliberate harm is the principle of double effect.[78] That corollary holds that one may, under certain conditions, do something good even though that good action will produce a harmful effect, as long as one does not *intend* that effect.[79]

Courts therefore do not declare a use abusive unless they have no way to judge the use rational. They are reticent to employ the abuse of rights principle where the actor can be seen to act out of mixed motivations. The purpose of mediated dominion is to insulate the owner's deliberations from outside criticism. The principle of double effect enables courts to honor the presumption that use rights establish by assuming that the owner's motivations were reasonable unless they are conclusively shown not to be. Knowledge that harm is likely, or even certain, to result from one's conduct does not in itself render one's decision to engage in the conduct culpable.

Actions that promote no intelligible interest

Perillo's second category of abuses – actions that are motivated by no cognizable interest of the actor – refers to actions that are not merely unreasonable but actually irrational. In these cases the property owner acts in such a way that no one, including the property owner, realizes any intelligible good, and the one against whom the right is exercised loses something valuable, i.e., suffers harm. In these cases, the owner's error is in acting on the basis of some sub-rational motivation, such as impulse or spite. The owner has chosen for himself an end that has no intelligible value, either in itself (as a basic good) or as an instrumental means of realizing some more fundamental good. The owner might think that he is doing something rational, but he is mistaken.

[77] Discussing *Riggs* v. *Palmer*, 22 NE 188 (NY 1889), Henry Smith observed, "Notice that the standard for the maxim to apply to avoid the straightforward application of the wills act is absurdity or (manifest) unreasonableness." Smith, "Law Versus Equity," 29.

[78] See Dworkin, *Justice for Hedgehogs*, 293–95; Germain Grisez, "Toward a Consistent Natural-Law Ethics of Killing" (1970) 15 *American Journal of Jurisprudence* 64; Joseph M. Boyle, "Toward Understanding the Principle of Double Effect" (1980) 90 *Ethics* 527.

[79] On these conditions and the importance of double effect generally, see Christopher O. Tollefsen, "Moral Absolutes and the Moral Life" (November 21, 2011) *Public Discourse* www.thepublicdiscourse.com/2011/11/4294.

As we have seen, human goods are plural and various, but not infinitely so. Law protects a strong core of owner dominion in part because most choices about the use of things are rationally undetermined. In cases of undetermined choice, all other things being equal, it is the choice of the actor that makes a good a reason for one's future actions.[80] One can just as reasonably use one's land to grow crops as to educate children. The choice to be a farmer instead of a teacher, or a teacher instead of a farmer, is therefore made freely. In the realm of pre-moral choosing among possible instantiations of the good, one really does make one's own life, in the sense that Raz means when he speaks of the ideal of personal autonomy, or the sense in which we earlier discussed self-constitution in the order of the will.

By contrast, it is possible to compare basic goods with merely instrumental goods.[81] Human health has intrinsic value; money does not. The value of money is entirely contingent upon its instrumental usefulness for acquiring other goods. Money has no value on a desert island, or if issued by a failed state. Furthermore, it is possible to compare goods with non-goods. Knowledge has intrinsic value; ignorance does not. Friendship has intrinsic value; alienation does not. If someone prefers ignorance and alienation then we can say that that person is worse off for it. Thus evaluative judgment is possible between goods and non-goods.

Leaving aside the moral harm that one causes to oneself by acting irrationally, an irrational action that causes harm to others ought to be prohibited in law. Because there is no intelligible value in a life spent alienating one's neighbors, a decision to become a curmudgeon, made for no reason other than being curmudgeonly, is a choice lacking rationality. When it causes harm to others, this irrational choice is a matter of concern to the community. It impedes the realization of friendship and community. Where one chooses without regard for any intelligible goods and no one suffers any harm, the law might not concern itself. But the situation is different where a choice lacking in intelligible value negatively affects the community. In such cases, it does not matter whether the actor harbors an intention to cause harm. The actor has chosen wrongly not because he has acted in violation of a basic moral principle but because his choice lacks rational value altogether, and the law steps in because of the harmful effects of this irrational decision.

[80] See, generally, MOF, chapters 11–13; John Finnis, *Moral Absolutes: Tradition, Revision, and Truth* (Washington, DC: Catholic University Press 1991).

[81] George, *Defense of Natural Law*, 45–48; Ronald Dworkin, *Life's Dominion: An Argument about Abortion, Euthanasia, and Individual Freedom* (New York: Knopf 1993), 71–72.

Here again, mixed motives are not sufficient to give rise to liability. Even if the owner chooses to realize an instrumental good, such as the acquisition of money or other additional property, the abuse of rights doctrine should not intrude, because the owner should have the freedom to put the instrumental good to use for the more fundamental end that supplied the instrumental value. But if the owner cannot offer a rational explanation of his conduct, then it is abusive. Property law need not protect the rights of owners to impoverish human experience.

Compare *Flaherty* v. *Moran* and *Kuzniak* v. *Kozminski*, two spite-structure cases decided by the Michigan Supreme Court.[82] In Flaherty the evidence made it obvious that the spite fence served "no useful or needful purpose" and was built and maintained "out of pure malice and spite."[83] By contrast, in Kuzniak, the court found that the defendant's erection of a shed near the complainant's land so as to block light might have been the result of malice, but that the building also served "a useful purpose," and therefore did not constitute a nuisance.[84]

Actions outside the telos of the right

Perillo's third category – exercises of the right inconsistent with the purpose for which the right is recognized – encompasses errors about the nature of rights. Use rights are not absolute.[85] Rather, they are properly exercised in certain ways, for certain ends, and are limited according to the purposes for which they are recognized. Indeed, the only way to understand both of the competing intuitions at work in property law (the goal of this book) is to view use rights as means of achieving the common good. To understand how property norms promote the common good, it is more helpful to speak of duties and obligations than of rights;[86] one who is rightly oriented toward the common good of his community will be at least as attentive to what he should do as he is to what is due to him. This book has emphasized duties

[82] *Flaherty* v. *Moran*, 45 NW 381 (Mich 1890); *Kuzniak* v. *Kozminski*, 65 NW 275 (Mich 1895).

[83] *Flaherty* v. *Moran*, 45 NW at 381.

[84] *Kuzniak* v. *Kozminski*, 65 NW at 276.

[85] The natural *law* account that I am defending in this book allows for the contingent nature of property rights in a way that some versions of the natural *rights* account does not. This distinction will, I hope, be clearer in Chapter 7. On the important differences between natural law and natural rights theories, see NLNR, chapter 8; Randy E. Barnett, "A Law Professor's Guide to Natural Law and Natural Rights" (1997) 20 *Harvard Journal of Law & Public Policy* 655.

[86] See NLNR, 205–10.

and the common good for that reason. But this emphasis does not make rights superfluous. Rights specify who is to benefit from duties and obligations, and in what ways, and therefore help to direct the practical reasoning of those who are subject to duties.[87]

The most basic and least controversial purpose of rights is to protect human dignity. The core notion of right consists of what one is owed consistent with the requirements of practical reason. These requirements are directed toward human goods, the basic aspects of human flourishing in their plural and incommensurable forms. In order to do their job, rights must rule out actions that threaten harm to basic human goods – murder, theft, slavery. The general purpose of rights is to protect the equal and inherent dignity of all human beings from unjust assault by restraining people from acting willfully inconsistent with the inherent dignity of another person.[88]

General, universal, and absolute rights are those that secure respect for human being-ness, which is evidenced in the human capacity (though it persists even when a human lacks the *ability*) to reason. As Finnis has argued, the ontological foundation of rights is the radical (fundamental) human capacity to choose for reasons, and thus to author one's own life consistent with a mutual respect for the radical capacity of others to do the same. Rights derive from norms or principles of practical reason because, in the human capacity to be a person who respects other persons for their own sake, and not as mere means to one's own ends (together with the "truths about basic human goods"), one finds the basic equality of human persons as proper objects of equal concern. This is the foundation for "the duties whose correlatives are human rights – duties *to*, responsibilities *for*, persons."[89]

Beyond that, it is difficult to generalize about rights, particularly about usufructs. Usufructs are not as simple as the categorical rights which correlate with duties of self-exclusion. Unlike the right to exclude, or the right not to be killed or enslaved, a usufruct is highly contextual and contingent upon its being exercised in a practically reasonable way. Indeed, it might not be profitable to think of usufructs and other positive entitlements and liberties as rights in the same sense as negative liberties and claim-rights. This idea finds support in Justice Holmes' view of abuse

87 NLNR, 198–210.

88 John Finnis, "Equality and Differences" (2011) 56 *American Journal of Jurisprudence* 17 at 18–20.

89 Finnis, "Equality and Differences," 18–20. Compare Dworkin, *Justice for Hedgehogs*, chapter 11.

of rights, which he expressed while serving on the Massachusetts Supreme Judicial Court.

> At common law, a man has a right to build a fence on his own land as high as he pleases, however much it may obstruct his neighbor's light and air ... But it is plain that the right to use one's property for the sole purpose of injuring others is not one of the immediate rights of ownership. It is not a right for the sake of which property is recognized by the law, but is only a more or less necessary incident of rights which are established for very different ends. It has been thought by respectable authorities that even at common law the extent of a man's rights in cases like the present might depend upon the motive with which he acted.[90]

In this formulation, the ends "for the sake of which property is recognized by the law" exclude using "one's property for the sole purpose of injuring others."

Yet this cannot be entirely correct. In general, usufructs establish exclusionary reasons for the actions of those who would interfere with the owner's use, even without knowledge of the owner's purposes. The potential meddler need not know anything about the owner's plan of action for the thing to know that he has no right to meddle. Usufructs are not absolute, and yield when exercised to cause harm unreasonably. But even in those instances, they create strong burdens of justification for those who object to particular uses.

So use rights must be rights of some kind. Perhaps they are watered down, or peripheral instances of, rights as compared to negative rights such as the right to exclude or the right of bodily integrity. But they are performing considerable normative work. Potential meddlers may not demand that the owner justify his uses of property, much less that he demonstrate that his use is consistent with the purpose for which the

[90] *Rideout* v. *Knox*, 19 NE 390 at 391–92 (Mass 1889). Strikingly, Holmes offered this view only eight years before he delivered his famous speech at Boston University, in which he launched the movement to study law as a science, from the external perspective. The same man who would eradicate from law terms such as "malice," "intent" and other moral language, Oliver W. Holmes, Jr., "The Path of the Law" (1897) 10 *Harvard Law Review* 457 at 464, also insisted that the law is "the witness and external deposit of our moral life," the practice of which "tends to make good citizens and good men." Holmes, "Path of the Law," 459.

Michael Taggart has identified additional inconsistencies in Holmes' stated views of the role of malice in fixing rights. Taggart, *Victorian England*, 171–77. One is reminded of the late Benjamin Kaplan's succinct description of Holmes as an object of study: "the monument itself is changeful." Benjamin Kaplan, "Encounters with O.W. Holmes, Jr." (1983) 96 *Harvard Law Review* 1828.

use right is recognized in law. The most reasonable reading of Perillo's third category of cases is that the courts are concerned about those uses that directly threaten the common good by violating some duty. Specifying and securing duties is the very purpose for which rights are recognized.

So the third category that Perillo identified is redundant of the first two categories. For if the fundamental purpose of usufructs is to enable and allow uses that do not violate the owner's basic duties, then the category of actions outside the purpose for which usufructs are recognized might seem to be summed up in those actions that (1) are practically unreasonable because they are borne out of a will that is inconsistent with integral human fulfillment, or (2) have no grounding in an intelligible human good and cause harm.

The third category could conceivably refer to the purposes of rights in a narrower sense. Different rights protect and promote the realization of different goods, or promote the realization of goods in different forms. Religious liberties are designed to promote harmony between humans and sources of ultimate meaning, an immaterial end, whereas usufructs primarily enable the realization of the material conditions necessary for human well-being. Thus it is coherent to claim that a right is abused when used for a purpose other than the narrow end for which the law recognizes it. If such a claim were true then rights might be abused even when exercised for some good end. Property rights might be abused if used to connect humans to numinous experiences, and religious liberties might be abused if used to feed homeless people.

That simply cannot be. Just as religious liberty includes the rights of religious actors to meet material needs, property rights protect a core of owner sovereignty in which property owners promote human flourishing in all of its rich dimensions, including immaterial goods. Court should not be in the business of weighing the goods that rights secure, else rights are not rights.

Sketching a doctrine of abuse of rights

This review suggests a way to develop an abuse of rights doctrine in concrete cases. The first task is to define the culpable state of mind that constitutes an abuse of rights. Next, include it in jury instructions and leave the fact question to jurors. The jury is the common law's primary institution of practical judgment. Abuse of rights, like doctrines of equity, takes its substance from "everyday moral disapproval" of wrongful behavior.[91] It should not be a legal question, lest motives be abstracted from categories of actions and material consequences. So, even where these claims are no longer submitted to juries, the distinction between fact and law should be maintained.

As the cases illustrate, the instructions must identify the states of mind that will give rise to liability and those that will not. A property owner abuses his rights if he (1) insists upon his right for the sole purpose to do injury to another person, that is, if he acts "from a wicked and wanton purpose to do the plaintiff an injury."[92] Also, a defendant can be liable if he (2) cannot justify his action by reference to any intelligible benefit, and the only apparent motivation is to cause injury.[93] But if the owner acted with the purpose of realizing some valuable end for himself then he has not abused his rights, "even if he at the same time entertained hostility towards the plaintiff and a desire to injure her."[94]

[91] Smith, "Law versus Equity," 28.

[92] In that case, the Pennsylvania Supreme Court reversed a judgment for plaintiff, rejecting the abuse of rights doctrine and ruling that malicious motives "cannot make that wrong which, in its own essence, is lawful." *Jenkins* v. *Fowler*, 24 Pa 308 (1855).

[93] *Greenleaf* v. *Francis*, 35 Mass 117 (1836).

[94] *Greenleaf* v. *Francis*, 35 Mass at 118–19. The jury returned a verdict for Francis and the Massachusetts Supreme Judicial Court affirmed. *Greenleaf* v. *Francis*, 35 Mass at 123.

7

The nature of property rights

Rights and their limits

Concerned about the public health dangers of genetically modified (GM) crops, activists in the United Kingdom formed a group called GenetiX Snowball (GXS). GXS worried that GM crops carry unpredictable toxic and allergenic effects, enable the development of virulent viruses, undermine the autonomy of farmers, and threaten the common good in other respects. A strategy of the group was to engage in acts of civil disobedience to call attention to their concerns. A tactic was to enter farms where GM crops were being grown and, having summoned news media to witness, destroy from dozens to hundreds of plants.[1]

By these means, several members of GXS earned a trespass complaint from Monsanto plc, a GM crop producer whose trial plants GXS destroyed on farms belonging to Monsanto's business partners. Upon Monsanto's summons for summary judgment and a permanent injunction against future incursions, the GXS activists successfully argued that they should be allowed to defend at trial on the grounds that their actions were justified under the doctrine of necessity and for the public interest. They proposed to introduce expert witnesses to testify as to the dangers that GM crops posed to public health and small farmers. On the basis of that testimony the trial court would conduct a "balancing exercise" to determine whether the entry into the farm and destruction of the plants were proportionate to the danger.

The Court of Appeal allowed Monsanto's appeal, holding that GXS's actions were unjustified as a matter of law. The court reasoned that any balancing of the public health dangers against the unlawful entry and plant destruction would set for the law "a task which no court could possibly answer nor could the outcome of the case possibly be predicted by lawyers." The balancing approach would make it "impossible to advise

[1] *Monsanto* v. *Tilly* [2000] Env LR 313 at 315–18.

in any case whether the defence of justification would succeed," and it would undermine private property, public order, and public confidence in the rule of law.[2]

Rather than allowing a far-reaching balancing of reasons, the law allows unconsented entry into a private property only in "exceptional circumstances," to save from destruction a human life or (maybe) property. The danger to life must be "immediate and obvious" so that a reasonable person would conclude that she has no alternative but to enter or destroy without consent. To extend the common law doctrine of necessity beyond those limited circumstances would be to allow infringement of owners' "lawful rights." Therefore, the common law recognizes no necessity justification to promote the "public interest." The proper way to alter Monsanto's rights is through political channels, not by justifying in court one's own infringement of those rights. If GXS wants to change the law, the court concluded, it must do so "by lawful and not unlawful means."[3]

What roles are rights playing in this decision? That the doctrine of necessity exists in common law entails that not all owners enjoy a conclusive right to exclude in all cases; lawyers and jurists have the power to authorize what would otherwise be an unlawful entry in certain cases for a particular category of reasons – to preserve a human life against imminent peril. Yet this consideration of reasons is limited to the category, beyond which the owner has a right, and the right imposes a conclusive duty. Monsanto may exclude; GXS may not use or destroy these plants. And the conclusiveness of the right over countervailing reasons is necessary in part for the law to operate as law – to guide the deliberations of those who interact with things with reasons for or against proposed plans of action, and to preserve public order.

Chapter 6 made the case that a doctrine of abuse of rights can guide the practical deliberations of owners without working a wholesale importation of morality into law. Yet it left open the question as to how abuse of rights is possible. If use rights can be abused – used to violate the basic requirements of practical reasonableness – then it is not clear in what sense they can be viewed as rights. On a perfectionist conception of law, abuse of rights might be, strictly speaking, a contradiction.[4] A right is not prior to the good. Rather, a right specifies what is or is not required by the

[2] *Monsanto* v. *Tilly* [2000] Env LR at 323–24, 339.

[3] *Monsanto* v. *Tilly* [2000] Env LR at 324–30, 338–40.

[4] H. C. Gutteridge, "Abuse of Rights" (1933) 5 *Cambridge Law Journal* 22 at 47; Michael Taggart, *Private Property and Abuse of Rights in Victorian England* (Oxford:

principles and requirements of practical reasonableness. Therefore, one cannot conclusively and finally say whether an owner enjoys a right to make a use unless and until one first determines that the use is fully reasonable.

A right acts within practical deliberation as a conclusive reason for action, the result of reasoned deliberation about what should be done. In practical deliberations about law, a right specifies jural relations. So John Finnis thinks one

> may safely speak of rights wherever a basic principle or requirement of practical reasonableness, or a rule derived therefrom, gives to A, and to each and every other member of a class to which A belongs, the benefit of (i) a positive or negative requirement (obligation) imposed upon B (including, *inter alia*, any requirement not to interfere with A's activity or with A's enjoyment of some other form of good), or (ii) the ability to bring it about that B is subject to such a requirement, or (iii) the immunity from being subjected by B to any such requirement.[5]

When settled and specified, a right removes the reasons previously deliberated on – what Joseph Raz has called first-order reasons – from future consideration and thus acts as an exclusionary reason. It seems therefore that a use "right" that is not conclusive is not a right in fact. If usufructs are merely reasons for action to be weighed against competing reasons, then they do not by themselves tell one what one should or should not do. They do not perform the normative work that rights are supposed to perform.

So, Finnis has charged, "The introduction of the phrase 'abuse of rights' is a sign that the speaker is covertly deflating an inflated claim of right."[6] And yet, Finnis also allows that the abuse of rights doctrine developed in civil law jurisdictions is an "intelligible doctrine."[7] And an abuse of rights maxim, if not a fully developed abuse of rights doctrine, can be seen operating in the common law. So the topic of abuse of rights presents a special kind of challenge. In theory abuse of rights might seem to be impossible or nonsense. In practice, however, abuse of rights is a real phenomenon.

Furthermore, as the *Monsanto* case illustrates, rights and wrongs are not merely conclusions of reasoning in law; they also serve as premises

Oxford University Press 2002), 146; *Collected Essays of John Finnis, vol. IV: Philosophy of Law* (Oxford: Oxford University Press 2012), 387.

[5] John Finnis, *Natural Law and Natural Rights* (2nd edn, Oxford: Oxford University Press 2011), 205 [hereinafter NLNR].

[6] Finnis, *Philosophy of Law*, 387.

[7] Finnis, *Philosophy of Law*, 388 n §.

and as guides to the practical reasoning of lawyers and their clients. The challenge then is to explain what kind of reasons property rights are or, more precisely, in what sense usufructs and exclusion rights can be called "rights." This inquiry will bear fruit in the remaining chapters as we examine the specification of property rights and duties.

The short answer to the question of how abuse of rights is possible is that use rights are rights in one sense, though not in a complete sense. Usufructs are not rights in the central sense of final conclusions about what duties one owes or what one is owed. But they perform a lot of normative work. They identify an important aspect of human flourishing, namely freedom to use and manage things. They rule out categories of first-order reasons; sometimes all but one or two categories. They hide their justifications and narrow the category of reasons that may be considered against their exercise. They create presumptions of justification and persuasion. And they serve as general guides to the practical reasoning of owners in a world of imperfect information and legal change.

The contingency and inconclusiveness of use rights is a beneficial feature for these reasons, and for another reason. Final judgment on the reasonableness of uses of property is left to institutions of private ordering, such as families, local communities, juries, and so on. As those institutions deliberate and decide what uses are reasonable, they shape usufructuary rights according to basic requirements of practical reasonableness, what are commonly called moral norms. And this has moral benefits for those communities. The act of specifying rights according to the requirements of morality is for communities an act of self-constitution in at least two senses. It shapes the physical condition of a community by specifying what uses will and will not be allowed on land, and thus constitutes the community in Aquinas' first order (discussed in Chapter 4). Also, it constitutes the community in Aquinas' third order, the order of the will, in which the community deliberates and decides what purposes to pursue and what means to allow in pursuit of those purposes.

The normative force of rights

Rights as absolute and conclusive

To speak of rights as indeterminate premises of practical reason, which can be restricted or justifiably infringed, creates a number of related problems, which John Finnis, John Oberdiek, and Grégoire Webber, among others, have discussed.[8] Rights as premises are prematurely reified, which invests in them normative significance that they do not possess; rights are everywhere, but they control no one's deliberations; rights do not instruct right-holders (e.g., property owners) what they may do and should not do; they do not correlate with duties, such that everyone has rights but no one is obligated to honor or fulfill them. And this practice reverses the perspective of practical reason away from the internal perspective of the one who owes duties and wants to know what he or she should do to a focus on "the viewpoint of the 'other(s)' to whom something is owed or due, and who would be wronged if denied that something."[9] This shift of perspective produces a divorce between what is one's right and what is just, because it relates the concept of right exclusively to the beneficiary. Rights can thus be opposed to law, justice, and other rights.[10]

One problem is that infringement of non-absolute rights is not only permissible but actually required where the balance of reasons weighs against honoring the rights. A consequence is the devaluation of normative currency. Truly inviolable rights have the same status as "rights" that can and should be "infringed" or overcome by competing reasons.[11] So, the same term is used to describe the right of an innocent person not to be killed deliberately and the "right" to use one's property in ways that might cause harm to one's neighbor. The usufruct is trading on the prestige and normative force of the inviolable right.[12] Meanwhile, the normative force of the inviolable right is degraded.

Against the non-conclusive view of rights, Webber argues that rights serve their purpose by concluding deliberations about what should be

[8] Grégoire C. N. Webber, *The Negotiable Constitution: On the Limitation of Rights* (Cambridge: Cambridge University Press 2009), chapters 2 & 3; Grégoire Webber, "On the Loss of Rights" in Grant Huscroft, Bradley W. Miller, and Grégoire Webber (eds.), *Proportionality and the Rule of Law: Rights, Justification, Reasoning* (New York: Cambridge University Press 2014), 123–54; Oberdiek, John, "Specifying Rights Out of Necessity" (2008) 28 *Oxford Journal of Legal Studies* 127; John Oberdiek, "What's Wrong With Infringements? (Insofar as Infringements Are Not Wrong): A Reply" (2008) 27 *Law and Philosophy* 293. See also Finnis, *Philosophy of Law*, 375–88; Bradley W. Miller, "Justification and Rights Limitations" in Grant Huscroft (ed.), *Expounding the Constitution; Essays in Constitutional Theory* (New York: Cambridge University Press 2008), 93 at 94–101; Francisco J. Urbina, "A Critique of Proportionality" (2012) 57 *American Journal of Jurisprudence* 49 at 62–66.

[9] NLNR, 205. [10] NLNR, 205–10; Finnis, *Philosophy of Law*, 375–88.

[11] Finnis, *Philosophy of Law*, 388; Webber, *Negotiable Constitution*, 56, 121–22.

[12] Webber, *Negotiable Constitution*, 122; Miller, "Justification," 96.

done. By limiting rights according to the principles and requirements of reason, one specifies the rights to make them *consistent with* what is right and just. The "idea of limitation . . . instructs one to understand rights as conclusions to practical reasoning that take into account not only the 'interest,' 'value,' or 'principle' grounding the right, but also the plethora of other considerations that determine the justifiable scope and content of the right."[13]

Oberdiek has argued for fully specified rights, the content of which depends on context, and includes consideration of what is just and justifiable. Specification of a right combines both the content of the right and the right's normative implications into a single inquiry about "what is justifiable to do under the circumstances." The content of a right, on this account, is therefore specified so as not to conflict in the first place with justifiable behavior. As a result, "the central role of rights in moral argument is conclusory: fundamentally, one argues *towards* rights, not *from* them."[14]

The boundaries of a right are measured out by all of the considerations that are relevant to the common good. It bears repeating that these considerations cannot be reduced to a net collective good.[15] As we have seen, because the basic forms of human well-being are incommensurable, it is incoherent to speak of the greatest aggregate good.[16] The basic aspects of each member of the community's well-being are *all* considerations that define and limit rights by specifying the requirements of practical reasonableness and the duties of the community's members and its political authorities.[17] Once the right is properly limited and defined, there are no remaining reasons to consider; one knows what is right to do. Specified and limited in this way, the right is absolute. It follows that any reasons for action that are not conclusive and absolute are not rights.[18]

Property rights feature prominently in these arguments. Webber and Oberdiek discuss cases implicating the right to exclude, which present simpler problems than the problem presented by abusive exercises of

[13] Webber, *Negotiable Constitution*, 124.
[14] Oberdiek, "Specifying Rights," 128, 141 (emphasis original).
[15] NLNR, 213; John Finnis, *Collected Essays of John Finnis, vol. III: Human Rights & the Common Good* (Oxford: Oxford University Press 2012), 32–35.
[16] NLNR, 111–18; Philippa Foot, *Moral Dilemmas: and Other Topics in Moral Philosophy* (Oxford: Oxford University Press 2002), 76–77.
[17] NLNR, 214–21; Webber, *Negotiable Constitution*, 133–46.
[18] Webber, *Negotiable Constitution*, 116–46.

usufructs. Rights of exclusive possession are impersonal and good against the world. They impose the same duties on all outsiders (even if, as Webber and Oberdiek argue, those duties are not fully specified). But many of the lessons to be drawn about exclusive possession can be applied to more context-dependent rights such as usufructs. And it is helpful to begin with simpler illustrations anyway.

Joel Feinberg supplied one much-discussed hypothetical case, which implicates the right to exclude. A backpacker in the mountains is surprised by a blizzard that threatens his life. Upon discovering "an unoccupied cabin, locked and boarded up for the winter, clearly somebody else's private property," the backpacker breaks in and takes shelter, saving his own life.[19] The backpacker has not infringed or violated a property right, Webber and Oberdiek both argue. Rather, it is correct to say that the cabin owner never had a property right to exclude someone who was trying to save his life.[20]

John Finnis posited a hypothetical case implicating the right of exclusive use. A fire breaks out in a suburb. In order to prevent the fire from spreading, the fire brigade blows up one house, thus clearing a combustible from the fire's potential path. Finnis argued that the house's owner could complain of a violation of his rights if the choice of his house were unfair, or if the action were arbitrary, or if his children are killed, or if he is not compensated, but not simply because the fire brigade destroyed his house.[21] His property rights, "properly understood," never included the right not to have his house destroyed in an emergency.[22] Webber affirms this conclusion, observing that each of those preserved by destruction of the house "has a claim to be protected from the fire."[23]

In both cases, it would be premature in the view of Webber and Oberdiek to state that the owner has a property right before answering the question what should (not) be done – what is right, just, lawful to do – in the particular circumstance. But after one has reached a right conclusion about what should (not) be done, one can say not only what is right to do, but also whether the owner had a right to use or exclude in the circumstances. In this way, rights are consistent with all that is required by the good, just, and right.

[19] Joel Feinberg, "Voluntary Euthanasia and the Inalienable Right to Life" (1978) 7 *Philosophy & Public Affairs* 93 at 102; Webber, "*Negotiable Constitution*," 128–29.
[20] Webber, *Negotiable Constitution*, 129; Oberdiek, "Specifying Rights," 134–35.
[21] Finnis, *Human Rights*, 33–34. [22] Finnis, *Human Rights*, 34.
[23] Webber, *Negotiable Constitution*, 143.

Webber's and Oberdiek's conception of rights-as-conclusions finds support in the common law doctrines of private and public necessity, which reinforce the intuitions that Webber and Oberdiek expect their readers to bring to the hypothetical cases. Feinberg's cabin case would implicate private necessity.[24] Finnis' conflagration case would implicate public necessity.[25] Doctrines of private and public necessity justify what would otherwise be unlawful incursions on private property in violation of the owner's right to exclude. If Webber and Oberdiek are correct then it is not correct to say that the owner's right to exclude is justifiably infringed or overcome in such cases. Rather, the owner has no right to exclude in such cases. If that is so, then the in rem right to exclude is a fiction; the owner does not have a general right to exclude others from the thing. Only when the respective rights and duties are fully specified with respect to actions and omissions in particular cases can we say, in hindsight, whether the owner enjoyed the right to exclude.

So Webber and Oberdiek present a formidable challenge not only to the notion of abuse of rights but also to the understanding of usufructs as rights, perhaps even to the possibility of in rem rights. Can they be answered?

Some possible solutions

One possible answer is to concede that rights are conclusions and to argue that in rem, two-term property right claims are rights. This was the strategy of Richard Epstein in his influential book on the nature of property rights.[26] Jeremy Waldron also has argued that abstract property rights are absolute without consideration of all aspects of the common good. So, he claims that "private property gives a man rights which he may exercise rightly or wrongly, reasonably or unreasonably,"[27] exactly

[24] Mark Lunney, "Trespass to Land" in Ken Oliphant (ed.), *The Law of Tort* (2nd edn, London: Butterworths 2007), 506–07; Kevin Gray and Susan Francis Gray, *Elements of Land Law* (5th edn, Oxford: Oxford University Press 2009), 1269–70; Restatement (Second) of Torts §197 (1965).

[25] *Cope* v. *Sharpe*, [1910] KB 168 at 170; *Pennsylvania Coal Co.* v. *Mahon*, 260 US 393 at 415–16 (1922); Restatement (Second) of Torts §196 (1965).

[26] Richard A. Epstein, *Takings: Private Property and the Power of Eminent Domain* (Cambridge: Harvard University Press 1985). Compare Ernest Weinrib, *The Idea of Private Law* (Oxford: Oxford University Press 2012), 13–33. Weinrib's Kantian conception of right leads him to reject the idea of rights as conclusions of practical deliberations about human welfare. "Freedom, not welfare, is primary." Weinrib, *Idea*, 130.

[27] Jeremy Waldron, *The Right to Private Property* (Oxford: Clarendon Press 1988), 310.

the concept that the *Pickles* court endorsed.[28] (Indeed, Waldron has gone so far as to argue that one may have a *moral* right to do wrong.)[29]

This approach is unsatisfactory for at least two reasons. First, it yields the embarrassing result that property owners are free to act in practically unreasonable ways, and therefore to harm their neighbors and to constitute themselves as practically unreasonable people. Second, this embarrassment is unnecessary because the *Pickles* approach is not true to the general approach of the common law, which treats property rights, especially use rights, as not-fully-specified until the reasonableness of their exercise has been adjudicated in cases of conflict and harm.

A different solution might be to disaggregate use rights into their constituent jural relations. J. E. Penner has suggested something like this. The existence of powers, Penner has argued, "permits the law to recognize a version of the idea of 'abuse of rights,' without the problems of 'nonsense,' 'evasion,' or 'devaluation of moral currency' to which that particular formulation can lead."[30] Because powers might exist without liberties and immunities, one might properly be said to have a right – a power – to do an act without having a conclusive claim-right against others to be free of their interference with the act, or an immunity from liability for performing the act.

Yet this approach does not get us far. A power without an immunity from liability for exercising it would not resolve a legal dispute over the power's exercise. Consider a spite fence case. A power is a right to alter someone's legal status, but if the neighbor has a claim-right for damages or injunctive relief against erection of the fence then he is not liable to suffer the existence of the fence. The neighbor's claim-right vitiates the owner's power. Unless one knows whether the neighbor is entitled to damages or injunctive relief against the erection of the fence, one does not know in a full and meaningful sense whether the owner has the "right" to erect it.[31]

[28] *Bradford Corp.* v. *Pickles* [1895] AC 587.

[29] Jeremy Waldron, "A Right to Do Wrong" (1981) 92 *Ethics* 21. Contrast William A. Galston, "On the Alleged Right to Do Wrong: A Response to Waldron" (1983) 93 *Ethics* 320.

[30] J. E. Penner, *The Idea of Property in Law* (Oxford: Oxford University Press 1997), 20.

[31] Stephen Munzer argues that Bentham's conception of powers is more useful than Hohfeld's because it enables greater differentiation between powers to interfere physically with things or bodies, which are powers of "handling," and powers over the active faculties of persons, which are powers of "imperation" and "deimperation." Stephen R. Munzer, "A Bundle Theorist Holds on to His Collection of Sticks" (2011) 8 *Econ Journal Watch* 265 at 267–68. But this is not helpful for our purposes. Powers of handling

Rights grounded in interests

A more promising account can be built on Joseph Raz's idea of rights as exclusionary reasons.[32] But this will require separating the idea from Raz's broader interest theory of rights, in which it is found. Without some objective standards on which to evaluate the weight of individual interests, one cannot determine which interests legitimately ground rights and which do not. Thus, the interest theory cannot explain which uses are right and which are abusive.

For Raz, "A right is based on the interest which figures essentially in the justification of the statement that the right exists."[33] According to Raz, "'X has a right' if and only if X can have rights, and, other things being equal, an aspect of X's well-being (his interest) is a sufficient reason for holding some other person(s) to be under a duty."[34] Thus the special normative force of rights is grounded in those interests that are deemed sufficient to justify recognition of a duty in others.

The right is not just any reason for action, of equal normative force to the interests that justify it. On Raz's account, a right establishes an exclusionary reason for action.[35] Exclusionary reasons are second-order reasons, the nature of which is to rule out of consideration first-order reasons for action. Rights and duties, as exclusionary reasons, operate by preventing first-order reasons, such as interests, from directing the agent's deliberation. When one encounters a right-holder, one is not at liberty to judge whether the right-holder's claim is justified by a balance of first-order reasons. One is instead required to respect the right without considering more.

The varying strength of individual interests is one consideration that makes it possible for some right claims to have more normative force than others. Because interests vary in weight, it is possible to distinguish between those interests that justify a right and those that do not. Raz states that an interest will ground a right if among the premises that justify the right are those "supplying grounds *for attributing to it the*

would seem to require full specification by reference to their corresponding liabilities and immunities no less than powers of imperation and deimperation, and vice versa.

32 Joseph Raz, *The Morality of Freedom* (Oxford: Oxford University Press 1986) [hereinafter MOF], chapter 7; Joseph Raz, *Practical Reason and Norms* (Oxford: Oxford University Press 1999), 35–48, 73–89; Joseph Raz, *Practical Reasoning* (Oxford: Oxford University Press 1978), 128–43.

33 MOF, 169. 34 MOF, 166.

35 Raz, *Practical Reason and Norms*, 35–48, 73–89; Raz, *Practical Reasoning*, 128–43; Penner, *Idea of Property*, 7–16.

required importance, or for holding it to be relevant to a particular person or class of persons so that they rather than others are obligated to the right-holder."[36]

The interest theory also requires recognizing *external* limitations on rights-derived-from-interests, what Raz calls "conflicting considerations." Where conflicting considerations outweigh the right-holder's claim, no duty is derived from it.[37] Yet this is ambiguous. Is no duty derived from the right because it is not a right, or because it is a right the exercise or assertion of which is not permitted? In other words, in instances of limitation on a right, is there a right or not?

Furthermore, Raz does not supply an objective measure with which to weigh interests. Indeed, Raz does not distinguish between what a right-holder happens to want and what is actually good; for Raz, an "aspect of X's well-being" appears to be synonymous with "his interest."[38] And in another context Raz has claimed that all desires and interests constitute reasons for action.[39]

Jeremy Waldron and James Penner, who employ Raz's interest theory of rights, have both addressed this ambiguity in Raz's account. But both of them also decline to provide any way to evaluate the relative weights of interests. Observing that the "concept of interests is vexed and controversial in the literature of political philosophy," Waldron distinguished between accounts in which interests are derived from preferences on one hand, and objective accounts on the other, in which a person's interests are "determined essentially by his nature . . . while his desires or preferences are not." On these objective accounts it is possible to consider one's interests apart from one's desires or preferences, since people do not always desire what is best for them. Having thus set up the alternatives, Waldron expressly declined to choose one.[40]

Penner also observed that, by defining one's interests critically, one can differentiate between legitimate reasons for action and desires that are not legitimate as reasons. Our interests, Penner noted, "unlike our desires, are necessarily related to a critical understanding of values, i.e. of those things which are truly of worth and those which are not." But ultimately, like Raz and Waldron, Penner also declined to "discuss values as operative reasons for action."[41] In particular, he expressed agnosticism

[36] MOF, 181 (emphasis added). [37] MOF, 180–86; Raz, *Practical Reasoning*, 132.
[38] MOF, 166. Raz uses the terms interchangeably throughout his discussion of rights, duties, and interests.
[39] Raz, *Practical Reason and Norms*, 34. [40] Waldron, *Right to Property*, 87–90.
[41] Penner, *Idea of Property*, 10.

on the existence or force of any basic human goods. This leads to a dead end. In Raz's interest theory, the normative force of a right depends on the weight of the interests on which it is based and the weight of the conflicting considerations that might prevent the right from imposing a duty. But one has no way to evaluate the weight of those first-order reasons.

Property rights as rights

Property rights as peripheral instances of rights

Let us begin afresh, first by conceding that in rem rights are not fully specified rights in the sense that Oberdiek and Webber mean. That is, they are not rights in the same, strict sense as the right not to be killed or the right not to be enslaved. But it is still possible to insist that they perform normative work as exclusionary reasons of a particular kind. When they are identified in their two-term, in rem form (as what Oberdiek calls "general rights"),[42] property rights exert normative force in several important ways.

It might help to consider in rem rights as less central or focal instances of rights than inviolable rights. If the purpose of rights is to serve as fully conclusive reasons for action then absolute rights, such as the rights not to be killed, maimed, enslaved, and so on, would be the central or focal instances of what we call "rights." In comparison to those rights, an owner's right of exclusive possession is slightly less central, because it's less fully conclusive. It conclusively imposes on all non-owners who have no permission to possess the res a duty not to enter into the res, except in cases of private or public necessity to save a human life or a neighborhood, respectively. Use rights are more peripheral still because they are more dependent on context and open to further limitation in particular cases. Yet as we will see, it is still not nonsense to speak of them as rights.

In what sense then can property rights be understood as rights? In the first place, they identify an important aspect of human flourishing, and thereby signal that the goods served by private ownership should be accorded significant weight. Finnis observes that the two-term right statements so common in modern bills of rights identify the various aspects of the common good of the community. Taking the Universal Declaration of Human Rights as illustrative, he notes that Article 29 of

[42] Oberdiek, "Specifying Rights," 127.

that Declaration includes "property" among other enumerated rights, such as security of person and equality before the law. Together these statements sketch "the *outlines of the common good*, the various aspects of individual well-being in community." The rights-talk simply emphasizes that the common good requires "that *each* and everyone's well-being, in each of its basic aspects, must be considered and favored at *all* times by those responsible for co-ordinating the common life."[43]

We have now seen several ways in which the freedom to manage and use things in community with others enables owners, their collaborators, and their beneficiaries to constitute themselves as practically reasonable people. A statement that owners ought to be free to use their things is a conclusion drawn from the observation that private property use serves at least one important aspect of well-being. To secure this important aspect of human flourishing, use rights perform a few additional, normative tasks.

Categorical, exclusionary reasons

Property rights do more than simply signify the weight of the first-order reasons served by private ownership. The duty that correlates with a property right performs normative work by narrowing the categories of reasons that might be asserted in justification of some action with respect to a thing one does not own. Just as rights can be exclusionary reasons, wrongs can also be exclusionary reasons as Neil MacCormick noted.[44] The first job of the common law is to declare what is right and wrong, thought Blackstone.[45] And property, the first concern of the common law, specifies what reasons for action are right or wrong to consider as possible motivations for acting on things.

That an exclusionary reason excludes first-order reasons from consideration does not entail that it must exclude *all* first-order reasons. J. E. Penner has considered the possibility that exclusionary reasons perform a special role in practical reasoning by excluding certain *categories* of reasons, though not necessarily all categories of reasons. This possibility is supported by Raz's claim that sometimes conflicting first-order reasons, "while sufficient to show that some action cannot be

[43] NLNR, 214.
[44] Neil MacCormick, *Practical Reason in Law and Morality* (Oxford: Oxford University Press 2008), 47.
[45] William Blackstone, *Commentaries on the Laws of England* (1769), vol. 1, Introduction §II.

required as a duty on the basis of the would-be right, do not affect the case for requiring other actions as a matter of duty."[46]

Penner thinks that an exclusionary reason can exclude many first-order reasons from one's deliberations and yet not be an absolute reason. Indeed, he doubts that an exclusionary reason can serve as "an absolute guide to behavior, which covers all circumstances." He borrows an example from Raz. A military officer's order is an exclusionary reason for his subordinates' actions. A soldier must obey the order, ignoring other considerations about what he should do. "But if the order was to commit an atrocity, the exclusionary reason would not exclude the first-order reason, that of the sanctity and dignity of human life."[47]

Penner argues that property rights can be understood in these terms as exclusionary reasons for action in rem – with respect to things. The owner has interests, which are the operative reasons for the owner's actions. But those who interact with the owner's things need not concern themselves with the owner's interests; those reasons are excluded from the duty-holder's consideration. Indeed, one encountering an owned thing need not even know who the owner is; the duty of self-exclusion is the same even if ownership changes hands.[48] All the outsider needs to know is that he is under a duty not to interfere with the thing.[49]

So, property rights (and wrongs) serve not as absolute exclusionary reasons but rather as categorical exclusionary reasons. Though they do not rule all categories of first-order reasons out of consideration, they rule out most. Both Feinberg's cabin case and Finnis' suburban fire case tell against the force of abstract property rights only because lives and fortunes are at stake. Entry for private necessity is justified only to "preserve life" against a "great and imminent danger."[50] As Oberdiek concedes, conditions of private necessity are "quite rare," and absent such conditions, "it makes perfect sense to say – as everyone does – that such and such is someone's private property."[51] As the *Monsanto* case illustrates, grounds of public necessity are narrower still. Blowing up a house to save a neighborhood from a fire is an exceptional case, as Justice Holmes observed.[52]

[46] MOF, 183. [47] Penner, *Idea of Property*, 9.

[48] James Penner, "On the Very Idea of Transmissible Rights" in James Penner and Henry E. Smith (eds.), *Philosophical Foundations of Property Law* (New York: Oxford University Press 2013), 244.

[49] Penner, *Idea of Property*, 23–31.

[50] *Southwark LBC* v. *Williams* [1971] Ch 734 at 743.

[51] Oberdiek, "Specifying Rights," 136.

[52] *Pennsylvania Coal Co.* v. *Mahon*, 260 US 393 at 415–16 (1922).

Furthermore, the category of first-order considerations that might justify a non-owner's entry is limited to *imminent* threats to an ascertainable human life (or perhaps home). So, where antiwar activists in New Zealand damaged a government facility used for collecting signals intelligence, they were liable for trespass notwithstanding that the intelligence was used for war efforts in Iraq in which civilians were killed and property damaged. No danger was imminent.[53]

Only a few, very weighty reasons are allowed to inform one's deliberations about whether to exclude oneself from another's private property. A provisioned backpacker who comes across a locked cabin on a warm, sunny day would be violating the owner's rights if he trespassed. It would not be a sufficient justification to observe that the backpacker always wanted to live in a mountain cabin, or that the backpacker would leave the cabin in a better condition. It would not matter whether the owner uses the cabin 364 days each year and has made a temporary trip to town for supplies or instead uses it only once in a while. The backpacker is prohibited by his duty of self-exclusion (and the owner's correlative right to exclude) from evaluating the cabin owner's plan of action, and from comparing that plan for the cabin against his own.

Similarly, the reasons that will justify the fire brigade in destroying a suburban home are quite limited. The right of an owner to exclusive use (together with the corresponding duties not to steal or destroy) is the strongest of property norms. In a real emergency, to preserve the life of a human being, it can sometimes be justifiable to take or destroy private property. But those reasons for action do not present themselves on a routine basis during the thousands of interactions that each of us has every day with things that do not belong to us. Except in the most extreme cases, it is enough for non-owners (including political authorities, about which more discussions are presented in Chapter 9) to know that they do not own the thing and do not have permission to take it.[54] All other potential reasons for action are ruled out of consideration.

In short, all but a narrow category of first-order reasons are excluded from consideration when we encounter things we do not own. Unless some obviously weighty reason could justify acting on the thing – a human life is at stake, for example – it simply does not matter what reasons the owner has for controlling the thing and excluding others.

[53] *Leason* v. *Attorney-General* [2014] 2 NZLR 224.

[54] See Penner, *Idea of Property*, 75–76.

Thomas Merrill and Henry Smith have observed that we know our duties to abstain from things we do not own – "not to enter upon it, not to use it, not to take it, etc. And we know all this without having any idea who the owner of the thing actually is. In effect, these universal duties are broadcast to the world from the thing itself."[55] This normative work is indispensable. Non-owners need to know how they can and should act with respect to the thousands of things that they encounter on a daily basis.[56] Other than in rare cases of necessity, there is no weighing of reasons for and against an act of trespass or theft.

Two-term right statements

Guidance for practical deliberations

Usufructs operate on practical deliberations in a more complicated way than exclusion rights. They create different norms for property insiders – owners and their families, licensees, tenants, agents, and so on – than they do for outsiders, and they require more extensive and context-dependent specification. Nevertheless, for outsiders, including both non-owners whose interests potentially conflict with owners and judicial authorities who must resolve the conflicts, usufructs create presumptions of reasonable use, and therefore place on anyone challenging the owner's use the burden of justifying an interference with that use, or persuading a court that he is entitled to relief for suffering harm from the use.

Two-term usufruct statements also perform normative work for owners and their collaborators in the real world.[57] Finnis noted, "Lawyers frequently talk about rights, not as three-term relations between two persons and an act of a certain type, but as two-term relations between persons and one subject-matter or (in a broad sense) *thing*: for example, someone's right to £10 under a contract, or to a share in a specified estate, or to the performing rights of an opera."[58] Lawyers

[55] Thomas W. Merrill and Henry E. Smith, "What Happened to Property in Law and Economics?" (2001) 111 *Yale Law Journal* 357 at 359.

[56] Thomas W. Merrill and Henry E. Smith, "Optimal Standardization in the Law of Property; The Numerus Clausus Principle" (2000) 110 *Yale Law Journal* 1; Thomas W. Merrill and Henry E. Smith, "The Morality of Property" (2007) 48 *William & Mary Law Review* 1849.

[57] On the differences between two-term and three-term right statements, see NLNR, 199–205.

[58] NLNR, 201.

use these formulations in order to respond to a question with a simple answer. Of course, lawyers are very good at qualifying that simple answer by stating many ways in which it could turn out to be wrong in the actual case. But the client seeks guidance, and the lawyer tries to provide it.

The client's practical question is an important one for the client: generally speaking, allowing for the unpredictable ways in which my use might affect other people, the common law might develop, and legislators and land-use regulators might act in the future, what can I do with my property? This is a real concern for owners, as any lawyer can attest and as the *Monsanto* court recognized. And a complete Hohfeldian analysis of the jural relations among all persons and institutions that might take an interest in the use is worse than useless to address the client's concern. If one were to work out all of those possibilities, it would become clear that an assertion that O has a right to do x can have "hundreds if not thousands of possible legal meanings."[59]

Because the lawyer cannot determine in advance what all of the owner's rights and duties will be, she makes a two-term generalization: O may (or may not) make use x. The generalization is imperfect because it does not conclusively resolve the question whether O will turn out in fact to have rights to make use x against contrary claims by neighbors A, B, and C. But if it approximates an informed lawyer's best estimate, in light of the current state of the law and the conditions of the neighborhood, then O might reasonably rely on it.

Usufructs thus enable owners to act in the real world where they have incomplete information about the plans and interests of other people and cannot predict all of the legal consequences of their choices and actions. In these imperfect conditions, usufructs provide a good enough answer to the practical question whether an owner has liberty and authority to act in a particular way under extant legal standards and rules, even if they do not predict with certainty whether the owner might be held liable to an outsider for the action in the event of a lawsuit. The conclusive specification that takes place in cases of abuse of rights, nuisance, waste, and other doctrines that employ reasonableness standards, determines the extent of the user's liability to or immunity from a particular person, another right-claimant who has suffered harm as a result of the use. But not all uses result in these conflicts. And in the meantime, owners need some guidance as to what they may and may not do with their property.

[59] Finnis, *Philosophy of Law*, 385.

In short, owners need abstractions and generalizations. If it is a fiction to call these generalizations rights, then it is a very useful fiction. The idea that these generalizations have the normative force of rights is indispensably useful for owners, for non-owners, and for civil society. Insiders, the category that includes all who have ownership interests in a thing and permission to use the thing, need to know what they can and should do with their assets. These people need to be able to rely on shorthand conclusions without full information (which, in economic terms, is prohibitively costly) about all of the possible relations and conflicts that might arise with respect to things.

Two-term rights statements have their own teleology. A two-term abstraction enables practical reasoning and action to go on in a world of imperfect information and legal change. The owner needs to know whether it is on balance safe for him to build the fence, just as the soldier needs to know whether he should obey his officers when he doubts the full wisdom of their orders. The answer – yes – is not conclusive; the officers might command him to commit a heinous act against civilians, which he has a moral obligation to disobey; the fence might turn out to be a nuisance. But the actor must act; he cannot afford to be paralyzed by all the possible contingencies.

Presumptions for outsiders and courts

On the other hand, it is not entirely a fiction to call these abstractions rights; they perform real normative work for non-owners and legal authorities. For non-owners and for judicial authorities who must resolve conflicts about use, usufructs establish presumptions – burdens of justification – in favor of the owner's use. They place on anyone challenging the owner an initial burden of persuasion, and they limit the reasons that the challenger may bring forward against the use. Unless the owner has caused harm, we do not require the owner to provide any reasons for the use; he is simply at liberty to make the use.

Even if the owner does cause harm, it is not a sufficient complaint to allege that he has not maximized the value of his asset, or that he might have made some more reasonable or beneficial use, or that his use benefits the wrong member of his family, or . . . One challenging the use must come forward with an allegation of unreasonable harm. The usufruct rules out of consideration all other reasons that might be asserted against the use. This normative work is far from insignificant. Though use rights are not fully specified in advance, they settle the question in the absence of a showing that they have been used unreasonably to cause harm.[60]

This normative work is on display in common law doctrines such as nuisance, waste, and riparian consumption. These doctrines treat usufructs as rebuttable presumptions in favor of the owner's use. Though an owner is not required to demonstrate the reasonableness of every use of his property, if a neighbor comes forward with proof of harm and a recognized reason to disallow the use, the owner must emerge from his zone of freedom and explain the reasonableness of his use. The presumption in favor of the owner is stronger in abuse of rights cases. Only if it is shown that the owner has acted for no reason other than an intention to cause harm (and has caused harm) will he be called to account. These facts signal that the owner is acting not in pursuit of objectively intelligible values but rather from some other motive, such as spite or an intention to harm. Any valuable reason for the owner's action will suffice to insulate his use from additional scrutiny and from liability.

Conclusive as remedial rights

Finally, two-term right statements can be, and often are, conclusive for remedial purposes. The distinction between property rules and liability rules, made clearly by Calabresi and Melamed,[61] reminds the lawyer that the absence of a duty not to enter, destroy, or use is not the same as the absence of a duty to compensate the owner for entry, destruction, and use. Owners might not enjoy a right to control or exclude in cases where destruction of their property is necessary to preserve a neighborhood, human lives, or national defense, but they are nevertheless owed compensation for their loss.

Oberdiek denies that compensation is due because, in the absence of a duty of self-exclusion or abstention, there can be no duty to compensate.[62] But he neglects to consider that the duty to compensate can rest on a different justification than the duty to exclude oneself.[63] Compensation

[60] Oberdiek is thus mistaken to claim that a right that imposes a prima facie duty is *merely* question-begging. Oberdiek, "Infringements Are Not Wrong," 299–300.

[61] Guido Calabresi and A. Douglas Melamed, "Property Rules, Liability Rules, and Inalienability: One View of the Cathedral" (1972) 85 *Harvard Law Review* 1089.

[62] Oberdiek, "Specifying Rights," 140–44; Oberdiek, "Infringements Are Not Wrong," 300–07.

[63] James E. Krier and Stewart J. Schwab, "Property Rules and Liability Rules: The Cathedral in Another Light" (1995) 70 *NYU Law Review* 440.

is neither a "second-best way of heeding" an obligation to exclude oneself, as Oberdiek supposes,[64] nor even a sufficient way to do so.[65]

This is why public authorities are subject to just compensation duties for takings and expropriations despite their eminent domain and police powers. Though the owner of the suburban home does not enjoy an absolute right to exclude the fire brigade in case of emergency, he does enjoy a right to compensation for the loss. Compensation for deprivations justified by public necessity appears to have been a common law requirement since the Revolution Settlement of 1688.[66] At common law, the government has no right to deprive the owner of property that existing law has not already denied to the owner, unless the government pays just compensation, even if it lawfully exercises a recognized power.[67]

The Supreme Court of the United States has ruled that under the Fifth Amendment of the US Constitution, a state's slightest violation of an owner's right to exclude, such as draping a wire over a building, constitutes a taking.[68] Compensation is not owed for battle damage to private property in an act of war,[69] nor in some cases of public necessity.[70] But those rulings were predicated on the mistaken assumption that the common law imposes no duty of repair or compensation on one who lawfully invokes the defense of necessity. Had the Court better understood the rule, it still might have limited the scope of the written Constitution's compensation requirement as it did, but maybe not. Property within public takings jurisprudence is the ensemble of rights specified and limited by those background principles of state law which already restrict land ownership prior to the contested state action.[71] The Court has long defined limits of the state's powers according to the state's

64 Oberdiek, "Specifying Rights," 129,

65 See *Jacque* v. *Steenberg Homes, Inc.*, 563 NW 2d 154 (Wis 1997).

66 *Burmah Oil Company Ltd* v. *Lord Advocate Respondent* [1965] AC 75.

67 *Attorney General* v. *De Keyser's Royal Hotel Ltd.* [1920] AC 508; *Manitoba Fisheries Ltd.* v. *The Queen*, [1979] 23 NR 159, 1 SCR 101; *Sinnickson* v. *Johnson*, 17 NJL 129 (NJ 1839); *The People* v. *Platt*, 17 Johnson's 195 (NY 1819); *Gardner* v. *Newburgh*, 2 Johnson's Chancery 162 (NY Ch).

68 *Loretto* v. *Teleprompter Manhattan CATV Corp.*, 458 US 419 (1982).

69 *United States* v. *Caltex (Philippines) Inc.*, 344 US 149 (1952).

70 *Bowditch* v. *Boston*, 101 US 16 (1879). Yet the requirement of necessity is strict, and requires a showing that alternative means of meeting an imminent danger were not available. *Trinco Investment Co.* v. *United States*, 722 F 3d 1375 (Fed Cir 2013).

71 *Lucas* v. *South Carolina Coastal Council*, 505 US 1003 at 1029–30 (1992); James R. Stoner, *Common-Law Liberty: Rethinking American Constitutionalism* (Lawrence: University Press of Kansas 2003), 146–47.

common law obligations.[72] The categorical duties that written constitution impose on governments are codified common law duties of self-exclusion and non-interference.[73]

Use rights complicate the state's duty because of the context-dependence of their specification. If the government must show that an owner's two-term liberty would not be specified as a three-term use right under existing law, then any deprivations of use that do not merely codify extant property rules will constitute takings for which compensation is owed. That is the rule in the United States. The state may not assert private law duties of the owner that are not already specified by existing property law; it must not destroy the owner's liberty to use without compensation.[74] If on the other hand the presumption is that the owner has no liberties unless and until specified by positive law, then compensation will never be owed for burdens on use, unless a regulation deprives an owner of the entire estate. That is the law in Canada.[75]

The United Kingdom and the European Court of Human Rights have taken neither position, but their rulings tend toward the latter. The rule of *France Fenwick & Company* v. *The King* is that an intention to expropriation without compensation will not be read into an act burdening use unless expressly stated, and that owners must therefore be compensated for deprivations of property unless their lost uses are already "unlawful acts" under existing law.[76] But in dicta the Court of King's Bench opined that the common law right of compensation does not apply to a "mere negative prohibition, though it involves interference with an owner's enjoyment of property."[77] Modernly under the Human Rights Act 1998 and the European Convention for the Protection of Human Rights, expropriation cases involve balancing tests and assessments of public necessity, which seem to come out nearly always in favor of the government and against the existence of any liberties of use.[78] A deprivation of

[72] *Pumpelly* v. *Green Bay & Mississippi Canal Co.*, 80 US 166 at 176–78 (1871); *Kansas* v. *Walruff*, 26 F 178 (Cir Ct Kan 1886).

[73] *Pumpelly* v. *Green Bay*, 80 US at 178.

[74] *Pennsylvania Coal Co.* v. *Mahon*, 260 US 393 at 415 (1922); *Lucas* v. *South Carolina Coastal Council*, 505 US 1003 (1992).

[75] *Mariner Real Estate Ltd* v. *Nova Scotia (Attorney General)* (1999) 177 DLR (4th) 696 (NS Ct App); *Steer Holdings Ltd.* v. *Manitoba* (1992) 21 RPR (2d) 298 (Manitoba Ct App).

[76] [1927] 1 KB 458 at 465.

[77] *France Fenwick & Company* v. *The King*, [1927] 1 KB at 467.

[78] See the discussion in *Trailer and Marina (Leven) Ltd* v. *Secretary of State for the Environment, Food and Rural Affairs* [2005] 1 WLR 1267.

use will give rise to a compensation claim only if it is so thorough that it constitutes "de facto expropriation."[79] This practice is found throughout the Commonwealth countries, which now tend not to require compensation for regulation of use.[80]

The reasons in favor of compensation requirements are plain, but they are seldom stated alongside the paeans to the benevolent regulatory state that are so common in contemporary compensation claim cases. Governments stand in freer position than private citizens to enter, interfere with, or damage the property of others. They are entrusted with the police powers and the power of eminent domain, and those powers are backed by the state's monopoly on force and violence, coercive powers that private citizens lack. If they are also authorized to define the scope of the owner's liberties through their positive laws then owners have no secure liberties. It is a more grievous outrage when a big, powerful corporation uses its political influence to take private property than when an individual trespasses. For the same reason, a state's exercise of its coercive power on behalf of the majority against the private rights of a minority ought to pique concern.

The Supreme Court expressed the concern this way:

> It would be a very curious and unsatisfactory result, if . . . it shall be held that if the government refrains from the absolute conversion of real property to the uses of the public it can destroy its value entirely, can inflict irreparable and permanent injury to any extent, can, in effect, subject it to total destruction without making any compensation, because, in the narrowest sense of that word, it is not *taken* for the public use. Such a construction would pervert the constitutional provision into a restriction upon the rights of the citizen, as those rights stood at the common law, instead of the government, and make it an authority for invasion of private right under the pretext of the public good, which had no warrant in the laws or practices of our ancestors.[81]

This is not to suggest that states should be deprived of police and eminent domain powers. A political authority owes duties not only to this property owner but also to the other members of the political community, to the preservation of goods that the members share as a community, the sharing of which constitutes the political community as a community. And it must often adopt and execute plans of action in satisfaction of

[79] *Papamichalopoulos* v. *Greece* (1993) 16 EHRR 440.

[80] Thomas Allen, *Right to Property in Commonwealth Constitutions* (New York: Cambridge University Press 2000), 162–200.

[81] *Pumpelly* v. *Green Bay*, 80 US at 177–78.

those duties, sometimes at the expense of this property owner, all subject to the requirements of justice (prohibiting irrational plans of action, favoritism, absolute prohibitions against killing and enslaving, etc.).[82] But internalizing the costs of new legal duties that it creates is often one of those demands of justice.

The residential conflagration cases discussed by Holmes and Finnis illustrate the limited and absolute nature of property rights asserted against the state. One does not enjoy a property right to prevent the fire department from blowing up one's house to save others. In this sense, even the right to control, the most categorical of property norms, is not fully specified in the abstract as against the political community. But rights to just compensation are absolute in a different way. They direct political authorities to act to the detriment of owners, but require them to pay compensation for any burden this action places on rights that have not already been limited at common law or by states' legislative exercises of the police powers.[83]

So, the state's duties are more limited than the duties that private citizens owe to owners. But so limited, they cannot be infringed, and they should not be infringed. The absolute nature of these rights is a necessary protection against the power that the political community can exercise through its government. Justice Holmes warned that the exceptional case of the "blowing up of a house to stop a conflagration" might tempt the political community to improve its condition "by a shorter cut than the constitutional way of paying for the change."[84] There exists a special danger in giving the state the power to frustrate the plans of action of private owners without paying compensation.

Put differently, the right to compensation can be understood to reach an accommodation by imposing on the state a categorical duty to pay in consideration of the state's authority to act in satisfaction of its duties to others. The owner has fewer rights against the state but is compensated for the difference. This is one way to answer to the public takings paradox: if property rights precede public powers and the public interest then one would expect the owner's consent to be required before the public can take property; if property rights are nothing but the results of public actions on and regulations of property, then one would not expect

[82] Finnis, *Human Rights*, 34.
[83] Finnis and Webber both allow that compensation might be required in law and justice. Finnis, *Human Rights*, 34; Webber, *Negotiable Constitution*, 143.
[84] *Pennsylvania Coal Co.* v. *Mahon*, 260 US 393 at 415–16 (1922).

the public to owe the owner compensation for a putative expropriation.[85] The answer is that two-term property "rights" can precede political action, though they are not always fully determinate and absolute. Or, more precisely, they can be absolute in one sense and for one purpose but not-fully-specified in another sense and for other purposes.

The dangers of abstraction

Despite the benefits of two-term abstractions, a danger lurks within them. A two-term abstraction is necessarily indeterminate. O cannot know for sure whether he will turn out to have a right to build the fence until he knows all the circumstances of neighbors A, B, C, the uses that they plan to make of their land, the potential effects of the fence on them, and so on. Does A benefit from an unrecorded equitable servitude, which prevents fences on neighboring lots? Would it be unreasonable, and therefore a nuisance, in light of the particular circumstances of B's use, for O to erect a fence next door? Does the scope of C's easement conflict with the placement of a fence there? Before we can attribute conclusory force to the statement, *O has a right to build a fence*, the two-term abstraction "must be translated into specific three-term relations."[86]

This can only be done within the context of the community of which O is part. One cannot say in the abstract where the boundaries of use rights are fixed because they are not fixed in the abstract. Rather, the boundaries are settled within particular communities. So the normative force of two-term right statements should not be overstated. Nor should the authority of the community to specify the boundaries of the right be usurped by the individual who is asserting the abstract right claim. The individual properly stands in relation to others as a participant in the common good.

[85] Alan Brudner states the paradox concisely: "It would seem that a distribution-blind duty to compensate must reflect a property preceding any collective distribution. But then why is consent not required for a discretionary public use of someone's resources?" Alan Brudner, "Private Property and Public Welfare" in James Penner and Henry E. Smith (eds.), *Philosophical Foundations of Property Law* (New York: Oxford University Press 2013), 69.

[86] NLNR, 218.

8

The contours of property rights

The nature of property norms

Mediated domains of private ownership enable individuals and communities of individuals - families, religious associations, charities, educational institutions, business enterprises - to employ the use of things in their acts of self-constitution and thus to realize, among other goods, the basic good of practical reasonableness. But because of conflicts and the possibility of practically unreasonable conduct, the exercise of freedom within the domains of private property must be mediated by those same institutions of private ordering and, where necessary, political authorities. Institutions of ordering, both political and private, must enable members of the community to coordinate their uses and management of things. To do this, they need to endorse and establish norms that will operate with binding force on the practical deliberations of those who own interests in property and those who encounter property. Moral norms are thus promulgated and specified as legal norms.

As discussed in Chapter 2, property law engages different authorities to guide practical reason according to whether it is guiding owners, non-owners, co-owners, etc., and to allow or eliminate from consideration those reasons that are important to consider or not to consider. The different authorities produce different norms. In the classical conception, property norms are divided into categories of impersonal and personal - in rem and in personam. In rem rights are good against the world, while in personam rights are contingent on and binding within particular relationships. This study will not follow exactly that orthodox taxonomy. Building on the claims of Chapter 7, it distinguishes between categorical norms and context-dependent norms. That approach will better lead to understanding the operation of property norms upon practical deliberations and judgment.

The moral foundations of legal norms

Many property scholars have noted that property law takes an interest in morality, character, and virtue. Scholars who are interested in the economic implications of property law laud property's affirmation of simple moral intuitions.[1] Compliance with the moral duty to exclude oneself from things belonging to others produces material benefits. Lockeans understand natural rights to (productive) labor to be pre-political and, at least in that sense, moral.[2] Meanwhile, critics of the classical and new essentialist conceptions, especially the authors of the Progressive Statement of Property, have argued that law has a role to play in promoting the virtue of owners.[3]

One also finds agreement on particular normative principles the force of which is not attributable (entirely) to law. One ought not dump used motor oil in the swamp; one ought not smash the windows of automobiles parked outside the baseball stadium for no compelling reason (e.g., to rescue a child trapped in a car in hot weather); one ought to share excess resources with those in need. The consensus on moral principles does not entail complete consensus on which norms should, or even can, give rise to legal obligations. But it should be uncontroversial to observe that law plays a role in enforcing some moral norms, even controversial norms. It was both necessary and reasonable for the US Congress to promulgate the Fair Housing Act precisely because not all landlords assented to the moral norm against discriminating on the basis of race. This is not to deny that the work of deriving legal rules from abstract moral principles is always difficult and often controversial. It is simply to observe that the work is always important and often unavoidable, especially when controversial.

The use of the term "moral" in property scholarship is varied and often ambiguous. Among the various meanings that can be ascribed to moral norms, I will focus here on two. First, the term can pick out those norms that are extra- or pre-legal, in the sense of deriving their normative force

1 For example, Merrill and Smith appreciate the economic benefits that flow from property law's affirmation of simple moral intuitions. The moral significance of property, as they call it, makes property possible. Thomas W. Merrill and Henry E. Smith, "The Morality of Property" (2007) 48 *William & Mary Law Review* 1849.

2 For example, Eric R. Claeys, "Productive Use in Acquisition, Accession, and Labor Theory" in James Penner and Henry E. Smith (eds.), *Philosophical Foundations of Property Law* (New York: Oxford University Press 2013), 13.

3 Gregory S. Alexander, Eduardo M. Peñalver, Joseph William Singer, and Laura S. Underkuffler, "A Statement of Progressive Property" (2009) 94 *Cornell Law Review* 743 at 743–44; Eduardo M. Peñalver, "Land Virtues" (2009) 94 *Cornell Law Review* 821.

from some source (God, natural law, promise, custom . . .) other than law. Second, the term can be used to describe norms that have reflexive implications for those agents of practical reason who use and rely on them in making practical judgments; these are norms taken into one's deliberations and choices, and thereby into one's character, as lasting reasons for action.

The norms considered in this chapter are moral norms in the second sense. Many of them were moral norms in the first sense but have now been brought into law by some legal institution and now have normative force as legal reasons. So, for example, where a local custom is adopted by a court as binding on members of the community, a norm that was moral in the first sense becomes a legal norm, and thereafter employs normative influence over the members of the community as a law, even though it continues to have moral implications in the second sense.

How extra-legal moral norms come into private law is a very interesting question, but is beyond the scope of this book. Many years ago, Henry Hart and Albert Sacks noted that the role of private ordering in the formation of private law has not received sufficient attention.[4] That insufficiency will not be remedied here. It must suffice to observe that lawyers reasonably take as a given that when they practice private law they are practicing law.

Influential accounts of private law presuppose that property norms are static (unlike private-law liability norms, which are dynamic).[5] But that presupposition is not necessary to the argument that private law is autonomous. It can be divorced from the insight that private law has its own norms and its own ways of reasoning, and that any attempt to examine private law exclusively from outside of it must result in an "infinite regress" of skepticism; the external perspective from which the normative truths of private law are skeptically viewed can be debunked from a perspective external to it.[6] It is therefore a mistake to view private law purely, or even primarily, as instrumentally useful for achieving some collective goal of public-law or political institutions. (Ernest Weinrib calls this external approach "functionalism.")

[4] Henry M. Hart, Jr. and Albert M. Sacks, *The Legal Process: Basic Problems in the Making and Application of Law* (Westbury, NY: Foundation Press 1994), chapter 2.

[5] Ernest Weinrib, *The Idea of Private Law* (Oxford: Oxford University Press 2012), 2; Charles Harpum, Stuart Bridge, and Martin Dixon, *Megarry & Wade: The Law of Real Property* (London: Sweet & Maxwell 2012), 2.

[6] Weinrib, *Idea of Private Law*, 17. Compare C. S. Lewis, *God in the Dock: Essays on Theology and Ethics* (Grand Rapids: Eerdmans 1970), 212–15. "[Y]ou can step outside one experience only by stepping inside another. Therefore, if all inside experiences are misleading, we are always misled."

Indeed, private law can be autonomous from public law, political institutions, and collective goals precisely because public law makers and other bodies of collective decision-making are not the only shapers of rights and duties. Within institutions of private ordering, the wisdom and choice required to translate context-dependent norms into exclusionary reasons for action emerge through the deliberations and judgments of an individual or community of individuals. Those judgments are either ratified by courts as lawful and reasonable or not. So the legal duties that are derived from abstract, contingent norms partake of practical wisdom acquired from the judgments of institutions of legal ordering; through the use of standards of reasonable acquisition, use, and disposition, which create fact questions for juries to resolve according to their own practical judgment; from judges ruling according to the standards of the common law and specific rules; and from legislatures.

The role of courts in this process is often misunderstood. The willingness of courts to ratify reasonable judgments and their refusal to ratify unreasonable judgments import into law the best practical judgments of private actors and keep out of law those judgments that law cannot endorse without being corrupted. An example is the limited freedom that owners and their lawyers have enjoyed over the centuries to create new estates and future interests (and formerly, tenures) of ownership. Within the confines of the numerus clausus principle, the common law has ratified the creation of many different estates and interests, which private property owners have severed out of the fee simple (or, in England, out of tenures held in land owned by the Crown[7]) in order to provide for friends, family members, and other grantees and beneficiaries. Common law actors – owners, their lawyers, judges, and legislatures – collaborated both to create and to standardize the complex of ownership estates. The resulting complex of forms permits owners wide latitude to dispose their assets according to individuated plans of action, consistent with the demands of information costs and legal institutions.[8]

[7] Harpum et al., *Megarry & Wade: The Law of Real Property*, chapter 2.

[8] The common law classification of estates and future interests:

> tells us a great deal about what it is like to be governed by rules. On the one hand, the categories are sufficiently numerous and the operating principles sufficiently flexible that they can accommodate virtually any set of intentions. Consequently, the system promotes individual autonomy in determining how property will be distributed after death. . . . On the other hand, the system is complex and difficult to master. Only a lawyer can maneuver through the somewhat arcane rules with confidence.

So, grantors have authority to act as private law makers, specifying the rights and duties, and the limitations on rights and duties, which will attach to the dominions of their grantees. But their power to limit the dominion of grantees is not unlimited. As important as the ratification of novel estates is the law's refusal to enforce putative rights and duties that are unreasonable. The common law does not enforce unreasonable restraints on alienation. It does not recognize any forms of ownership outside the standardized forms. Nor does it give effect to perpetuities.

Some property duties and rights cannot be ratified because they are inconsistent with the requirements of practical reasonableness, what we often call moral norms. Slavery and racial discrimination are obvious examples. Others are more subtle. A donor who attempts to convey a gift causa mortis, in anticipation of impending death, cannot complete the gift by a volitional act of suicide.[9] The law will not ratify the attempt to vest rights in a donee by an intentional act that is inconsistent with respect for human life.

More dramatically, property law ratifies trespass against a practically unreasonable owner who is not making use of a resource. Under the doctrines of prescription and adverse possession, an outsider's action that would otherwise violate the categorical duty to exclude oneself is ratified after the fact as lawful if the possessor has entered openly and notoriously, against the true owner's dominion, and remains continually (or, in the case of prescription, repeatedly makes the use) throughout the statutory period.

Strikingly, the doctrine of adverse possession is not always concerned with the culpability of the adverse possessor at the time of that person's entry. In the United Kingdom good faith belief of entitlement is a condition qualifying one to register title gained by adverse possession,[10] while the common law rule for unregistered title requires the squatter to know that his plans for the land are inconsistent with the future plans of the true owner.[11] American states are not unanimous on the intent required to gain title by adverse possession. Some states require innocent

Thomas W. Merrill and Henry E. Smith, *The Oxford Introductions to U.S. Law: Property* (New York: Oxford University Press 2010), 95–96.

[9] *Agnew* v. *Belfast Banking Co.* [1892] 2 IR 204 at 211; *In Re Fanning* [1922] 3 DLR 925 at 926 (Ontario); *Ray* v. *Leader Federal Savings & Loan Association*, 292 SW 2d 458 at 467 (Tenn Ct App 1953); *In Re Dudman* [1925] Ch. 553 at 555.

[10] Land Registration Act 2002, schedule 6, s. 5(4)(c). Adverse possession is insufficient to affect the title of the owner of registered land. Land Registration Act 2002, s. 96(1). It establishes title only as against other claimants. Harpum et al., *Megarry & Wade*, 1494–96.

[11] *Buckinghamshire County Council* v. *Moran* [1990] Ch. 623 at 627–28.

good faith. Some have required bad faith, that is, the trespasser must know that he is trespassing, while many states make the adverse possessor's intent irrelevant.[12]

On the other side, adverse possession can be understood to concern the practical deliberations of original owners. Though the true owner's intention is de jure irrelevant, as a matter of fact only negligent or disinterested owners are likely to fall prey to adverse possession. An owner who fails to take any interest in his land, and thus does not notice, or takes no action against, the possessor who is putting the resource to productive use is not acting fully practically reasonably with respect to the asset. The adverse possessor, though a trespasser, makes use for an extended period of time, and the law awards him title. Thus the common law goes so far in condemning hoarding of unused resources as to ratify a violation of the simplest of in rem property norms.

In this way, the doctrines of prescription and adverse possession give particular shape to the context-dependent norms against hoarding and in favor of good stewardship. There is no one uniquely right answer to the question as to how much land one should have. Nor is there one uniquely right standard for judging an owner's efforts to develop, exploit, and maintain the resources that he or she owns. A judgment of adverse possession is a practical judgment that the adverse possessor made a reasonable use of the resource – acted the way a reasonable owner would have acted, in the language of the law – and strongly suggests that the original owner did not.

Another ratification strategy is a state's use of its police power to prohibit ex ante those uses that are most likely to be ruled outside the owner's right post facto by common law institutions of adjudication. So, for example, a regulation prohibiting the operation of brick kilns in residential neighborhoods simply states in advance what the contours of the landowner's rights are likely to turn out to be after the use has been challenged in a private action.[13] The legislature is in such a case simply codifying the rules that the common law institutions have developed.

There is a danger here. Ex ante regulation is sometimes characterized as a norm-making strategy akin to the common law of wrongs. But this characterization deserves scrutiny. Ex ante rules foreclose discretion about what one should do, at least as to one option or one class of options. Ordinances and statutes are designed to avoid use conflicts

[12] Merrill and Smith, *Oxford Introductions: Property*, 35.
[13] See *Hadacheck* v. *Sebastian*, 239 US 394 (1915).

before they arise. They achieve this goal by ruling out potential reasons for action from the practical deliberations of owners and lawful users. They eradicate from the owner's scope of action potential uses that the owner might otherwise have freedom to make, and reasons that the owner would otherwise have freedom to consider.

By contrast, common law doctrines are generally applied post facto and their application is particularized to the circumstances of each case. Furthermore, determinations of reasonableness are made by juries as a matter of fact, not by judges as a matter of law. Thus, a determination of unreasonableness in one case need not control a later case. In short, private law is attuned to the incommensurability of human goods and the open-endedness of practical reasoning.

This is not to suggest that regulatory restrictions on property are never justifiable. To the contrary, the case in favor of the common law conception of property entails the common law police powers.[14] At the very least, states have an obligation to legislate in protection of common law rights, including property rights, which property owners might jeopardize by their actions. Authority is often needed to coordinate action toward a common good. And not all regulations change the law in a substantive sense. Regulations that merely codify common law protections are restatements of the boundaries of property owner sovereignty, and thus do not rule out of consideration any actions that were available to owners in the first place.

Having earlier examined the role that property law plays in self-constitution, we are in a position to see one reason why it is uncontroversial to claim that property law ought to take account of moral principles, in the *second* sense of "moral" identified above. Practically reasonable people tend to act in practically reasonable ways. An owner who is in the habit of giving charitably makes herself into (constitutes herself as) a charitable person. States have rational interests in the practical reasonableness of users of property partly because they have interests in governing reasonable people. So law should both free and encourage owners and their collaborators to use things in practically reasonable ways.

Similarly, law has reason to deflect some unreasonable choices and actions. Because practical reasoning is a reflexive activity, choosing and acting contrary to the principles of practical reasonableness makes one

[14] James R. Stoner, Jr., *Common Law and Liberal Theory: Coke, Hobbes, and the Origins of American Constitutionalism* (Lawrence: University Press of Kansas 1992), 131–36.

unreasonable. Unreasonable people cause harm to their neighbors. They threaten, as where they exercise property rights abusively, to implicate legal institutions in their unreasonable actions. And they cause harm of a different, but important, sort to themselves. Those who accustom themselves to acting without regard for the requirements of practical reasonableness will be less likely to consider those requirements in the future. An owner who hoards becomes a hoarder.

Practical reasonableness has value not only instrumentally but also in itself. Even leaving aside the material benefits of practically reasonable conduct (reduced conflict among neighbors, avoidance of waste, etc.), states have an interest in the practical reasonableness of those who interact with property because states have an interest in the well-being of citizens. If a citizen is practically reasonable then he is well off. And the communities and associations of which a practically reasonable person is part are better off than they would have been if he had shaped himself into an immoral person.[15]

Property norms and practical reason

Categorical and context-dependent norms

The normative force of property rights and duties varies according to the scope of the reasons that such rights and duties exclude from practical deliberation. This is a spectrum, and what follows should not be understood as a complete taxonomy. For simplicity it will divide property norms into two categories, then work out a few finer gradations. We will begin by distinguishing between categorical norms and context-dependent norms.

Categorical norms, including absolute norms (their strongest instances), rule whole categories of reasons out of consideration, and make particular circumstances irrelevant to the question what one should do or not do. Categorical norms are negative norms – they prohibit actions, such as murder, rape, theft, and slavery, which are inconsistent with the right-holder's inherent dignity as an agent of practical reason. Because they impose negative duties of self-exclusion and abstention, they are easy to understand. They can be easily translated from general norms into absolute conclusions, and easily universalized from a particular person to all persons who are similarly situated.

[15] See, generally, Robert P. George, *Making Men Moral: Civil Liberties and Public Morality* (New York: Oxford University Press 1993).

Context-dependent norms guide deliberation toward more reasonable choices and actions and away from less reasonable choices. But they cannot resolve practical deliberations unless and until they are specified as three-term conclusions of practical reason. Application of context-dependent norms – choosing one from among many possible solutions to a problem – requires deliberation and wisdom and leaves much to discretion. Until specified as rights and wrongs in particular cases – right and wrong answers to particular questions – context-dependent norms are necessarily open-ended and contingent. Unlike categorical (especially absolute) norms, they can be either prohibitive or affirmative, but not conclusive until specified.

Categorical norms

As we saw in Chapter 7, an absolute right is a correct conclusion of practical reason about what should be done. It supplies a conclusive and fully exclusionary reason to the one considering what to do and thereby imposes an absolute duty. The duty that corresponds to the right admits of no exceptions, and is not to be weighed against competing reasons. It can be stated in three terms, which together identify the actor, the action, and the subject, leaving nothing to the imagination or discretion of the person deliberating. But some negative, absolute rights can be generalized as two-term abstractions. The strongest of categorical, two-term right statements are the absolute rights, such as the rights not to be enslaved, maimed, or purposefully killed. It is sufficient to state that this particular human being has a right not to be enslaved. It is not necessary to further state that some other human being has a duty not to enslave her.

Generalized, abstract, or two-term statements of negative rights exercise normative force in part by ruling out, if not all possible reasons for action other than the duty, then entire categories of reasons. How is this possible? Two-term right statements do not specify who holds the correlating duty. Nor do they specify any particular action. But categorical, two-term statements can apply to easily discernible categories of persons (e.g., all persons or non-owners of this thing) and can require those persons to comply by doing nothing (e.g., not maiming or not taking the thing or using it). They perform this normative work by signaling to duty bearers certain categories of actions (maiming, taking) that may not be performed on certain categories of objects (human beings, things that do not belong to me), in some cases for certain categories of reasons (no taking except to save a human life), and in other cases for any reason (no maiming, period).

One often owes absolute and categorical duties to persons by virtue of the status – ontological or conferred – of those persons, without needing to know more. Absolute two-term duties – I must not kill, enslave, maim, rape – are owed to beings that have the ontological status of human beings. Categorical, two-term duties that are not absolute are owed to persons whose status is not inherent in their nature but rather is conferred on them. I must obey my superior officers because they are my superior officers. They hold the office of officer and I do not. I must not take or trespass on this thing because it does not belong to me. Someone holds the office of owner over this thing and I am not that someone.

Yet the analogy between absolute duties and property duties should not be taken too far. A property duty is not owed to the thing – an owned automobile, for example does not have a right not to be taken. Duties are owed to persons. Two-term duties give rise to two-term rights – absolute or categorical – in the person to whom the duty is owed.

Categorical, two-term rights being good against the world, they necessarily correlate with negative duties, duties of non-action or non-interference. A positive right can never be a fully specified, binding conclusion of practical judgment until the duty-holder is specified who must satisfy it and the precise requirements of the duty are fully identified. By contrast, a negative right can be good against the world – enforceable against everyone on the same terms – precisely because it is a negative right. To function categorically, two-term duties must be prohibitive, rather than affirmative, because only a duty *not* to do some act can be obeyed in a wide variety of circumstances. Thus claims to discern affirmative, moral obligations in property, such as Gregory Alexander's statement that "an owner is morally obligated to provide to the society of which the individual is a member those benefits that the society reasonably regards as necessary for human flourishing,"[16] are incomplete at best.

Of course, affirmative duties can be specified and promulgated (e.g., posited or adopted by custom) as categorical norms. A business owner instructs her maintenance crew to drop everything else and fix that machine as soon as possible. A government commands its citizens to pay income taxes no later than April 15. But unlike norms that are deduced from the basic principles and requirements of

[16] Gregory S. Alexander, "The Social-Obligation Norm in American Property Law" (2009) 94 *Cornell Law Review* 745 at 774.

reason, which are universal and morally required, these enactments are determinations of the lawmaker and therefore are particular and contingent. If the business owner's machine is suddenly made obsolete by a new technology or technique then the boss might reasonably rescind her instruction with no negative moral consequence. And no moral principle requires that governments require payment of income taxes, much less that those taxes be paid in a certain percentage on April 15. Any moral force attending the command is supplied by the (negative) categorical prohibition against disobeying not-unjust commands of those who exercise lawful authority.

The inherently negative nature of two-term categorical norms is most clearly seen in their most forceful instances, moral and legal absolutes.[17] Absolute norms, such as the prohibitions against murder and rape, are norms that hold without exception. They are categorical because their application is not contingent on personal factors. One need not know anything at all about the personal history, commitments, or practical deliberations of any person one encounters to know that one has no right to kill or rape her. These norms can be conclusive and exceptionless precisely because they require no affirmative actions. Each person can comply with such norms simply by choosing not to act where action would violate one of the norms. Affirmative norms must allow discretion to consider in which circumstances the duties apply; moral absolutes do not.[18]

In law, moral absolutes generally find expression in criminal prohibitions. But moral absolutes find their way into property law when enforcement of a private property right would sanction an intrinsically unjust act. This was the situation in *Riggs* v. *Palmer*, discussed in Chapter I.[19] Elmer Palmer prevented his grandfather from disinheriting him by murdering the man. Common reason dictated that property law should not operate "in favor of one who murdered his ancestor that he might speedily come into the possession of his estate." Other moral absolutes have come into property law from external sources, such as the US Constitution's Thirteenth Amendment, which prohibits slavery.

In the common law tradition, negative categorical norms such as these are often expressed as wrongs.[20] As Neil MacCormick pointed out,

[17] John Finnis, *Moral Absolutes: Tradition, Revision, and Truth* (Washington, DC: Catholic University Press 1991), 27–29, 104–05.

[18] See Finnis, *Moral Absolutes*, 27–29, 104–05.

[19] *Riggs* v. *Palmer*, 22 NE 188 at 189 (NY 1889).

[20] William Blackstone, *Commentaries on the Laws of England* (1769), vol. 1, §II.

wrongs can be derived from positive norms, but the positive commandments are not the wrongs themselves. MacCormick gave a few examples of wrongs that appear to require action, such as, "It is wrong to disobey the referee or ignore his decisions," and, "It is wrong for parents to neglect the upbringing of their minor children."[21] The first norm forbids an action – disobedience of the referee – and therefore is a negative norm, even though the referee's instruction in a particular case may require some affirmative action, such as leaving the field of play. The action norm is not categorical in its abstract form. It requires further specification, which cannot be done except in context. Similarly, there are no actions that parents would be negligent to fail to perform always and in all circumstances, or for all but a narrow category of reasons. It is negligent to let one's children go hungry, but that does not entail a categorical obligation to feed them. Indeed, to feed them in some circumstances might itself be negligent, as where they are already well-fed and one is trying to teach them the virtue of temperance. It is negligent not to show affection to one's children, but that does not entail that one must always hug them. And so on.

Wrongs are sometimes conflated with in rem norms. In rem norms have sometimes been understood to be necessarily negative norms, imposing duties of non-action (abstention, non-interference, etc.).[22] This mistake is understandable. In rem norms are often, though not necessarily, categorical. But the fit between in rem and negative norms is not as close as that between categorical and negative norms.

Contrast two typical requirements of a landmark designation. A law authorizing local government to designate a privately owned building as a historic or aesthetic landmark will often impose two duties on the landowner: (1) a negative prohibition against changing the structure and (2) an affirmative obligation to maintain the premises in a reasonably fit and pleasing condition. Both of these duties are in rem. One is categorical and negative; the other is contextual and affirmative. The owner can comply with the first duty by doing nothing, and the duty can be specified in two-term statements; the owner has a duty not to change anything. The second duty, being affirmative and context-specific, is incomplete as a two-term statement. How fit must the premises be? Must the owner repaint the walls every two years or every ten years?

[21] Neil MacCormick, *Practical Reason in Law and Morality* (Oxford: Oxford University Press 2008), 47–53.

[22] J. E. Penner, *The Idea of Property in Law* (Oxford: Oxford University Press 1997), 28.

Must he replace rotted clapboards with identical wood or can he substitute a cheaper alternative where the difference will not be apparent to non-experts? And so on.

The clearest and simplest of two-term categorical norms is the duty of self-exclusion from things one does not own. The norm is neither open-ended nor contextual. Though not absolute, it can be outweighed by very few reasons. Apart from cases of necessity, such as a threat to human life, one cannot justify entering or taking on a balance of reasons. And violation of the norm is treated with severe disapprobation. An intentional trespass can be punished with punitive or exemplary damages.[23] In the United States, if the government infringes the right to exclude, it is liable under the Takings Clause, no matter how minimal the intrusion.[24]

The categorical duty to exclude oneself from others' things is derived from the moral norm that one ought to respect the plans of action that others adopt. I am subject to a duty not to take or trespass against others' things not because, and not to the extent that, I have judged others' plans for those things as superior to my own. The duty arises out of the respect that I owe to the owner as a fellow human or community of humans, not out of any judgment about the moral validity of the owner's plans. Thus the duty prevents me from substituting my own judgment for the deliberations and choices of the owner. All I need to know is that the owner is a human being or community of humans and therefore capable of adopting reasons and plans of action. By excluding myself from things that others own, I honor the owners as agents of practical reason.

Stephen Munzer is correct that one can exercise self-restraint by not interfering in prohibited ways with collective property.[25] But the virtue of temperance is not the only aspect of practical reasonableness with respect to things, nor even the most valuable. There is something uniquely valuable in developing the habit of excluding oneself from private

[23] See *Jacque* v. *Steenberg Homes, Inc.*, 563 NW 2d 154 (Wis 1997), and the discussion of that case in *The Oxford Introductions to U.S. Law: Property* (New York: Oxford University Press 2010), 68–70; and Merrill and Smith, "The Morality of Property." Though exemplary damages were once allowed in the UK in cases of intentional trespass, see *Williams* v. *Currie* (1845) 135 All ER 774; *Loudon* v. *Ryder* [1953] 2 QB 202, their allowance is now limited to cases of official action, motivation to profit, and statutory rights. *Rookes* v. *Barnard* [1964] AC 1129; Mark Lunney, "Trespass to Land" in Ken Oliphant (ed.), *The Law of Tort* (2nd edn, London: Butterworths 2007), 534.

[24] *Loretto* v. *Teleprompter Manhattan CATV Corp.*, 458 US 419 (1982).

[25] Stephen R. Munzer, *A Theory of Property* (Cambridge: Cambridge University Press 1990), 129. Munzer uses the term "communal property," but the context suggests that he means to refer to property that is owned collectively and controlled by political authorities.

property. The reason for that action, as opposed to self-exclusion from assets generally, can be, and in practically reasonable people will over time become, respect for the plans of action of another human being (or private community of human beings) who is (are) employing the resource in projects of self-constitution.

So some categorical duties are completely exclusionary reasons, others are more contingent and allow for consideration of other reasons. A spectrum suggests itself.[26] The strongest duties are moral absolutes, such as the prohibitions against killing, maiming, and enslaving. The rights that correlate with those duties – the rights to life and bodily integrity – are therefore the strongest rights. They are rights in the strict sense, absolute rights; there can never be a sufficient reason to violate them. Slightly less forceful is the duty not to steal. The right that correlates with that duty is the right to control. The right to control one's property is almost as strong as absolute rights, but not quite. Further along the spectrum is the duty not to enter, which correlates with the right to exclude. Finally, the duty not to interfere correlates with the right to use. As we have seen, use rights create strong presumptions for the deliberations of outsiders and judicial authorities, but those presumptions can be overcome.

All of these norms are in rem in the sense that lawyers use that term: they refer to things and are good against the world. And yet only the absolute norms are entirely opaque, exclusionary reasons for action. The others do not allow discretion in general or in the first instance. But they might yield to context-specific reasons in particular circumstances and on specific conditions. Nevertheless, those circumstances must be few, and the conditions strictly confined.

Context-dependent norms

The benefit of context-dependent norms is that they can be adapted according to the specific needs that people will encounter around the use and management of things. Of course, that is also what makes context-dependent norms so difficult to universalize. This is why affirmative norms particularly, and context-dependent norms generally, are seldom appropriate products of generally applicable regulations. They are best developed and specified into rights (and wrongs) within those domains and communities of people whom they are designed to govern.

[26] Compare Claeys, "Productive Use."

Context-dependent norms are necessary because we must often take action. Our negative duties do not exhaust our moral obligations to each other; every choice and action must respect all of the basic requirements of practical reasonableness. We should honor our obligations, which arise out of our relationships, promises, and commitments.[27] We should favor, and therefore act to promote, the common good of our communities. We should develop a coherent plan of life, and remain committed to our own plans of action. And so on.

Abstract, context-dependent norms are non-conclusive because one cannot decide what should be done in the abstract. To state just a few of the basic requirements of practical reasonableness is to reveal that conflicts will often arise between any norms that require action. And resolution of those conflicts requires wisdom and discretion. Does favoring the common good of one's community mean that one must sell all one has and give to the poor, or should one instead honor one's prior commitment to finish college? A husband has good reasons to buy flowers for his own wife rather than another woman, yet he might occasionally buy flowers for his employees to show his gratitude for their loyalty and diligence. Who has a stronger claim to the inheritance of a rich, childless widow, a distant-but-deserving cousin whom she has never met or her alma mater? There is no one, uniquely right answer to the question of what one should do with one's things.

So, norms that give rise to affirmative obligations are necessarily contingent. Though they must be borne in mind at all times and in all circumstances, they are directive only in certain circumstances. If my conscience is well formed, I will feel obliged to help the poor when I am able. But that does not entail that I must feed every hungry person that I meet, much less that I must feed all hungry people without exception. Affirmative duties must be contingent because of the inherent limitations of human nature and the open-endedness of lived human experience. For this reason, it would be hasty to jump to the conclusion that law should mandate those actions that lawmakers discern to be practically reasonable.[28]

There are other reasons to doubt the wisdom of translating context-dependent norms, especially affirmative ones, directly into *legal* rights

[27] John Finnis, *Natural Law and Natural Rights* (2nd edn, Oxford: Oxford University Press 2011), chapter 11.

[28] This is another problem with the so-called social obligation norm proposed by Gregory Alexander. See Alexander, "Social Obligation Norm."

and duties.[29] The possibility that owners will use property for ends that are not fully reasonable is not alone a *sufficient* reason to allow law to intrude into the owner's domain. Not all less-than-desirable states of affairs are equal. Some are worth accepting in exchange for the goods that private property produces. For another thing, lawmakers are not inherently better than private owners at identifying and selecting human goods. Indeed, because basic goods are all equally basic, most selections of one good state of affairs at the expense of another by a political authority on behalf of the community must necessarily be arbitrary. Furthermore, even if lawmakers always were able to identify the best ends, there remains in deliberation about each action the question of the most efficacious means, which will often be quite context-specific.[30]

Even leaving all of those considerations aside, there remains a much more fundamental danger inherent in the use of law to direct the practical deliberations of owners toward particular actions. Because they eradicate discretion, binding affirmative norms foreclose practical deliberation. Thus, they have the potential to destroy the possibility of practical deliberation, and using them to promote the virtue or practical reasonableness of property owners will generally be counter-productive. As a good that is realized through acts of self-constitution, practical reasonableness cannot be realized except through the exercise of free deliberation and choice. As John Finnis has remarked, "Aristotle indicated that chosen actions make an important difference not only to the matters which agents are trying to achieve or avoid but also, willy-nilly, to the agents themselves (and in another way, to anyone who admires them or adopts their principles of action)."[31] Just like self-constitution through pre-moral choosing, practical reasonableness also requires free choice. Without the freedom to make a choice, one cannot constitute oneself as a practically reasonable person.[32] Thus, if law supplies a conclusive reason for action, which is binding on the actor's deliberation and choice, then the actor is deprived of the opportunity to choose to be reasonable.

Practical reasonableness is both expensive and fragile. To be sure, the law must attend to the requirements of practical reasonableness, and

[29] Consider, in addition to what follows, Hart's observations about the open texture of law. H. L. A. Hart, *The Concept of Law* (3rd edn, Oxford: Clarendon Press 2012), chapter 7.

[30] Henry E. Smith, "Mind the Gap: The Indirect Relation between Ends and Means in American Property Law" (2009) 94 *Cornell Law Review* 959.

[31] Finnis, *Moral Absolutes*, 22. Compare Andrew M. Yuengert, *Approximating Prudence* (New York: Palgrave MacMillan 2012), 95–119.

[32] Finnis, *Moral Absolutes*, 20–24, 58–59; George, *Making Men Moral*, 176–77.

should where possible guide citizens consistent with those requirements. But it must also where possible avoid substituting itself for the requirements of morality. The law should serve practical reasonableness, but should encourage citizens to make practical reasonableness, rather than fear of the consequences of noncompliance with legal rules, their guide for action. It should, in short, leave the specification of context-dependent norms to reasoning agents as much as possible.

The challenge for property law is to develop affirmative norms so that they guide practical deliberations as much as possible without threatening the freedom of owners and their collaborators to choose what to do with property. Property law must take cognizance of the possibility that owners may exercise their freedom in ways that cause harms. But the core of owner sovereignty must be left intact if owners are to be free to develop into practically reasonable people.

What about usufructs?

We are now in a position to pick up the inquiry into the nature of usufructs. Usufructs act differently on the practical reasoning of different people, depending on where they stand in relation to the thing. This discussion will break usufruct into claim-rights against interference, powers, immunities, and liberties.

Usufructs operate as exclusionary reasons for action on the practical deliberations of outsiders, creating for those who have no interest in the thing a duty not to interfere or meddle with the use of the thing. The outsider looking at a strawberry field does not need to know who the people are working in the field. They might be owners. They might be invitees whom the owners allow to pick their own strawberries. They might be employees of the owners who are hired to harvest the berries. It does not matter. Just as he bears a duty not to enter without permission, he bears a duty not to interfere with the harvesting operation. To the outsider, the usufruct is a categorical, exclusionary reason for action, which owners and licensees have a claim-right to enforce.

Yet the usufruct is not *merely* the claim-right not to be interfered with. To those in the field, it matters a lot whether they are fee simple owners, with complete discretion to make whatever use of the field they like, or rather licensees, easement holders, or others whose freedom is more limited. In part they will want to know what powers they enjoy while present in the field, and what powers they do not enjoy. To serve its function as a source of authority, the power may be under-determined. If the owner is obligated to exercise the power for particular ends, in particular ways, or for the benefit of particular people, then the norm is less of a power because it *constrains* the scope of the owner's authority. But to guide deliberations, powers must specify at least some content. Those inside the domain of ownership need to know what they may and may not do specifically to alter the legal relations. May I fish from that stream? May I withdraw this sum? May I invite my brother? Those who enjoy interests in the thing must enjoy broad discretion to arrange their respective rights and entitlements for the well-being of the community as a whole. Yet they also need guidance. Easements, covenants, servitudes, bailments, licenses, and other sources of power provide that guidance.

Liability and immunity are also parts of the usufruct. If a rancher allows his cattle to trespass on his neighbor's field, then the parties will want to know the extent of the rancher's liability. Under the English rule the rancher is strictly liable.[33] In an open-range jurisdiction, the rancher's immunity creates a presumption that he is not required to pay for unintended costs that his activities generate.[34] But if he acts unreasonably and causes intentional harm then he can be called to account. A jury will pass moral judgment on his conduct – declare it intentional or unintentional – and he will be liable or not liable according to the "characteristic mode of reasoning" used in private law.[35]

Even accounting for the constituent elements of claim-right, power, and immunity for use, the usufruct has an additional essence, which is not safely described as an affirmative right. The difficulty of capturing the essence of the thing is well known. Lawyers refer to it as a use right, but we have seen how fraught that idea is. Philosophers have referred to it as positive liberty but that is inadequate. Let us stick to the jurisprudential concept of a liberty-right and briefly mention its most salient implication.

To Hohfeld's insight that a liberty correlates with a no-right, Finnis has added the clarification that it entails a no-duty.[36] The liberty is "surrounded by a perimeter of supporting claim-rights," but neither the existence nor the absence of the claims rights is a condition of the

[33] *Fletcher* v. *Rylands* [1866] 1 LR Ex 265. [34] *Comerford* v. *Dupuy*, 17 Cal 308 (1861).

[35] Weinrib, *Idea of Private Law*, 5.

[36] Wesley Newcomb Hohfeld, *Fundamental Legal Conseptions as Applied in Judicial Reasoning* (New Haven: Yale University Press 1919), 38–39; John Finnis, *Collected Essays of John Finnis, vol. IV: Philosophy of Law* (Oxford: Oxford University Press 2012), 375–88. Compare Simon Douglas and Ben McFarlane, "Defining Property Rights" in James Penner and Henry E. Smith (eds.), *Philosophical Foundations of Property Law* (New York: Oxford University Press 2013).

existence of a liberty.[37] In property, a liberty is the absence of relevant, conclusive legal reasons for action about what (not) to do with a resource. That does not mean that the exercise of a liberty is unconstrained or unguided. Choices and actions are always motivated. Some motivations – fear, hunger – are sub-rational. Others – avarice, spite – are even immoral. But many are reasons, including morally-justifiable reasons. A property liberty frees its holder to act for reasons of her own choosing, or even of her own creation. It carves out a domain of freedom within which to create reasons, and thereby to fashion a part of oneself according to one's own creative design as a being who advances a particular instantiation of the common good. It is the place within which one can make choices that have meaningful effects in the material world and in one's character, the space within which, as C. S. Lewis said of the present moment, humans have an experience analogous to God's experience of reality as a whole – "in it alone freedom and actuality are offered them."[38] If property has a moral core, then the liberty is it.

[37] Finnis, *Philosophy of Law*, 377.
[38] C. S. Lewis, *The Screwtape Letters* (London: MacMillan 1962), chapter 15.

9

Settling property rights in law

Specifying rights

Who decides what rights owners will and will not have, and what duties will correlate with them? This question matters because the agent who specifies the rights and duties of a society's members gets to decide what ends the society will pursue, and what projects will be employed to pursue those ends. If we have a society that consists of various and plural institutions of ordering and policy making, then we will have varied and plural projects of human flourishing. If by contrast policy making is performed only to satisfy individual preference, or only to satisfy the collective end chosen by political decision-makers, then the common good is impoverished and diminished.

Institutional questions such as this are of particular importance to property law, but the complexity of the questions is not reflected in many attempts to answer them. Many suppose a zero-sum conflict between the individual and the state. So-called bottom-up accounts of property teach that government powers – eminent domain, taxation, police powers, and enumerated powers of governments with written constitutions – must be always and everywhere exercised at the expense of absolute and settled, individual property rights. Top-down theories suppose that property rights are established by government actions, so that a property right is simply whatever is left over after the government is done regulating, like the hole in the middle of a donut.

Further complicating matters in the United States, the project is beset by the tendency to approach the problem through the lens of the Takings and Due Process clauses of the Fifth Amendment to the Constitution. This is understandable. Americans have a written constitution and property is a central term in those provisions. Our Bill of Rights and Fourteenth Amendment both identify property rights as limitations on the powers of governments. Nevertheless, property rights are not reducible to protections against state action. Indeed, property rights and duties emerge primarily to govern relations between non-state actors. And the duties that political authorities owe to owners are not all the same as the duties that private owners owe to each other. The property duties that a political authority owes to a private property owner are complicated by the duties that it owes to other citizens.

The practice of reading property rights through the lens of Takings clause jurisprudence in particular begets at least two unfortunate consequences. First, this approach creates twin opportunities to misunderstand the reach of the Takings clause. On one side is the danger of making private use rights depend on the nature of the government action at issue.[1] The state is then free to infringe property rights and harm the practical reasonableness of citizens as long as it uses the proper terminology. On the other side, usufructs and other two-term right abstractions can be viewed as more definitive and absolute than they really are, especially for purposes of private law. As a result, public law might be seen to secure rights that owners would not enjoy in private law.

Second, this approach tends to reduce property to a mechanism for resolving conflicts between individual preferences and state interests. It is blind to the intermediary institutions and private communities that order civic and private affairs toward a common good. As we have already seen, this reductionism is true neither to the exercise of practical reason nor to the common law, which both require a pluralist deference to pre-moral choices among basic goods – a precondition jeopardized by regulations that rest on an illusory "collective good" – and support for norms of practical reasonableness, which often require subordination of individual preferences.

The common good is most thoroughly realized in intermediary institutions within which families, associations, and other groups of people pursue plural and incommensurable goods in acts of communal and individual self-constitution. Specification of duties and other exclusionary reasons within these communities is best attuned to the requirements of practical reasonableness and to the good of all concerned. True, these communities sometimes fail to account for the good of outsiders, who are not part of their communities. But private law has institutions of ordering to mediate those failures too.

The common good is instantiated as plural and incommensurable, but not infinitely plural, basic goods that provide reasons for action to all

[1] Then-Justice Rehnquist, writing in dissent, criticized Justice Brennan for committing this error in *Penn Central Transportation Company* v. *City of New York*, 438 US 104 (1978).

individuals and communities of individuals. To reduce the common good to either individual preference or a single-measure "collective good" is to fail to respect the practical reasonableness of human beings. It is also to deny the possibility of self-constitution of private communities and associations, which is realized in collaborative enterprises directed toward plural and incommensurable goals.

Against both top-down and bottom-up theories of property, this chapter sketches a middle-out account, in which individuals and collective decision-makers both play a secondary role in specifying property rights and duties. Rights and duties emerge in the first instance from communities and institutions of private ordering, such as the family, the local community, and the jury; from customs; from judicial actors applying common law maxims and rules and thereby deferring to ancient wisdom; and from agents' obedience to the requirements of reason. Indeed, common law property norms are well suited to the requirements of practical reason in part because they are products of private ordering. Private property law can be autonomous from political institutions – those authorities who exercise the police and eminent domain powers – without being completely reduced to first appropriation. And the pluralism and reasonableness of private property law are reasons for political authorities to act first on a principle of not causing harm to those institutions out of which private property law arises.

Indeed, it is more than possible; it happens throughout the law of property.

- An owner of a unique building or beautiful landscape voluntarily accepts the imposition of a conservation easement, which prevents alteration of the resource and preserves it for others to enjoy without any state action.
- A business owner takes bailment of a van for benefit of his business. The van breaks down. An automobile mechanic fixes the van and asserts an artificer's (mechanic's) lien to secure payment. The mechanic enjoys a right of exclusive possession by operation of the authority that was conferred on him by the bailee to perform the repairs, "and its exercise requires no intervention by the courts."[2]
- A local community has a long and general custom of public use of the dry-sand area of a beach, exercised without interruption for so long that the memory of man runneth not to the contrary. By common

[2] *Tappenden* v. *Artus* [1964] 2 QB 185, [1963] 3 All ER 213.

consent and uniform practice, the custom creates legally enforceable duties in adjacent landowners not to interfere with the public's use, even without any authoritative pronouncement, much less promulgation by a legal authority.[3]

- Meshake, an indigenous Canadian, travels to the tribal land of his common law wife and there hunts a moose without a license. The customary law of the tribe, the Lac Seul Band, contains a kinship exception to trespass liability, for which Meshake qualifies. This private right to hunt on Lac Seul Band land entitles Meshake to shelter under the Lac Seul Band's treaty rights, which exempt them from public hunting laws within their territory. Therefore, Meshake cannot be held criminally liable for his unlicensed hunt.[4]

Individualist and collectivist accounts

In order to understand the significance of institutions of private ordering in specifying use rights, it will be helpful to consider the shortcomings of both individualist and collectivist accounts. The false dichotomy between individual preferences and collective interests matters because it can produce errors about what use rights are, and how they come about.

Epstein and absolute property rights

Of recent bottom-up theories, perhaps none has been more prominent than Richard Epstein's neo-Lockean account. For Epstein, property rights are pre-political and absolute as two-term abstractions. Epstein draws from this the primary implication that all burdens that the state places on private ownership give rise to just compensation liability under the Takings Clause of the Fifth Amendment.[5] Thus, Epstein would not have property rights depend on the nature of the government power being asserted or the state's duties to other citizens. In his original work he concluded, "*All* regulations, *all* taxes, and *all* modifications of liability

[3] *State of Oregon ex rel. Thornton* v. *Hay*, 462 P 2d 671 (Or 1969).

[4] *R* v. *Meshake* [2003] OJ No 202 (Ontario Court of Justice), reversed by 85 OR (3d) 575 (Ontario 2007).

[5] Richard A. Epstein, *Takings: Private Property and the Power of Eminent Domain* (Cambridge: Harvard University Press 1985); Richard A. Epstein, "Bundle-of-Rights Theory as a Bulwark Against Statist Conceptions of Private Property" (2011) 8 *Econ Journal Watch* 223.

rules are takings of private property prima facie compensable by the state."[6]

For Epstein, an owner has an abstract, pre-political, natural right to property, grounded in appropriation and conceived as a two-term right abstraction: O has a right to x. The rights are concretized at this abstract stage of specification so that O has a right to x that is good against the world without further conditions or limitations.[7] Epstein embraces Blackstone's off-hand description of property as the owner's despotic dominion.[8]

Principles of first appropriation play a significant role in shaping many property rights, especially in the western states within the United States. And as we have seen, it is not nonsensical to speak of many two-term right abstractions as rights. Indeed, many categorical, two-term right statements are essential to the normative work that private property performs. Yet not all of them are. And appropriation does not by itself supply the degree of specification one finds in the common law. As Thomas Merrill and Henry Smith have observed, tying rights to appropriation results not in a single property right but rather in a "mosaic of acquisition principles."[9]

Epstein's Lockean account is usefully compared with that of Eric Claeys. Claeys argues that Locke should be understood as identifying an ideal state, not fully specified rights.[10] On Claeys' interpretation, Locke's theory justifies usufructs for productive labor but does not directly justify rights of exclusive control. Other principles are needed to complete specification of the owner's rights and duties. Specification is particularly complicated with usufructs and cannot be done in the abstract. The ideal state commends simple, legal forms embodied as commands. But those provide only a first cut at specifying the norms of property. Practical wisdom is required to specify rights and duties further. Many reasonable solutions can be derived from the same principles, and not all lawmakers are reasonable; many are subject to passion and interest.

6 Epstein, *Takings*, 95.
7 Epstein concedes the failure of Locke's theory of consent; he substitutes a theory of forced exchanges. Epstein, *Takings*, 14–15.
8 Epstein, *Takings*, 22.
9 Thomas W. Merrill and Henry E. Smith, *The Oxford Introductions to U.S. Law: Property* (New York: Oxford University Press 2010), 40.
10 Eric R. Claeys, "Productive Use in Acquisition, Accession, and Labor Theory" in James Penner and Henry E. Smith (eds.), *Philosophical Foundations of Property Law* (New York: Oxford University Press 2013), 13 at 45.

Someone needs to specify rights of use. Epstein resists the idea that the state is the source of property rights and duties. That resistance has much to commend it. But property rights need not be settled only by individual action to provide meaningful protection against government action. At least some of the work of specifying property rights is performed *neither* by individual acts of appropriation *nor* by state action, but rather in the complex deliberations and interactions among members of plural and overlapping, private communities and intermediary institutions. Those institutions are not active agents in Epstein's account. At most, they transfer or assign rights that have already been created and fully specified by individual or collective action. The purpose of constitutional protections for property, Epstein argues, is to govern the relationship between the individual and the state.[11] Where individual acts of appropriation fail to produce sustainable rights, as where first-appropriation rights threaten common pool resources, Epstein is happy to allow that "collective solutions are required."[12]

Water rights

Epstein's elision shows up prominently in his discussion of water rights. He wants to understand norms of land use as extending "with equal force" to rights to use water.[13] He concedes that the initial distribution of rights in water cannot be specified as precisely as rights in real or personal property, but he resists the idea that water rights are whatever a reviewing court or other state actor says they are. His solution is to apply a Lockean first-appropriation doctrine to questions of water use. Yet to view exclusive appropriation as the ground of water rights and duties is to miss important nuances in the common law tradition's treatment of riparian ownership.

Appropriation came late to play a role in the development of the common law governing water[14] and still does little normative work in riparian disputes. Water law is concerned primarily with use, and between and among riparian owners water usufructs are governed by the more open-ended standard of reasonable use.[15] As one court summarized it, the essence of the common law doctrine is that a riparian owner "may not use the water in any manner that is unreasonably harmful to another riparian owner."[16]

[11] Epstein, *Takings*, 3. [12] Epstein, *Takings*, 218. [13] Epstein, *Takings*, 67–73.

[14] See, generally, Joshua Getzler, *A History of Water Rights at Common Law* (Oxford: Oxford University Press 2004).

[15] *Lockwood* v. *Brentwood Park Investments Ltd*, 1 NSR (2d) 669 (NS 1970).

[16] *Mattaponi Indian Tribe* v. *Commonwealth*, 72 Va Cir 444 (2007).

The norms of water law arose out of actions sounding in nuisance,[17] which give rise to in personam and context-dependent duties. Neither priority of appropriation nor the natural condition of a watercourse settles the rights and duties by itself. "Reasonable use is the touchstone for determining the rights of the respective parties."[18] The context-dependent nature of this standard prevents one from viewing two-term abstractions about water rights as conclusive. Water rights and duties are the conclusions of judgment about reasonable use in particular cases, not the premises from which judgment is derived.[19]

In his influential decision in *Tyler* v. *Wilkinson*, Justice Story stated that a riparian landowner "has no property in the water itself; but a simple use of it, while it passes along."[20] He almost certainly did not intend this simplified expression to be taken as a complete statement of the law. Riparian owners enjoy exclusive, categorical rights as against non-riparian owners. So if a landowner owns all of the riparian land around the water, then he owns exclusive title to the water.[21] And water may not be taken for purposes not related to the riparian tenement.[22] But the common law does not specify in the abstract or categorically the particular rights that each riparian owner enjoys as against every other riparian. As a result, "no proprietor has a right to use the water to the prejudice of another."[23] Justice Story's "principle of forbearance of itself could provide no bright line between acceptable encroachment and wrongful invasion of others, rights."[24]

Owners of riparian or littoral land adjacent to a single water resource are members of a community in a loose sense, who own the resource in a quasi-commons.[25] They may exclude the rest of the world, but they must cooperate with each other. Riparian owners are expected to work things out among themselves, to deliberate together, to take others' reasons for

[17] Getzler, *Water Rights*, 52–63. [18] *Lancey* v. *Clifford*, 54 Me 487, 490 (1867).

[19] Getzler relates the resolution of an early nuisance claim under the assize of novel disseisin in 1213 "for diversion of water from a mill, where the nuisance to the mill was abated by specifying rights of the parties to the water flow for particular times and places along the stream, and assigning duties for the maintenance and repair of the watercourse." Getzler, *Water Rights*, 55.

[20] *Tyler* v. *Wilkinson*, 24 F Cas 472, 474 (Cir Ct RI 1827).

[21] *Holker* v. *Porritt* (1875) 10 Exch 59.

[22] *McCartney* v. *Londonderry and Lough Swilly Railway Company, Ltd* [1904] AC 301.

[23] *Tyler* v. *Wilkinson*, 24 F Cas at 472–74. [24] Getzler, *Water Rights*, 274–76.

[25] This concept of quasi-commons was of course not unknown to Locke, who wrote of land that is held in common within a community but is joint property as against "all mankind" outside the community. John Locke, *Second Treatise on Government*, Book V §35.

action into each owner's deliberations, and, above all, to act reasonably toward each other. The system of riparian property is, as one court recently observed, a "self-regulating system."[26] The river is therefore not merely a physical resource but also an opportunity for owners to exercise practical reason.

Private acts of coordination and negotiation among riparian owners have both settled rights and duties in the first instance and redistributed those rights and duties by contract and exchange. Of course, the settlements of riparian owners are not immutable. A longstanding use, uninterrupted for the required period, can establish title to future use as against those riparian owners who failed to interfere with the use, and a grant or consent by all other interested riparian owners can have the same result.[27] But that is simply another way of saying that usufructs can be extinguished by adverse possession, and that they can be conveyed; in other words, they are property. It is not to deny that usufructs can be specified in the first instance through collaborative deliberations and judgments of those concerned.

Joshua Getzler relates the settlement of usufructs in a stream to which Charles, Duke of Rutland and the early industrialist Richard Arkwright both laid claims. Without any established usage or custom, or any clear rules, the parties quarreled for three and a half years, but they never went to court and eventually settled on a distribution that was satisfactory to both sides. Getzler remarks that this resolution "demonstrates how bargaining could result in a new allocation of property rights in water, without there being any clear pre-existing idea of the legal rights of the parties." The settlement was achieved "to create a mechanism for co-operation and for aligning the differing objectives of the parties, not to divide the profits of an economic enterprise."[28]

Private ordering is not always sufficient by itself to settle usufructs. Conflict is inevitable; cooperation within the quasi-commons breaks down in times of stress. In riparian cases, stress has generally come in the form of drought, industrialization, or both. Where the number of riparian owners is large, where they do not have reasons to care about each other's well-being, and especially where commercial rivalries incentivize appropriations at the expense of competitors, cooperation often fails. In those instances practical judgment must come from outside the

26 *Mattaponi Indian Tribe* v. *Commonwealth*, 72 Va Cir 444 (2007).
27 *Tyler* v. *Wilkinson*, 24 F Cas at 474; *Pratt* v. *Lamson*, 84 Mass 275 (1861); *Van Sickle* v. *Haines*, 7 Nev 249 (1872).
28 Getzler, *Water Rights*, 32–33.

community of owners. When the practical deliberations of the riparian owners break down, those owners must call upon the practical deliberations of common law judges and juries to establish a settled rule, an exclusionary reason for action that will resolve future disputes by foreclosing all but one solution.

Still, hard and fast rules settling water rights and duties among riparian owners came relatively late. The House of Lords got around to specifying the right of a riparian owner to natural flow in 1859,[29] many decades after the Industrial Revolution in England got going, and then for the purpose of excluding percolating water from the right. Getzler reports that the Lords then "had the greatest difficulty in deciding what the law was." He concludes that the complexity and confusion in riparian entitlements lends "little support [to] the theory that clear and distinct property rights and their efficient legal protection were an essential precondition of the Industrial Revolution."[30]

Even the rules announced by common law courts have tended to look more like maxims than rules. So, in affirming a jury verdict against a riparian owner whose agents diverted water from a stream to operate a mill, the Illinois high court opined that a riparian landowner may use enough water to satisfy his "natural wants," which include quenching thirst and watering cattle, but has no right to make "artificial" uses, such as manufacturing.[31] In England the standard is no use for "extraordinary purposes," which includes spray irrigation.[32]

With this background, the first appropriation doctrine that the western states in the United States have adopted looks less Lockean and more like a way to manage the deliberations of riparian owners in conditions of constant stress. States that suffer perpetual drought, in which long rivers supply the needs of vast expanses of land and in which riparian owners may never meet, cannot count on riparian owners to act reasonably toward each other. In Epstein's terms, the costs of common pool management come to outweigh the benefits of freeing riparian owners to deal with each other.[33] So the clearest possible rule is used to divide up the rights appurtenant to various estates and the rights are made severable from the riparian land in order to incentivize and allow the most productive use of the water.

[29] *Chasemore* v. *Richards* (1859) 7 HLC 349, 11 ER 140.

[30] Getzler, *Water Rights*, 43.

[31] *Evans* v. *Merriweather*, 4 Ill 492 (1842).

[32] *Rugby Joint Water Board* v. *Walters* [1967] 1 Ch 397.

[33] On the costs of common pool management, see Epstein, *Takings*, 216–28.

None of this suggests that Epstein is mistaken about the constitutional implications of government interference in water use rights. Riparian rights are estates in the use of water as against non-riparian owners, and can be enforced as such.[34] Water rights can be taken subject to the compensation duty, and if a state actor interferes with their enjoyment, the state cannot avoid liability on the ground that it is using the water for a public good.[35] The riparian owners control the sum of rights as against non-riparian landowners and non-owners, including the state, even if each particular share of the right cannot be defined abstractly or a priori.

Taxation as taking

Epstein's argument that taxation constitutes a taking begins with the recognition that depriving many owners of their rights is no less a taking of property than depriving one owner. "If the state takes property from A, then that property is still taken even if the state also takes property from B through Z." Epstein proceeds to argue that taxation under threat of force is "scarcely different" from the confiscation of assets. "The thief who says, 'your money or your life' has given his victim a choice, but he cannot keep the money on the grounds that the victim gave it to him. The thief's threat of force transforms giving into taking."[36] It is no different if the state demands a tax, which the owner may satisfy from whichever assets he chooses. Of course, there is no common law right to be free of taxation, as Epstein recognizes. But he observes that the consequence for refusal to pay a tax is attachment of a lien to one's property. Thus, he insists, one cannot claim that taxes are outside the reach of the Takings clause, "when their effectiveness precisely depends on coercive power clothed in official garb."[37]

So, for Epstein a tax is a taking because of the threat of a taking. But even if the coercive possibility of a lien were sufficient to establish Takings clause liability, it is not clear that the lien is an infringement of a property right. A laborer who files a mechanics lien to secure payment for services rendered on real estate is acting lawfully because landowners enjoy no right to be free from lien liability for debts that they incur. An unpaid tax is in this sense not distinguishable from an unpaid bill for services rendered.

[34] *Hite* v. *Town of Luray*, 8 SE 2d 369, 373 (Va 1940).

[35] *Town of Purcellville* v. *Potts*, 19 SE 2d 700 (Va 1942).

[36] Epstein, *Takings*, 99.

[37] Epstein, *Takings*, 100.

It is important to return to our earlier observation that a political community is a community. The earlier discussion stressed the differences between political authorities and private institutions for the purpose of demonstrating how each can affect practical deliberations. But one should also observe their similarities. Living within a political community produces benefits and gives rise to obligations. That the ratio of obligations to benefits for any particular citizen is not equal or proportionate to the ratio of other citizens is not in itself an infringement of property rights. The powers and obligations of governments established by constitutions determine the rights of owners in part, just as the obligations of private citizens determine the rights of other citizens. Whatever the status of regulatory burdens under the Takings clause, it seems that it should be uncontroversial to view taxes as "a proper price of communal citizenship."[38]

Property rights as collectivist solutions

At the other end of the spectrum from Epstein stands the *Statement of Progressive Property* and the school of thought out of which it arises.[39] Though expressions of the progressive view differ in some respects, progressive accounts share two foundational claims: (1) that owners are subject in justice to affirmative distributive obligations and (2) that those obligations are properly specified by political authorities – bodies of collective decision-making – so that property is what is left over after the state has finished distributing rights and duties (for now). Some iterations of the view find distributive obligations in the police powers.[40] Some would view those obligations as property norms.[41] Some ground the relevant norms in fairness, others in a collective good. On all of these accounts, the rights and duties of property are products of, or accommodations reached through, political decision-making.

[38] Jeremy Paul, "The Hidden Structure of Takings Law" (1991) 64 *Southern California Law Review* 1393 at 1406.

[39] Gregory S. Alexander, Eduardo M. Peñalver, Joseph William Singer, and Laura S. Underkuffler, "A Statement of Progressive Property" (2009) 94 *Cornell Law Review* 743.

[40] Gregory S. Alexander, "Takings, Narratives, and Power" (1988) 88 *Columbia Law Review* 1752 at 1753. Compare Hanoch Dagan, "Takings and Distributive Justice" (1999) 85 *Virginia Law Review* 741.

[41] Gregory S. Alexander, "The Social-Obligation Norm in American Property Law" (2009) 94 *Cornell Law Review* 745; Eduardo M. Peñalver, "Land Virtues" (2009) 94 *Cornell Law Review* 821.

This view of property owes much to Frank Michelman. In an influential article, he insisted that it is "a mistake to see property . . . as something categorically apart from . . . political action."[42] He articulated the view that private property rights are "determined by existing conditions of economic resource employment within [the owner's] social universe – call it society, community, state."[43] Michelman used those last three terms interchangeably. In this account, the rights and correlating duties that comprise property norms are determined by political authorities as matters of positive law.

For Michelman, one principle guides and constrains the state's power to specify rights and duties: fairness.[44] The alternative to "collective action" is, in Michelman's account, the operation of the "market-expressed preferences" of individual owners, and the chief rival to fairness is efficiency.[45] Michelman's influential account thus made no room for incommensurable goods, for irreducible requirements of practical reasonableness, or for the intermediary institutions and institutions of private ordering that shape and justify property rights while mediating between the individual and the state.

This approach creates a problem for public law if the domain of property ownership is to receive constitutional protection. Jeremy Paul has called this the "problem of positivism." As Paul framed it, "[H]ow can government simultaneously be responsible for establishing the property rights of the citizenry and also be entrusted not to render its constituents helpless when conditions dictate defining property rights so as to benefit public officialdom?"[46] That is the positivism problem's political component. It has a jurisprudential component, too. Property can impose no duties on the state unless it has a determinate meaning for, and binding authority on, the state's deliberations and actions. If the state is the source of rights and duties then property cannot do that work.

The positivism problem is not peculiar to contemporary progressives. Any account of property that holds that property emanates from the state will raise this difficulty, as did the work of Felix Cohen and other legal realists.[47] Entailed in Cohen's view, Henry Smith points out, is that "the

[42] Frank I. Michelman, "Property as a Constitutional Right" (1981) 38 *Washington & Lee Law Review* 1097 at 1112.

[43] Frank I. Michelman, "Property, Utility, and Fairness: Comments on the Ethical Foundations of Just Compensation Law" (1967) 80 *Harvard Law Review* 1165 at 1167.

[44] Michelman, "Utility and Fairness," 1171–72.

[45] Michelman, "Utility and Fairness," 1172–83.

[46] Paul, "Hidden Structure," 1411.

[47] Felix S. Cohen, "Dialogue on Private Property" (1954) 9 *Rutgers Law Review* 357.

state could always withdraw or alter its endorsement of an owner's decisional power."[48] Nor is the problem peculiar to American lawyers. Leading authorities on property in the United Kingdom rather casually take property to owe its existence to the state, as where the editors of Megarry and Wade locate the origins of property law in "judge-made rules" and statutes.[49] This is not true to the common law ideal, in which "judges are to discover law rather than create it, and particularly to discover it in the customs of the people, especially as expressed in case precedents."[50]

The positivist view is expressed in striking fashion in Gray and Gray's *Elements of Land Law*, where private ownership is such a tenuous concept that possessory terms are placed within quotation marks. In a passage contrasting the "modern view" of property against the "historic view" of "property absolutism," they describe property as "a socially derived privilege of use": "'Property' in land means no more and no less than what the state actually permits an individual to do with 'his' or 'her' land." Property is therefore only forms of use, which the state permits people to exercise "and which can be varied or withdrawn at the sole discretion of, and on terms dictated by, the state." Rights and duties settled by private action can be completely defeased "where they cease to serve the public interest."[51]

Yet, progressive accounts also create a separate, even more fundamental problem than the problem of positivism. Because basic human goods and the basic requirements of practical reasonableness are incommensurable, a conceptual incoherence sits at the heart of any theory that would ground affirmative distributive obligations in a single requirement of reason, such as fairness, or in a collective good. To claim that general norms of charity and equality require uniform, state-specified, and affirmative obligations is to go beyond what reason can accomplish. And without leaving to owners the discretion of deliberating on the personal and contextual considerations that must guide any decision to distribute or reallocate entitlements, it is to threaten the possibility of practical

48 Henry E. Smith, "Emergent Property" in James Penner and Henry E. Smith (eds.), *Philosophical Foundations of Property Law* (New York: Oxford University Press 2013), 327.

49 Charles Harpum, Stuart Bridge, and Martin Dixon, *Megarry & Wade: The Law of Real Property* (London: Sweet & Maxwell 2012), 8.

50 David VanDrunen, "Natural Law, Custom, and Common Law in the Theology of Aquinas and Calvin" (2000) 33 *University of British Columbia Law Review* 699.

51 Kevin Gray and Susan Francis Gray, *Elements of Land Law* (5th edn, Oxford: Oxford University Press 2009), 109–12 & 112 n 2.

reasonableness as a guide for promoting the common good with material resources.

Fairness is a necessary, but not a sufficient, guide to direct distributive choice and action. Because the "all-round flourishing of human beings in community is indefinitely many-sided," John Finnis has observed that no one, universally applicable criterion can resolve questions of just distribution.[52] Specifying duties of just distribution and provision requires one to "assess what practical reasonableness *requires* of particular people (in their dealings with other people)."

> And what is thus required of particular persons depends essentially on what responsibilities they respectively have, whether by virtue of voluntary commitments (eg assumption of rulership) or by virtue of past or present receipt of benefits from another (eg as children, in relation to their respective parents), or by virtue of the dependence of others upon them (eg as parents, in relation to their own children), or by virtue of a network of relationships of actual and potential interdependencies.[53]

Claims to assistance arise out of human relationships. Each of one's duties to one's wife, neighbor, children, fellow worshipper, and so on correlates with a *personal* right. Right and duty correlate exactly because they arise on opposite sides of the same relationship, and their contours are specified by the nature of that relationship. One owes to one's children, in addition to love, the material benefits they need to grow and flourish. They have a right to receive those benefits. They have those rights, and their parents have the correlative duties, because they are their parents' children. One does not owe the same duties to anyone other than one's children because every other relationship one has is different than the relationship with one's children.

Abstract duties of fair distribution do not conform to the contextual nuances of human relationships. In theory, political authorities could assign to each adult a number of dependents. That duty might be analogous to the duty of support that one naturally owes to one's children. But the specification of that duty would be arbitrary, and more than a little creepy. So perhaps it is no surprise that many legal "rights" to consume and use resources are stated in the abstract, with no correlative duty assigned to anyone in particular.

52 John Finnis, *Natural Law and Natural Rights* (2nd edn, Oxford: Oxford University Press 2011) [hereinafter NLNR], 174.

53 NLNR, 175.

Cooperative human practices and institutions of private ordering are able to take into account all of the requirements of practical reasonableness, and their countless possible contextual applications, in ways that political authorities cannot. The myriad and complex human obligations out of which rights and duties of provision arise, and the complex, irreducible demands that practical reason makes on persons in those relationships, are best considered and specified within context, not by a uniform rule.

Also, by defining property norms as affirmative *obligations* of altruism, the progressive proposals make it impossible for owners to take admirable reasons into their deliberations, and thus into their character. A legal obligation, backed by coercion, supplants the pre-moral and moral reasons for action in the agent's deliberations. The agent no longer acts for the well-being of another human being but rather in order to avoid the coercive action of the state.

An equally acute problem arises on the Progressive Statement account, in which distributive obligations are justified on the basis of an authoritative calculation of the greatest good for the greatest number, i.e., the collective good. In this account, the owner's duties run to the collective whole.[54] Gregory Alexander argues for "a constitutional norm predicated on the idea that private ownership entails obligations to act (or refrain from acting) for the purpose of promoting the collective good of the community."[55] Peñalver has stated that collective decision-making should be understood to override the decisions of private owners where it "is likely to yield better (that is, more morally correct) decisions about how the land ought to be used."[56] And many progressive accounts invoke the "average reciprocity of advantage" that all owners supposedly realize when the state regulates property, such that no owner has grounds for complaint when a positive law deprives her of assets or uses because she receives in-kind compensation from the collective benefits of the regulatory scheme taken as a whole.[57]

[54] Michelman adumbrated this approach with his appeal to the "sum total of goods" produced by the exercise of property rights. Michelman, "Utility and Fairness," 1167.

[55] Alexander, "Social Obligation Norm," 757. [56] Peñalver, "Land Virtues," 849, 870.

[57] For a robustly statist expression of this view, see Gray and Gray, *Elements*, 1398. The quoted phrase is from *Pennsylvania Coal Co.* v. *Mahon*, 260 U.S. 393 at 415 (1922), but in that case the Supreme Court vindicated the property rights at stake, which were settled and specified by institutions of private ordering, and required the state to pay compensation.

In order for these claims to be coherent, there must be some collective good to provide a unitary standard of moral good. But there is none. Because basic human goods are not commensurable with each other, most plans of action and states of affairs cannot be measured against each other on a common scale. So, for example, Brian Angelo Lee has demonstrated that average reciprocity of advantage is realized only in the very rare circumstance where a posited law solves a coordination problem between two owners whose uses are identical or commensurable in a common currency.[58] Because owners often make radically different uses based on different and incommensurable plans of action, those conditions will seldom obtain.

Nor are health, safety, morals, public order, the general welfare, and the other grounds for the police powers reducible to a single, ideal state of affairs.[59] As Philippa Foot put it, "there is simply a blank where consequentialists see 'the best state of affairs.'"[60] There are better and worse *states* of affairs, in a plural sense, because people can succeed in achieving their good goals or fail to do so (and can succeed or fail in pursuit of evil goals). But there is no univocal meaning of good, and therefore no single state of affairs in which all of the good of all other possible states of affairs is realized, plus something more. Injunctions to choose the state of affairs that will yield the greatest collective good are "not so much false as senseless."[61] To posit an aggregate collective good, or general utility, as the justification for specifying rights and duties is to speak of a nothing. Any rights or duties specified on such grounds are not grounded in reasons but only in the will of the lawmaker.

The Progressive Statement itself affirms that human goods are plural and incommensurable.[62] One Progressive Statement author, Eduardo Peñalver, quotes with approbation John Finnis' illustration of incommensurability, that the "injunction to maximize net good is senseless, in the way that it is senseless to try to sum up the quantity of the size of this page, the quantity of the number six, and the quantity of the mass of this book."[63]

[58] Brian Angelo Lee, "Average Reciprocity of Advantage" in James Penner and Henry E. Smith (eds.), *Philosophical Foundations of Property Law* (New York: Oxford University Press 2013), 99–127.

[59] Lee, "Average Reciprocity," 215–18.

[60] Philippa Foot, *Moral Dilemmas: and Other Topics in Moral Philosophy* (Oxford: Oxford University Press 2002), 76–77.

[61] NLNR, 112. [62] Alexander et al., "Progressive Statement," 743.

[63] Peñalver, "Land Virtues," 858, quoting NLNR, 113.

It is, as Peñalver rightly affirms, senseless to try to sum up the goods that property serves within a society on any collective scale. Joseph Raz has articulated the test of incommensurability as a failure of transitivity. "Two valuable options are incommensurable if (1) neither is better than the other, and (2) there is (or could be) another option which is better than one but is not better than the other."[64] Neither of the first two options is better than the other, but they are not of equal value. Any attempt to calculate their relative values is pointless. Because ultimate ends are incommensurable, there is no collective good of the community, no collective values, no more or less morally correct decisions about which aspects of human flourishing to pursue for the political community as a whole. Incommensurability renders any such calculation impossible. Peñalver et al. fruitfully use the incommensurability thesis to expose the blind spots of economic accounts of private property. But the same implications undermine their own project. Any attempt to reduce all values to one scale must necessarily result in the frustration of many admirable and charitable plans of action.

The problem inheres not in the particular criterion that progressives have selected but rather in the selection of a criterion and the promulgation of a rule, an exclusionary reason for action. The arbitrariness (Michelman) and incoherence (Alexander and Peñalver) of theories that suppose the state to be the source of property norms are not functions of the particular requirement (fairness) or value (collective good) chosen to specify those norms. They are rather costs of the necessary choice of *a* requirement or value at the expense of others equally basic. And this problem is unavoidable for such theories.

There are, of course, occasions when the state must choose and promulgate an exclusionary reason for action, as where it must in justice codify moral absolutes and other categorical norms (e.g., against slavery and theft) because the prohibited actions are *never* or almost never reasonable options. And there are a few instances where the right norm can be calculated from commensurable options, as where state action secures reciprocity of advantage. Otherwise, the choice of a norm is under- or un-determined. There are also cases where the state should choose a norm in order to coordinate actions, especially where such coordination will disrupt no vested rights or duties already settled and specified (e.g., the selection of a speed limit or initial zoning of an

[64] Joseph Raz, *The Morality of Freedom* (Oxford: Oxford University Press 1986) [hereinafter MOF], 325.

undeveloped town). That choice might (or might not) have a rational basis, but it cannot be said to be morally required.

So it is no answer that variations of the realist and progressive accounts use different terms to describe the norms on which redistributive obligations are supposed to be based: social responsibility, social values, social obligation, civic virtue, and even practical reason.[65] In all of these accounts, the norms are identified, articulated, and enforced through political action, which leaves domains of private ordering at the mercy of zero-sum political contests and their resultant rules, which are morally undetermined.

Private ordering: specifying rights for the common good

Communal and individual self-constitution accrues to the benefit of the political community. The state has a strong interest in the development of practically reasonable citizens. Private property law lays a foundation for public law not only by establishing baseline expectations for commercial and legislative action, but also by securing the conditions within which citizens exercise civic virtues, and in particular learn to deliberate together, to share reasons for action and to become habituated to pursuing a common and pluralistic good.

Communal self-constitution by specification

Property rights must be specified. The common law maxim that one must use one's property so as not to interfere unreasonably with another's use and enjoyment is open-ended. It must be given specific content to solve real problems. Someone must do the work of settling what uses are legally permissible within the various contexts in which disputes might arise. Viewed one way, this is a problem; viewed another way, it is an opportunity. The open-endedness of usufructs (and, to a lesser extent, rights of exclusion, gift, and alienability) give communities opportunities to constitute themselves in commitment to reasons. Use rights take shape on a case-by-case basis and are settled as legally enforceable rights within the context of lived relations among human beings. This specification and settling is done primarily by institutions of private ordering and

[65] Compare Alexander, "Social Obligation Norm"; Peñalver, "Land Virtues"; Dagan, "Distributive Justice"; and Frank Michelman, "Takings, 1987" (1988) 88 *Columbia Law Review* 1600 at 1629.

secondarily through legislative bodies. As the authorities of private law settle the boundaries of use rights, they constitute their communities both in material ways and in the moral sense seen in earlier chapters.

Use rights emerge first from plans of action grounded in basic reasons, then from uses for those reasons, and finally from the judgments of communities and institutions of private ordering about what uses are unreasonable. The general requirement that a life estate holder must not commit waste is given specific shape as a prohibition against cutting down *that* tree by the condition of the land at the commencement of the estate, the life tenant's intentions and plans, local customs and past practices of others who own estates and interests in the land, any express terms that are lawfully imposed on the tenancy, and the vetoes of future interest holders.

The impatience of politicians (and lawyers)

The expansion of the police powers in the United States throughout the last century, and the growing incoherence of regulatory takings law, was made possible in part because courts lost sight of the primary role of private ordering. As the Supreme Court made express in *Mugler* v. *Kansas*[66] and *Miller* v. *Schoene*,[67] but allowed to drop from view in *Village of Euclid* v. *Ambler Realty Co.*,[68] the justification for the police powers is grounded in a real and substantial relation to the prevention of harm, not the creation of a single best state of affairs (a goal that, as we have seen, is incoherent because no such state of affairs exists). Furthermore, the state retains obligations to those on whom it acts and those on whose behalf it acts. Owners remain owners of their own things and moral agents with a capacity to exercise practical reason, even as they are also non-owners of other peoples' things.

Just as private property law must be attuned to all of the demands of practical reasonableness when it specifies the rights of ownership, so must political actors. Positive law has sometimes drawn the boundaries badly wrong, as when common law states and nations enacted laws to create rights of slavery, and the radical response of public law to that injustice – the Slavery Abolition Act 1833 in Great Britain, the Thirteenth and Fourteenth Amendments in the United States – was not merely justifiable but required by the common law maxim that nothing that is

[66] *Mugler* v. *Kansas*, 123 US 623 (1887). [67] *Miller* v. *Schoene*, 276 US 272 (1928).
[68] *Village of Euclid* v. *Ambler Realty Co.*, 272 US 365 (1926).

contrary to reason is lawful. No matter how essential a slave might be to the slaveowner's plan of action, and no matter how admirable that plan might otherwise be, it is simply unreasonable to consider another human being as an object of ownership. This conclusion is entailed in a moral absolute, which necessarily follows from the kind of being a human being is, and therefore gives rise to an absolute, two-term duty – one must never enslave ... anyone – in reason.

Slavery was for a long time unknown at common law, and its rise in positive law derogated common law rights and duties.[69] The story of slavery is a story of lawmakers first departing from, then returning to, common law norms. That Section 4 of the Fourteenth Amendment prohibits debts and takings claims for the emancipation of slaves is consistent with the idea that slaves were never really property, and that it was a mistake of both morality *and law* to treat them as property.

The distance of legislators from the applications of property norms, which made them especially incompetent to adjudicate the question of slavery, prevents them from discerning other types of distinctions. Private law's ordering of these distinctions should be disturbed with caution.[70] The norms of property should be specified by those who are familiar with the facts on the ground. The special powers of political authorities are justified in their responsibility to preserve civic order and the other preconditions that are necessary for individuals and communities to bring about good states of affairs. Put differently, the state exists primarily to act on behalf of those whose harm is not prevented by private ordering and to coordinate those necessary actions that institutions of private ordering cannot perform without direction. Yet ex ante regulation is a second-best means of ordering the political community. Private law has its own mechanisms for producing and preserving order.[71]

Regulation does its best work by suppressing disorder.[72] It often does more harm when it tries to create order. A century of experience with nearly unfettered land-use regulation should be sufficient to establish

[69] James R. Stoner, *Common-Law Liberty: Rethinking American Constitutionalism* (Lawrence: University Press of Kansas 2003), 130–31; *Prigg* v. *Pennsylvania*, 41 US 539 (1842).

[70] So, for example, the common law disfavors, and requires strict construction of, any novel restraints that legislatures place on rights of exclusion, use, and alienability. *Phillips* v. *Pembroke Real Estate, Inc.*, 819 NE 2d 579 (Mass 2004).

[71] Robert C. Ellickson, "Alternatives to Zoning: Covenants, Nuisance Rules, and Fines as Land Use Controls" (1973) 40 *University of Chicago Law Review* 681.

[72] Nicole Stelle Garnett, *Ordering the City: Land Use, Policing, and the Restoration of Urban America* (New Haven: Yale University Press 2010), 28.

that legislators are anything but superior sources of practical judgment about ordering the community. Zoning and central planning might well be justifiable as a coordinating device when regulators are writing on a clean slate, before a municipality has been developed. That was the situation in *Village of Euclid*. But central planning appears much less justifiable once land uses have taken shape. Having had zoning codes in place for many decades, today's land-use planners frequently make exceptions, amendments, and exemptions in particular cases, and they enter into bilateral agreements with private developers, often with little or no advance public input.[73] Not surprisingly, these practices give rise to widespread corruption and arbitrary decision-making. Sometimes land-use regulators engage in outright discrimination.[74]

The police powers need not conflict with property. As described by Blackstone, the police powers were exercised to prohibit common nuisances, those "being either the doing of a thing to the annoyance of the king's subjects, or the neglecting to do a thing which the common good requires."[75] Because an owner of property has no right at common law to commit a nuisance, an exercise of the police powers to prohibit a nuisance does not deprive anyone of property rights. Though avoiding conflicts of rights was advanced as the primary justification for the police power into the nineteenth century,[76] it was not always exercised to secure vested rights. Clear rules were not always available. Where they were lacking and needed in order to coordinate civic conduct, a state enjoyed the power to clarify the boundaries of common law rights and duties and to promulgate protections for them.[77] James Stoner thus understands the police power as one that "perfects the common law or adjusts it to the

[73] Daniel P. Selmi, "The Contract Transformation in Land Use Regulation" (2011) 63 *Stanford Law Review* 591 at 594, 600–01.

[74] These problems are now well documented. See, e.g., *Carruth* v. *Madera*, 233 Cal App 2d 688 at 695–96 (1965); David Callies and Julie Tappendorf, "Unconstitutional Land Development Conditions and the Development Agreement Solution: Bargaining for Public Facilities After Nollan and Dolan" (2001) 51 *Case Western Reserve Law Review* 663 at 664; Alejandro Camacho, "Mustering the Missing Voices: A Collaborative Model for Fostering Equality, Community Involvement and Adaptive Planning in Land Use Decisions Installment One" (2005) 24 *Stanford Environmental Law Journal* 3; Patricia E. Salkin, "Ethical Considerations in Land Use Decision Making: 2006 Annual Review of Cases and Opinions" (2006) 38 *Urban Lawyer* 669 at 683; Daniel R. Mandelker and A. Dan Tarlock, "Shifting the Presumption of Constitutionality in Land-Use Law" (1992) 24 *Urban Lawyer* 1 at 2, 5–6.

[75] William Blackstone, *Commentaries on the Laws of England* (1769), vol. 4, 167.

[76] Stoner, *Common-Law Liberty*, 127–31.

[77] See *Commonwealth* v. *Alger*, 61 Mass 53 at 95–96 (1851).

circumstances of a modern commercial society, but it begins from common-law rights and duties."[78]

Since the police power has come unmoored from its common law foundation,[79] its exercise is justified not by reference to the ends of private law or civic order but only on the basis of legislative authority. In *Harbison* v. *City of Buffalo* and similar cases, the state action was not aimed at prohibiting unlawful use. To allow the landowner to assert her vested right against the government would "constitute an unwarranted restriction upon the Legislature" in its "effective administration" of land-use regulation.[80] The exercise of state power is self-justifying, without reference to the ends of private rights and duties, and can be used to eradicate vested property rights without due process and without just compensation.

Violations of the state's categorical duties have often been justified as necessary restraints on absolute property rights. But the Lockean, absolute right is a bogeyman, a result of mistaking two-term abstracts for fully specified and conclusive rights. The oversimplified conception of private property as an abstract right of exclusive use does a disservice to institutions of private ordering; it makes private rights seem far more unyielding and threatening than they really are. By ignoring the role of private law in producing and mediating between domains of private ownership, courts have made regulation pursuant to the police powers seem more necessary than it really is, portraying the police power as the only protector of public goods.

Consider the *Schoene* case. Schoene, the State Entomologist of Virginia, ordered the destruction of Miller's ornamental cedar trees under the authority of a state law enacted to protect nearby apple orchards from a disease that the cedar trees carried, which threatened destruction of the apple trees. The Supreme Court ruled that the law and its execution did not deprive Miller of property without due process of law.[81] To reach this holding, the Court assumed a conflict between absolute private rights, for which legislation was the only solution. It then untied the state's obligations from the common law, insisting that it was irrelevant whether the infected cedars constituted a nuisance at common law. "For where, as here, the choice is unavoidable, we cannot

78 Stoner, *Common-Law Liberty*, 129.

79 Stoner's discussion of the case law in this period is illuminating. Stoner, *Common-Law Liberty*, 133–45.

80 *Harbison* v. *City of Buffalo*, 152 NE 2d 42 (NY 1958).

81 *Schoene*, 276 US at 277–81.

say that its exercise, controlled by considerations of social policy which are not unreasonable, involves any denial of due process."[82]

The Court perceived a conflict that might not have existed; we'll never know whether Miller enjoyed a vested right to keep his cedar trees. This impatience was enabled by the Court's caricature of property as a two-term, abstract, and absolute right of Miller to keep diseased trees. On the basis of that error, the Court was able to portray the choice facing the state legislature as "a choice between the preservation of one class of property and that of the other wherever both existed in dangerous proximity."[83] Perhaps the legislature's impatience was justified by the exigencies of the circumstances. If so, the legislature's action should have been justified on that ground and compensation should have been paid. Or a defense of necessity should have been asserted, in which case no compensation was due. Because they do not interfere with any common law property rights, regulations that simply codify rights and duties that were previously settled by common law norms do not give rise to takings claims.[84]

Similarly, the *Village of Euclid* Court portrayed the police power in an overly broad way because it needlessly assumed that property rights were at stake. It would have been enough for the Court to note that Ambler Realty was bringing a facial challenge to a newly enacted zoning ordinance, and to reverse the judgment in Ambler Realty's favor on that ground alone, without engaging in an extended discourse about the vicissitudes of modern urban life and the police powers necessary to combat them. Ambler Realty had made no actual use of its land and had no specific plans for development when it filed its claim. Thus it was not possible to discern what Ambler Realty's use rights might turn out to be.

The problems that these cases created for constitutional law have proven intractable largely because the decisions were premised on false conceptions of what property is. The source of the difficulty for takings law is that legislators and regulators do not wait for property institutions to settle the respective rights and duties of owners and their neighbors. That does not entail that legislators *should* wait in all cases. There are often good reasons to regulate property use. But lawmakers should be clear about what they are doing.

82 *Schoene*, 276 US at 280. 83 *Schoene*, 276 US at 279.

84 *Lucas* v. *South Carolina Coastal Council*, 505 US 1003 at 1029–30 (1992); Epstein, *Takings*, 112–21; *Wilson* v. *First County Trust Ltd* [2004] 1 AC 816 at 854; Harpum et al., *Megarry & Wade*, 17–18.

The reasoned development of property rights

This does not mean that common law rights should be defined with reference to the state of the law at the close of the nineteenth century. The common law tradition is one of self-correction. Laws that prohibit racial discrimination in public accommodations codify the common law doctrine, which required reasonable access to premises opened to the public.[85] That the posited enactments required segregation during Jim Crow does not entail that those rules were reasonable or consistent with common law.

A common law institution of property need not fall into either indeterminacy or fossilized adherence to discredited biases, as Margaret Jane Radin has supposed.[86] It is not an abstract, pre-political right vindicated in principles of first appropriation. It is a domain of ownership mediated by standards of reasonableness. Well-formed judgments that employ those standards are grounded in immutable principles, but must remain open to the maturation of practical judgment and the correction of past mistakes in accordance with those principles. The common law mediates principles of practical reason in historical contexts through an organic process of private ordering and, where necessary, legislation. Where legislative bodies call the common law to reconcile itself to its own principles, they are acting on the same authority as that which they exercise when they codify established, common law doctrines.

Even the common law's failures reveal the reasoned principles on which it depends. The doctrine of coverture was unjust in large part because it excused married women from responsibility for their contracts and dispositions. All that was required to expose the injustice was to hold femme coverts to the consequences of their dealings, as the common law already required of unmarried women and of men.[87] The abolition of coverture was a correction that reconciled the common law tradition with itself. The case of slavery, which Radin supposes is problematic, is even easier. Slavery was abolished on the ground that it is inherently immoral and unjust, *and therefore always has been wrong*, to own another human being.

And what is the alternative? Radin addresses the positivism problem by positing the "progressive naturalist," who perceives a best conception

[85] See *Ferguson* v. *Gies*, 46 NW 718 (Mich 1890).

[86] Margaret Jane Radin, *Reinterpreting Property* (Chicago: University of Chicago Press 1993), 100–05.

[87] *Jones* v. *Taylor*, 7 Tex 240 (1851).

of property, which we have not yet attained. Radin supposes that the "history of changing property notions is describable as a history of rejecting bad parts of the institution and substituting better ones – a process that can continue indefinitely."[88] But among other problems, Radin's conception is betrayed by history. There is no reason to suppose that newer doctrines are always, or even generally, better than older ones, or that the progression of posited law is always one of improvement. Certainly, the progression from feudalism to slavery was not an improvement.[89] The history of law's development is one of deterioration alongside improvement. The challenge is to avoid chronological snobbery and to discern which of the recent innovations in law will turn out to be a mistake.

Law, morality, and social practice sometimes come apart in ways that reflect better on private citizens, local communities, and intermediary institutions than on public lawmakers and social engineers. Robert Ellickson's landmark study of ranchers and farmers in Shasta County, California, revealed a community that largely ignored posited legal rules and instead coordinated their actions on the basis of a conscious commitment to a general norm of "cooperation among neighbors." Ellickson reports that residents were governed by "the general obsession with neighborliness."[90] Ranchers whose animals caused harm to others' property considered themselves responsible for the damage even where the rules gave them immunity from liability. Yet trespass victims did not insist on compensation for their losses, even when they were legally entitled to it, and victims who invoked their formal, legal rights by demanding compensation or (worse) retaining a lawyer were treated as social deviants. And a rancher who found others' cattle in his own herd would often tend the cattle until they could be returned to their owners, almost always without seeking reimbursement of feeding expenses.

Ellickson offered economic explanations for these behaviors. The lumping of losses produced a reciprocal advantage; everyone saved the transaction costs of negotiation and litigation. Neighbors would prefer to

[88] Radin, *Reinterpreting Property*, 103.

[89] On the respective rights of freemen, villeins, and tenants of ancient demesne, see *Iveagh* v. *Martin* [1961] 1 QB 232 at 260–72.

[90] Robert C. Ellickson, "Of Coase and Cattle: Dispute Resolution among Neighbors in Shasta County" (1986) 38 *Stanford Law Review* 623 at 672, 677; Robert C. Ellickson, *Order Without Law: How Neighbors Settle Disputes* (Cambridge: Harvard University Press 1991), 48, 57. Ellickson's account accords with my own experience working as a farm hand in Maine as a boy and young man.

suffer a loss than incur a debt to someone in order to retain leverage over that person. And because knowledge of law is expensive to obtain, residents used informal, simple, moral norms instead. In short, residents used wealth-maximizing norms.

This seems a perfectly sound explanation from the external perspective of science, but Ellickson's economic interpretation does not fully account for the way that Shasta County residents regarded their own reasoning. From the internal perspective of the average resident, the primary reason to take responsibility even when one is not liable, or to refrain from seeking remedies to which the law entitles one, is to act like, and therefore to be, a virtuous person. What Ellickson terms the "puzzle of cooperation" is not mysterious to those who consider themselves obligated to treat other members of their community well. The residents whom Ellickson interviewed expressed their governing norms in terms of moral obligation, right and wrong, and moral esteem.[91]

It is no accident that such virtues are rooted in the customs of a local community, and in property ownership within that community. Promulgation of moral norms by action, for oneself and for one's community, changes one's nature in the order of the will. Participating in private property institutions gives one opportunities and incentives to become practically reasonable. Practical reasonableness is not the only reason to favor private property, but perhaps it is possible to gain material prosperity and one's soul, as well.[92]

[91] Ellickson, "Coase and Cattle," 673; Ellickson, *Order without Law*, 53.

[92] Mark 8:36: "For What shall it profit a man, if he shall gain the whole world, and lose his own soul?"

BIBLIOGRAPHY

Ackerman, Bruce A., *Private Property and the Constitution* (New Haven: Yale University Press 1977).

Alexander, Gregory S., "The Social-Obligation Norm in American Property Law" (2009) 94 *Cornell Law Review* 745.

"Property's Ends: The Publicness of Private Law Values" (2014) 99 *Iowa Law Review* 1257.

"Takings, Narratives, and Power" (1988) 88 *Columbia Law Review* 1752.

Alexander, Gregory S., Peñalver, Eduardo M., Singer, Joseph William, and Underkuffler, Laura S., "A Statement of Progressive Property" (2009) 94 *Cornell Law Review* 743.

Alexander, Gregory S. and Peñalver, Eduardo M., "Properties of Community" (2009) 10 *Theoretical Inquiries in Law* 127.

"Introduction" in *Property and Community* (New York: Oxford University Press 2010) 1.

Alkire, Sabina, "The Basic Dimensions of Human Flourishing: A Comparison of Accounts" in Nigel Biggar and Rufus Black (eds.), *The Revival of Natural Law: Philosophical, Theological and Ethical Responses to the Finnis-Grisez School* (Burlington: Ashgate 2000).

Allen, Thomas, *Right to Property in Commonwealth Constitutions* (New York: Cambridge University Press 2000).

Amar, Akhil Reed, "Forty Acres and a Mule: A Republican Theory of Minimal Entitlements" (1990) 13 *Harvard Journal of Law & Public Policy* 37.

Andreoni, James, "Impure Altruism and Donations to Public Goods: A Theory of Warm-Glow Giving" (1990) 100 *Economic Journal* 464.

Aquinas, Thomas, *Commentary on Aristotle's Nicomachean Ethics*, C. J. Litzinger (trans.) (Notre Dame: Dumb Ox 1993).

Aristotle, *The Politics*.

Nicomachean Ethics.

Austin, Lisa, "Possession and the Distractions of Philosophy" in James Penner and Henry E. Smith (eds.), *Philosophical Foundations of Property Law* (New York: Oxford University Press 2013), 182.

Balotti, R. Franklin and Hanks, Jr., James J., "Giving at the Office: A Reappraisal of Charitable Contributions by Corporations" (1999) 54 *Business Lawyer* 965.

Barnett, Randy E., "A Law Professor's Guide to Natural Law and Natural Rights" (1997) 20 *Harvard Journal of Law & Public Policy* 655.

Barros, D. Benjamin, "Home as a Legal Concept" (2006) 46 *Santa Clara Law Review 255.*

"Property and Freedom" (2009) 4 *NYU Journal of Law & Liberty* 36.

Berger, Peter L. and Neuhaus, Richard John, *To Empower People: From State to Civil Society* (2nd edn, Washington, DC: AEI Press 1996).

Berry, Wendell, *The Gift of Good Land* (San Francisco: North Point Press 1981).

Bigelow, Melville M., *Papers on the Legal History of Government* (Boston: Little, Brown & Co. 1920).

Blackstone, William, *Commentaries on the Laws of England* (1769).

Blumenthal, J. A., "To Be Human: A Psychological Perspective on Property Law" (2009) 83 *Tulane Law Review* 609.

Boyle, Joseph M., "Toward Understanding the Principle of Double Effect" (1980) 90 *Ethics* 527.

Bratman, Michael E., *Faces of Intention* (Cambridge: Cambridge University Press 1999).

Bridge, M. G., *Personal Property Law* (Oxford: Oxford University Press 2002).

Bridge, Michael et al., *The Law of Personal Property* (London: Sweet & Maxwell 2013).

Brooks, Arthur C., *The Road to Freedom* (New York: Basic Books 2012).

Brudner, Alan, "Private Property and Public Welfare" in James Penner and Henry E. Smith (eds.), *Philosophical Foundations of Property Law* (New York: Oxford University Press 2013).

Buckle, Stephen, *Natural Law and the Theory of Property* (Oxford: Clarendon Press 1991).

Byers, Michael, "Abuse of Rights: An Old Principle, a New Age" (2002) 47 *McGill Law Journal* 389.

Calabresi, Guido and Melamed, A. Douglas, "Property Rules, Liability Rules, and Inalienability: One View of the Cathedral" (1972) 85 *Harvard Law Review* 1089.

Callies, David and Tappendorf, Julie, "Unconstitutional Land Development Conditions and the Development Agreement Solution: Bargaining for Public Facilities after Nollan and Dolan" (2001) 51 *Case Western Reserve Law Review* 663.

Camacho, Alejandro, "Mustering the Missing Voices: A Collaborative Model for Fostering Equality, Community Involvement and Adaptive Planning in Land Use Decisions Installment One" (2005) 24 *Stanford Environmental Law Journal* 3.

Carrese, Paul O., *The Cloaking of Power: Montesquieu, Blackstone, and the Rise of Judicial Activism* (Chicago: University of Chicago Press 2003).

"Common Law" in Mark Bevir (ed.), *Encyclopedia of Political Theory* (Thousand Oaks: Sage 2010).

Chused, Richard H., "Married Women's Property Law: 1800–1850" (1983) 71 *Georgetown Law Journal* 1359.

Claeys, Eric R., "Property 101: Is Property a Thing or a Bundle?" (2009) 32 *Seattle University Law Review* 617.

"Virtue and Rights in American Property Law" (2009) 94 *Cornell Law Review* 889.

"Bundle-of-Sticks Notions in Legal and Economic Scholarship" (2011) 8 *Econ Journal Watch* 205.

"Productive Use in Acquisition, Accession, and Labor Theory" in James Penner and Henry E. Smith (eds.), *Philosophical Foundations of Property Law* (New York: Oxford University Press 2013), 13.

Coase, Ronald H., "The Problem of Social Cost" (1960) 3 *Journal of Law & Economics* 1.

Cohen, Felix S., "Dialogue on Private Property" (1954) 9 *Rutgers Law Review* 357.

Cohen, Morris R., "Property and Sovereignty" (1928) 13 *Cornell Law Quarterly* 8.

Dagan, Hanoch, "Takings and Distributive Justice" (1999) 85 *Virginia Law Review* 741.

"The Social Responsibility of Ownership" (2007) 92 *Cornell Law Review* 1255.

Property: Values and Institutions (Oxford: Oxford University Press 2011).

"Pluralism and Perfectionism in Private Law" (2012) 112 *Columbia Law Review* 1409.

"The Public Dimension of Private Property" (2013) 24 *King's Law Journal* 260.

Demsetz, Harold, "Toward a Theory of Property Rights" in Robert C. Ellickson, Carol M. Rose, and Bruce A. Ackerman (eds.), *Perspectives on Property Law* (3rd edn, New York: Aspen 2002), 135.

Dennison, Mark S., "Bailee's Liability for Damage, Loss, or Theft of Bailed Property" in 46 *American Jurisprudence Proof of Facts 3d* (New York: West 1998), 361.

Donohue, Kevin F., "Crossroads in Hospital Conversions – A Survey of Nonprofit Hospital Conversion Legislation" (1999) 8 *Annals Health Law* 39.

Douglas, Simon and McFarlane, Ben, "Defining Property Rights" in James Penner and Henry E. Smith (eds.), *Philosophical Foundations of Property Law* (New York: Oxford University Press 2013).

Dukeminier, Jesse et al., *Property* (6th edn, New York: Aspen 2006).

Dworkin, Ronald, *Taking Rights Seriously* (Cambridge: Harvard University Press 1978).

Life's Dominion: An Argument about Abortion, Euthanasia, and Individual Freedom (New York: Knopf 1993).

Justice for Hedgehogs (Cambridge: Harvard University Press 2011).

Ekins, Richard, *The Nature of Legislative Intent* (Oxford: Oxford University Press 2012).

Ellickson, Robert C., "Alternatives to Zoning: Covenants, Nuisance Rules, and Fines as Land Use Controls" (1973) 40 *University of Chicago Law Review* 681.

"Of Coase and Cattle: Dispute Resolution among Neighbors in Shasta County" (1986) 38 *Stanford Law Review* 623.

Order without Law: How Neighbors Settle Disputes (Cambridge: Harvard University Press 1991).

"Property in Land" (1993) 102 *Yale Law Journal* 1315.

Epstein, Richard A., *Takings: Private Property and the Power of Eminent Domain* (Cambridge: Harvard University Press 1985).

"Causation – In Context: An Afterword" (1987) 63 *Chicago Kent Law Review* 653.

Design for Liberty (Cambridge: Harvard University Press 2011).

"Bundle-of-Rights Theory as a Bulwark against Statist Conceptions of Private Property" (2011) 8 *Econ Journal Watch* 223.

Feinberg, Joel, "Voluntary Euthanasia and the Inalienable Right to Life" (1978) 7 *Philosophy & Public Affairs* 93.

Finnis, John, *Natural Law and Natural Rights* (2nd edn, Oxford: Oxford University Press 2011).

Moral Absolutes: Tradition, Revision, and Truth (Washington, DC: Catholic University Press 1991).

"Equality and Differences" (2011) 56 *American Journal of Jurisprudence* 17.

Collected Essays of John Finnis, vol. I: Reason in Action (Oxford: Oxford University Press 2012).

Collected Essays of John Finnis, vol. II: Intention & Identity (Oxford: Oxford University Press 2012).

Collected Essays of John Finnis, vol. III: Human Rights & The Common Good (Oxford: Oxford University Press 2012).

Collected Essays of John Finnis, vol. IV: Philosophy of Law (Oxford: Oxford University Press 2012).

Foot, Philippa, *Moral Dilemmas: and Other Topics in Moral Philosophy* (Oxford: Oxford University Press 2002).

Friedman, Milton, *Capitalism and Freedom* (Chicago: University of Chicago Press 2002).

Galle, Brian, "Keep Charity Charitable" (2010) 88 *Texas Law Review* 1213.

Galston, William A., "On the Alleged Right to Do Wrong: A Response to Waldron" (1983) 93 *Ethics* 320.

Garnett, Nicole Stelle, *Ordering the City: Land Use, Policing, and the Restoration of Urban America* (New Haven: Yale University Press 2010).

Garnett, Richard W., "The Story of Henry Adams' Soul: Education and the Expression of Associations" (2001) 85 *Minnesota Law Review* 1841.

George, Robert P., *Making Men Moral: Civil Liberties and Public Morality* (New York: Oxford University Press 1993).

In Defense of Natural Law (New York: Oxford University Press 1999).

"The Common Good: Instrumental but Not Just Contractual" (May 17, 2013) *Public Discourse*.

Gergen, Mark P., Golden, John M., and Smith, Henry E., "The Supreme Court's Accidental Revolution? The Test for Permanent Injunctions" (2012) 112 *Columbia Law Review* 203.

Getzler, Joshua, *A History of Water Rights at Common Law* (Oxford: Oxford University Press 2004).

"Plural Ownership, Funds, and the Aggregation of Wills" (2009) 10 *Theoretical Inquiries in Law* 241.

Ginson, George D., "Corporate Contributions to Charity and Enabling Legislation" (1959) 14 *Business Lawyer* 434.

Glazer, Amihai and Konrad, Kai A., "A Signalling Explanation for Charity" (1996) 86 *American Economic Review* 1019.

Glendon, Mary Ann, *The New Family and the New Property* (Toronto: Butterworths 1981).

Gray, John Chipman, *The Rule against Perpetuities* (3rd edn, Boston: Little, Brown, and Company 1915).

Gray, Kevin and Gray, Susan Francis, *Elements of Land Law* (5th edn, Oxford: Oxford University Press 2009).

Green, Thomas Hill, "The Right of the State in Regard to Property" in MacPherson (ed.), *Property: Mainstream and Critical Positions* (Toronto: University of Toronto Press 1978), 103.

Grisez, Germain, "The First Principle of Practical Reason" in Kenny Anthony (ed.), *Aquinas: A Collection of Critical Essays* (Notre Dame: University of Notre Dame Press 1969).

"Toward a Consistent Natural-Law Ethics of Killing" (1970) 15 *American Journal of Jurisprudence* 64.

Gutteridge, H. C., "Abuse of Rights" (1933) 5 *Cambridge Law Journal* 22.

Harpum, Charles et al., *Megarry & Wade: The Law of Real Property* (London: Sweet & Maxwell 2012).

Hart, H. L. A., *The Concept of Law* (3rd edn, Oxford: Clarendon Press 2012).

Hart, Jr., Henry M., and Sacks, Albert M., *The Legal Process: Basic Problems in the Making and Application of Law* (Westbury, NY: Foundation Press 1994).

Harris, J. W., *Property and Justice* (Oxford: Oxford University Press 1996).

Hayek, F. A., *The Constitution of Liberty* (Chicago: University of Chicago Press 1960).

Himmelfarb, Gertrude, "Welfare as a Moral Problem" (1996) 19 *Harvard Journal of Law & Public Policy* 685.

Helmholz, R. H., "Bailment Theories and the Liability of Bailees: The Elusive Uniform Standard of Reasonable Care" (1992) 41 *University of Kansas Law Review* 97.

Hogue, Arthur R., *Origins of the Common Law* (Bloomington: Indiana University Press 1966).

Hohfeld, Wesley Newcomb, *Fundamental Legal Conceptions as Applied in Judicial Reasoning* (New Haven: Yale University Press 1919).

Holmes, Jr., Oliver W., "The Path of the Law" (1897) 10 *Harvard Law Review* 457.

Honoré, Tony, *Making Law Bind* (Oxford: Oxford University Press 1987).

Johnson, Paul, *Modern Times: The World from the Twenties to the Nineties* (New York: HarperCollins 1992).

Jones, Jeffrey Douglas, "Property and Personhood Revisited" (2011) 1 *Wake Forest Journal of Law & Public Policy* 93.

Kaplan, Benjamin, "Encounters with O.W. Holmes, Jr." (1983) 96 *Harvard Law Review* 1828.

Katz, Larissa, "Exclusion and Exclusivity in Property Law" (2008) 58 *University of Toronto Law Journal* 275.

"Spite and Extortion: A Principle of Abuse of (Property) Right" (2013) 122 *Yale Law Journal* 1444.

Kelly, Daniel B., "Strategic Spillovers" (2011) 111 *Columbia Law Review* 1641.

Kent, James, *Commentaries on American Law* (New York: Halsted 1827).

Klein, A. S., "Validity of Charitable Trust to Promote Change in Laws or Systems or Methods of Government" (2011) 22 *American Law Reports 3d* 886.

Klick, Jonathan and Sitkoff, Robert H., "Agency Costs, Charitable Trusts, and Corporate Control: Evidence from Hershey's Kiss-Off" (2008) 108 *Columbia Law Review* 749.

Korsgaard, Christine M., *The Constitution of Agency* (Oxford: Oxford University Press 2008).

Kraybill, Donald B., "Opting Out: How the Amish Have Survived in America" (March 7, 2014) 141(5) *Commonweal* 13.

Krier, James E. and Schwab, Stewart J., "Property Rules and Liability Rules: The Cathedral in Another Light" (1995) 70 *NYU Law Review* 440.

Kurtz, Sheldon F., *Moynihan's Introduction to the Law of Real Property* (5th edn, St. Paul: West 2011).

Lawson, F. H. and Rudden, Bernard, *The Law of Property* (Oxford: Clarendon Press 1982).

Lee, Brian Angelo, "Average Reciprocity of Advantage" in James Penner and Henry E. Smith (eds.), *Philosophical Foundations of Property Law* (New York: Oxford University Press 2013), 99.

Lee, Patrick and George, Robert P., *Body-Self Dualism in Contemporary Ethics and Politics* (New York: Cambridge University Press 2008).

Lehavi, Amnon, *The Construction of Property: Norms, Institutions, Challenges* (Cambridge: Cambridge University Press 2013).

Lewis, C. S., *The Abolition of Man* (San Francisco: Harper Collins 1944).

The Screwtape Letters (London: MacMillan 1962).

"Meditation in a Toolshed" in *God in the Dock* (Grand Rapids: Eerdmans Publishing 1970).

Loftin, Lisa, "Protecting the Charitable Investor: A Rationale for Donor Enforcement of Restricted Gifts" (1998) 8 *Boston University Public Interest Law Journal* 361.

Lundrigan, Robert A., "The Cy Pres Doctrine" (1955) 1 *Alberta Law Review* 598.

Lunney, Mark, "Trespass to Land" in Ken Oliphant (ed.), *The Law of Tort* (2nd edn, London: Butterworths 2007).

MacCormick, Neil, *Practical Reason in Law and Morality* (Oxford: Oxford University Press 2008).

MacLeod, Adam J., "The Mystery of Life in the Laboratory of Democracy: Personal Autonomy in State Law" (2012) 59 *Cleveland State Law Review* 589.

MacPherson, C. B., "The Meaning of Property" in MacPherson (ed.), *Property: Mainstream and Critical Positions* (Toronto: University of Toronto Press 1978), 1.

"Liberal Democracy and Property" in MacPherson (ed.), *Property: Mainstream and Critical Positions* (Toronto: University of Toronto Press 1978), 199.

Madison, James, Hamilton, Alexander, and Jay, John, *The Federalist Papers*, Rossiter (ed.) (New York: Penguin Putnam 1961).

Mandelker, Daniel R. and Tarlock, A. Dan, "Shifting the Presumption of Constitutionality in Land-Use Law" (1992) 24 *Urban Lawyer* 1.

Marx, Karl and Engels, Friedrich, *Manifesto of the Communist Party*, Engels (ed.) (Chicago: Kerr & Co. 1906).

Marzen, Thomas J. et al., "Suicide: A Constitutional Right?" (1985) 24 *Duquesne Law Review* 1.

Mechem, Philip, "The Requirement of Delivery in Gifts of Chattels and of Choses in Action Evidenced by Commercial Instruments" (1926) 21 *Illinois Law Review* 341.

Merrill, Thomas W., "Property and the Right to Exclude" (1998) 77 *Nebraska Law Review* 730.

"The Property Prism" (2011) 8 *Econ Journal Watch* 247.

Merrill, Thomas W. and Smith, Henry E., "Optimal Standardization in the Law of Property; The Numerus Clausus Principle" (2000) 110 *Yale Law Journal* 1.

"What Happened to Property in Law and Economics?" (2001) 111 *Yale Law Journal* 357.

"The Morality of Property" (2007) 48 *William & Mary Law Review* 1849.

The Oxford Introductions to U.S. Law: Property (New York: Oxford University Press 2010).

Property: Principles and Policies (2nd edn, St. Paul: Foundation Press 2012).

Michelman, Frank I., "Property, Utility, and Fairness: Comments on the Ethical Foundations of Just Compensation Law" (1967) 80 *Harvard Law Review* 1165.

"Property as a Constitutional Right" (1981) 38 *Washington & Lee Law Review* 1097.

"Takings, 1987" (1988) 88 *Columbia Law Review* 1600.

Mill, John Stuart, "Of Property" in MacPherson (ed.), *Property: Mainstream and Critical Positions* (Toronto: University of Toronto Press 1978).

Miller, Bradley W., "Justification and Rights Limitations" in Grant Huscroft (ed.), *Expounding the Constitution; Essays in Constitutional Theory* (New York: Cambridge University Press 2008).

"Proportionality's Blind Spot: 'Neutrality' and Political Philosophy" in G. Huscroft, B. W. Miller, and G. Webber (eds.), *Proportionality and the Rule of Law: Rights, Justification, Reasoning* (New York: Cambridge University Press 2014).

Minnow, Nell, "Corporate Charity: An Oxymoron?" (1999) 54 *Business Lawyer* 997.

Minor, John B., *Institutes of Common and Statute Law* (2nd edn, Richmond: Anderson Bros. 1895).

Moore, Michael S., "Four Reflections on Law and Morality" (2006) 48 *William & Mary Law Review* 1523.

Morton, Peter, *An Institutional Theory of Law: Keeping Law in Its Place* (Oxford: Clarendon Press 1998).

Mossoff, Adam, "What Is Property? Putting the Pieces Back Together" (2003) 45 *Arizona Law Review* 371.

"The False Promise of the Right to Exclude" (2011) 8 *Econ Journal Watch* 255.

Munzer, Stephen R., *A Theory of Property* (Cambridge: Cambridge University Press 1990).

"Introduction" in *New Essays in the Legal and Political Theory of Property* (New York: Cambridge University Press 2010), 1.

"A Bundle Theorist Holds on to His Collection of Sticks" (2011) 8 *Econ Journal Watch* 265.

"Property and Disagreement" in James Penner and Henry E. Smith (eds.), *Philosophical Foundations of Property Law* (New York: Oxford University Press 2013), 289.

Murray, Charles, *The Happiness of the People* (Washington, DC: AEI Press 2009).

Nagel, Thomas, *The Possibility of Altruism* (Oxford: Clarendon Press 1970).

National Center for Charitable Statistics, "Quick Facts About Nonprofits," available at http://nccs.urban.org/statistics/quickfacts.cfm.

Novak, Michael, *The Spirit of Democratic Capitalism* (New York: Madison Books 1991).

Oberdiek, John, "Specifying Rights Out of Necessity" (2008) 28 *Oxford Journal of Legal Studies* 127.

"What's Wrong with Infringements? (Insofar as Infringements Are Not Wrong): A Reply" (2008) 27 *Law and Philosophy* 293.

Paul, Jeremy, "The Hidden Structure of Takings Law" (1991) 64 *Southern California Law Review* 1393.

Peñalver, Eduardo M., "Land Virtues" (2009) 94 *Cornell Law Review* 821.

Penner, J. E., *The Idea of Property in Law* (Oxford: Oxford University Press 1997).

"Potentiality, Actuality, and 'Stick'-Theory" (2011) 8 *Econ Journal Watch* 274.

"On the Very Idea of Transmissible Rights" in James Penner and Henry E. Smith (eds.), *Philosophical Foundations of Property Law* (New York: Oxford University Press 2013), 244.

Penner, James and Smith, Henry E., "Introduction" in James Penner and Henry E. Smith (eds.), *Philosophical Foundations of Property Law* (New York: Oxford University Press 2013), xv.

Perillo, Joseph M., "Abuse of Rights: A Pervasive Legal Concept" (1995) 27 *Pacific Law Journal* 37.

Perovich, John D., "Validity and Construction of Testamentary Gift to Political Party" (1972) 41 *American Law Reports 3d* 833.

Philbrick, Francis S., "Changing Conceptions of Property in Law" (1938) 86 *University of Pennsylvania Law Review* 691.

Pipes, Richard, *Property and Freedom* (New York: Vintage Books 1999).

"Human Nature and the Fall of Communism" (1996) 49 *Bulletin of the American Academy of Arts & Sciences* 38.

Porter, Jean, *Ministers of the Law: A Natural Law Theory of Legal Authority* (Grand Rapids: Eerdmans 2010).

Postema, Gerald J., "Classical Common Law Jurisprudence (Part I)" (2002) 2 *Oxford University Commonwealth Law Journal* 155.

Proudhon, Pierre-Joseph, *What Is Property?*, Donald R. Kelley and Bonnie G. Smith (eds. & trans.) (Cambridge: Cambridge University Press 1994).

Radin, Margaret Jane, "Property and Personhood" (1982) 34 *Stanford Law Review* 957.

Reinterpreting Property (Chicago: University of Chicago Press 1993).

Raz, Joseph, *Practical Reasoning* (Oxford: Oxford University Press 1978).

The Morality of Freedom (Oxford: Oxford University Press 1986).

Practical Reason and Norms (Oxford: Oxford University Press 1999).

"Liberty and Trust" in R. P. George (ed.), *Natural Law, Liberalism, and Morality* (New York: Oxford University Press 1996), 113.

"Facing Up: A Reply" (1989) 62 *Southern California Law Review* 1153.

Regan, Donald H., "Authority and Value: Reflections on Raz's Morality of Freedom" (1989) 62 *Southern California Law Review* 995.

Reich, Charles A., "The New Property" (1964) 73 *Yale Law Journal* 733.

Ripstein, Arthur, "Possession and Use" in James Penner and Henry E. Smith (eds.), *Philosophical Foundations of Property Law* (New York: Oxford University Press 2013), 156.

di Robilant, Anna, "Abuse of Rights: The Continental Drug and the Common Law" (2010) 61 *Hastings Law Journal* 687.

Rood, John R., *A Treatise on the Law of Wills* (Chicago: Callaghan & Co. 1904), 19.

Rose, Carol M., "Possession as the Origin of Property" (1985) 52 *University of Chicago Law Review* 73.

"Crystals and Mud in Property Law" (1988) 40 *Stanford Law Review* 577.

"Canons of Property Talk, or Blackstone's Anxiety" (1998) 108 *Yale Law Journal* 601.

"Psychologies of Property" in James Penner and Henry E. Smith (eds.), *Philosophical Foundations of Property Law* (New York: Oxford University Press 2013), 272.

Rose-Ackerman, Susan, "Altruism, Nonprofits, and Economic Theory" (1996) 34 *Journal of Economic Literature* 701.

Ryan, Alan, *Property and Political Theory* (Oxford: Basil Blackwell 1984).

Property (Minneapolis: University of Minnesota Press 1987).

Salkin, Patricia E., "Ethical Considerations in Land Use Decision Making: 2006 Annual Review of Cases and Opinions" (2006) 38 *Urban Lawyer* 669.

Sandel, Michael J., *What Money Can't Buy: The Moral Limits of Markets* (New York: Farrar, Strauss, and Giroux 2012).

Selmi, Daniel P., "The Contract Transformation in Land Use Regulation" (2011) 63 *Stanford Law Review* 591.

Sen, Amartya, *Development as Freedom* (New York: Knopf 1999).

Schwartz, Victor E., "Civil Liability for Causing Suicide: A Synthesis of Law and Psychiatry" (1971) 24 *Vanderbilt Law Review* 217.

Scruton, Roger, *The Meaning of Conservatism* (South Bend: St. Augustine's Press 2002).

Sheridan, L. A., "Charity versus Politics" (1973) 2 *Anglo-American Law Review* 47.

Singer, Joseph William, *Entitlement: The Paradoxes of Property* (New Haven: Yale University Press 2000).

"Original Acquisition of Property: From Conquest & Possession to Democracy & Equal Opportunity" (2011) 86 *Indiana Law Journal* 763.

Smith, Henry E., "The Language of Property: Form, Context, and Audience" (2003) 55 *Stanford Law Review* 1105.

"Mind the Gap: The Indirect Relation between Ends and Means in American Property Law" (2009) 94 *Cornell Law Review* 959.

"Community and Custom in Property" (2009) 10 *Theoretical Inquiries in Law* 5.

"Property Is Not Just a Bundle of Rights" (2011) 8 *Econ Journal Watch* 279.

"An Economic Analysis of Law Versus Equity" (2013), 3, available at www.law.yale.edu/documents/pdf/LEO/Hsmith_LawVersusEquity7.pdf.

"Emergent Property" in James Penner and Henry E. Smith (eds.), *Philosophical Foundations of Property Law* (New York: Oxford University Press 2013).

Sohm, Rudolph, *The Institutes: A Textbook of the History and System of Roman Private Law*, James Crawford Ledlie (trans.) (3rd edn, Oxford: Clarendon Press 1907).

Somin, Ilya, "The Limits of Backlash: Assessing the Political Response to Kelo" (2009) 93 *Minnesota Law Review* 2100.

de Soto, Hernando, *The Mystery of Capital: Why Capitalism Triumphs in the West and Fails Everywhere Else* (New York: Basic Books 2000).

Stoner, Jr., James R., *Common Law and Liberal Theory: Coke, Hobbes, and the Origins of American Constitutionalism* (Lawrence: University Press of Kansas 1992).

Common-Law Liberty: Rethinking American Constitutionalism (Lawrence: University Press of Kansas 2003).

Story, Joseph, *Commentaries on the Law of Bailments with Illustrations from the Civil and the Foreign Law* (9th edn, Boston: Little, Brown and Company 1878).

Taggart, Michael, *Private Property and Abuse of Rights in Victorian England* (Oxford: Oxford University Press 2002).

Mother Teresa, *Come Be My Light* (New York: Doubleday 2007).

de Tocqueville, Alexis, *Democracy in America*, Gerald E. Bevan (trans.) (New York: Penguin 2003).

Tollefsen, Christopher O., "Moral Absolutes and the Moral Life" (November 21, 2011) *Public Discourse*, www.thepublicdiscourse.com/2011/11/4294.

Tomasi, John, *Free Market Fairness* (Princeton: Princeton University Press 2012).

Ullmann, Walter, *Principles of Government and Politics in the Middle Ages* (London: Methuen 1961).

Underkuffler, Laura S., *The Idea of Property: Its Meaning and Power* (New York: Oxford University Press 2003).

Urbina, Francisco J., "A Critique of Proportionality" (2012) 57 *American Journal of Jurisprudence* 49.

VanDrunen, David, "Natural Law, Custom, and Common Law in the Theology of Aquinas and Calvin" (2000) 33 *University of British Columbia Law Review* 699.

Waldron, Jeremy, "A Right to Do Wrong" (1981) 92 *Ethics* 21.

"Welfare and the Images of Charity" (1986) 36 *The Philosophical Quarterly* 463.

The Right to Private Property (Oxford: Clarendon Press 1988).

"Community and Property – For Those Who Have Neither" (2009) 10 *Theoretical Inquiries in Law* 161 at 189–90.

Weaver, Richard M., *Ideas Have Consequences* (Chicago: University of Chicago Press 1948).

Webber, Grégoire C. N., *The Negotiable Constitution: On the Limitation of Rights* (Cambridge: Cambridge University Press 2009).

"On the Loss of Rights" in Grant Huscroft, Bradley W. Miller, Grégoire Webber (eds.), *Proportionality and the Rule of Law: Rights, Justification, Reasoning* (New York: Cambridge University Press 2014), 123.

Wehner, Peter and Brooks, Arthur C., *Wealth & Justice: The Morality of Democratic Capitalism* (Washington, DC: AEI Press 2011).

Wolfe, Christopher, "A Response to Joseph Raz" in R. P. George (ed.), *Natural Law, Liberalism, and Morality* (New York: Oxford University Press 1996).

Weinrib, Ernest, *The Idea of Private Law* (Oxford: Oxford University Press 2012).

Yiannopoulos, A. N., "Civil Liability for Abuse of Right: Something Old, Something New" (1994) 54 *Louisiana Law Review* 1173.

Yuengert, Andrew M., *Approximating Prudence* (New York: Palgrave MacMillan 2012).

INDEX

For EU product safety concerns, contact us at Calle de José Abascal, 56–1°,
28003 Madrid, Spain or eugpsr@cambridge.org.

www.ingramcontent.com/pod-product-compliance
Lightning Source LLC
Chambersburg PA
CBHW061136281026
53914CB00003BB/26
* 9 7 8 1 1 0 7 0 9 5 7 6 2 *